THE POLITICS OF ENGAGED GENDER RESEARCH IN THE ARAB REGION

THE POLITICS OF ENGAGED GENDER RESEARCH IN THE ARAB REGION

Feminist Fieldwork and the Production of Knowledge

Edited by

Suad Joseph, Lena Meari, and Zeina Zaatari

I.B. TAURIS
LONDON • NEW YORK • OXFORD • NEW DELHI • SYDNEY

I.B. TAURIS
Bloomsbury Publishing Plc
50 Bedford Square, London, WC1B 3DP, UK
1385 Broadway, New York, NY 10018, USA
29 Earlsfort Terrace, Dublin 2, Ireland

BLOOMSBURY, I.B. TAURIS and the I.B. Tauris logo are trademarks of
Bloomsbury Publishing Plc

First published in Great Britain 2022

Copyright © Suad Joseph, Lena Meari and Zeina Zaatari, 2022

Suad Joseph, Lena Meari and Zeina Zaatari have asserted their right under the Copyright,
Designs and Patents Act, 1988, to be identified as Editors of this work.

For legal purposes the Acknowledgments on pp. xvii–xviii constitute an extension
of this copyright page.

Cover design by Toby Way
Cover image: *NW21481*, by Etel Adnan, from Patrice Cotensin/Galerie Lelong

All rights reserved. No part of this publication may be reproduced or transmitted in
any form or by any means, electronic or mechanical, including photocopying,
recording, or any information storage or retrieval system, without prior permission
in writing from the publishers.

Bloomsbury Publishing Plc does not have any control over, or responsibility for,
any third-party websites referred to or in this book. All internet addresses given in this
book were correct at the time of going to press. The author and publisher regret any
inconvenience caused if addresses have changed or sites have ceased to exist,
but can accept no responsibility for any such changes.

A catalogue record for this book is available from the British Library.

A catalog record for this book is available from the Library of Congress.

ISBN: HB: 978-0-7556-4523-7
PB: 978-0-7556-4522-0
ePDF: 978-0-7556-4524-4
eBook: 978-0-7556-4525-1

Typeset by Newgen KnowledgeWorks Pvt. Ltd., Chennai, India
Printed and bound in Great Britain

To find out more about our authors and books visit www.bloomsbury.com
and sign up for our newsletters.

CONTENTS

Dedication viii
List of Contributors xi
Acknowledgments xvii

1. Introduction: Knowledge Production on Women and Gender in the Arab Region: Local Contexts 1
   Suad Joseph, Lena Meari, and Zeina Zaatari

2. The Politics of Training for Engaged Gender Research 33
   Suad Joseph

PART 1 MAGHREB (NORTH AFRICA)

3. Doing Fieldwork with Women Land Rights Activists in Morocco: Power Relationships within Feminism and Its Discursive Framework of Right 51
   Souad Eddouada

4. The Day I Became a Gentrifier: Narratives from the Outsider/Insider Ethnographer in the Field 69
   Reeham Mourad

PART 2 MASHRIQ (ARAB EAST)

5. Reflections on the Structural and Daily Realities of Field Research 87
   Rania Jawad

6 Fieldwork in the Palestinian Colonial Context: Searching for the Voices of Palestinian Women 101
Samar Kassis

7 The Fear Factor: Fieldwork Away from the Safety Blanket of Depoliticized Notion of Gender and Women's Issues 119
Sara Ababneh

8 Research in the Jordanian Child Welfare System: Navigating Taboo Subjects 139
Rawan W. Ibrahim

9 Conducting Research while Death Surrounds You: The Researcher, Gender, and War in Syria 151
Saja Al Zoubi

10 Feminist Researcher in a Conservative Islamic Society, Iraq 169
Ilham Makki Hammadi

PART 3 KHALEEJ (ARAB GULF)

11 Embeddedness in the Field: Navigating Familiarity 189
Sarah Shaer

12 Personality and Perception: Aspects of the Researcher's Identity and Their Impact on Field Research within Diverse Locations 201
Kholoud Al-Ajarma

This book is dedicated to:

Etel Adnan

1925–2021

Etel Adnan was many things to many people. To Suad Joseph, she was a friend and mentor, and "Aunti Etel" to her daughter Sara Rose. To the world, Etel Adnan was a Lebanese and an American poet, short storywriter, essayist, painter, tapestry designer, thinker, and philosopher. She was educated in Lebanon, France, and the United States and lived in all three countries for extended periods of time, all of which were home to her in different ways. Her mother was Greek; her father was from what was to become Syria, but was still under the Ottoman Empire for which he was a high-ranking officer. Educated in French schools in Lebanon, she moved to Paris to study at the Sorbonne, and then (1955) to the United States to continue her studies of philosophy at Harvard and the University of California, Berkeley.

During the period that she was teaching philosophy at Dominican College in San Raphael, California (1958–72), she joined the poets' protest movement against the war in Vietnam. She chose that moment to become "an American poet." Being an American poet was a connection to First Nations peoples, about and for whom she also wrote. She developed her work as a visual artist during this period. Moving back to Beirut in 1972, just before the Lebanese Civil War, she wrote what became her award-winning, classic war novel, *Sitt Marie-Rose*, as well as texts for documentaries about the war. She returned to California in 1977, remaining there until the last decade or so when she returned once again to Paris. During those many decades she became an iconic figure for artists, activists, thinkers in a swath of the world, including First Nations communities, queer communities, racial and social justice movements, progressives, and those for whom words and words visualized tell us critical stories.

Her poetry has been put to music; she wrote texts/scripts for theater; she published close to twenty books; some of her books were made into films; and her art was exhibited at innumerable shows in the United States, Europe, and the Middle East.

Etel Adnan was her words, her art, the music that accompanied her art, the stage that spoke her text, and more. She was deeply engaged in/with the world. She lived deeply the remnants of the nineteenth century, the fullness of the twentieth century, and the beginnings of the twenty-first century. History and time were companions with whom she conversed and argued. Everywhere she had companions—the fortunate folks with whom she reflected upon life worlds around her. She was present in the moment, always, and always brought more to the moment than those of us around her would grasp. Her presence was a gift of perception, connection, embodied relationality. And that she leaves with us her presence, in everything she wrote, spoke, painted, worked on or with, including her many companions.

Suad Joseph, Zeina Zaatari, Lena Meari

CONTRIBUTORS

Sara Ababneh just joined the University of Sheffield as a lecturer in the Politics and International Relations Department. Prior to that she was an associate professor at the University of Jordan's Center for Strategic Studies where she was the chair of the Political and Social Research Unit. In addition, she taught at and coordinated multiple US study abroad programs in Jordan. Ababneh earned her PhD in politics and international relations from St. Antony's College, University of Oxford. She wrote her dissertation on female Islamists in Hamas in occupied Palestine and the Islamic Action Front in Jordan. Ababneh was selected as the Carnegie Centennial Fellow at the Middle East Institute at Columbia University in New York. She also was a visiting scholar at the University of Tübingen. Ababneh has conducted research on Mandate Palestine, gender and Islamism, Muslim family laws, and labor movements. Her research interests include class, gender, and struggles for liberation, social justice, postcolonial and feminist IR theory, and economic sovereignty. Currently, Ababneh studies the popular Jordanian protest movement (*al-Hirak al-Sha'bi al-Urduni*).

Kholoud Al-Ajarma is a Palestinian anthropologist, award-winning photographer, and filmmaker. She holds a PhD in anthropology, theology, and religious studies from the University of Groningen (Netherlands) where she has worked as a lecturer until she joined Edinburgh University's Alwaleed Centre for the Study of Islam in the Contemporary World in January 2021. She is a graduate of Peace Studies and Conflict Resolution (MA), and Anthropology and Development Studies (MPhil). Al-Ajarma has also worked in the fields of migration, refugee rights, visual culture, knowledge production, and climate change in Palestine, the Mediterranean region, Europe, and Latin America. Parallel to her academic work, Al-Ajarma has continued volunteering with refugee communities and with many youth-led organizations in Palestine, developing innovative platforms for active youth participation within human rights research, media, conflict resolution, and environmental justice.

Saja Al Zoubi is a developmental economist whose research focuses on refugee's livelihoods and gender with a focus on Syrian refugees. Saja works as a researcher in Oxford Department for International Development. She designs and teaches tutorials of gender and forced migration, and Middle East politics in Christ Church, University of Oxford, UK, in addition to US universities' program in Oxford.

Al Zoubi's research has focused broadly on issues of gender and rural development, including issues of women's empowerment, and its role in rural development. Her book, *The Role of Women in Home Economics*, where she examined how women can play a significant role in different sectors (economic, agriculture, health, environment, education, etc.) through their efficient participation in household management, was the first academic reference in home economics published in Syria. It is still used in Syrian universities as a reference. Since the war broke out in Syria, her concern has been researching ways to improve the livelihoods and food security of affected households (IDPs and refugees), especially women-headed households, and supporting young people to educate, enhance capacity building, and find work opportunities. Currently, she researches how refugees' livelihoods are asffected by national and international policies and politics. As a socioeconomist for around 15 years, Al Zoubi has been working in academia, national and international institutions including UNHCR, Action against Hunger (ACF), Norwegian Refugee Council (NRC), and The Arab Centre for the Studies of Arid Zones and Dry Lands (ACSAD). She conducted research on the socioeconomic and demographic impacts of the war, with a focus on women. In addition, she conducted a comprehensive study about enhancing the livelihoods and food security of Syrian refugees in Lebanon for around two years in the Syrian camps in Bekaa valley with international organizations (International Center for Agricultural Research in the Dry Areas (ICARDA) and The World Academy of Sciences (TWAS)).

Al Zoubi was selected by The University of North Carolina at Chapel Hill (2016) and Cornell University (2017) for post-doc fellowships. She is the recipient of numerous awards from international and regional foundations.

Souad Eddouada is associate professor of English at Ibn Tofail University in Kenitra, Morocco. Her area of interests are: Islam, gender, human rights, land reform, and the commons. Eddouada was recently awarded a multiyear grant from the Moroccan Ministry of Education, Ibn Khaldoun Social Science Program, to support research and writing for her book project: *Women and Land Rights in Morocco: Privatization and Women's Protest in a Muslim-Majority Nation*. Eddouada's work on gender, human rights, and family law in Morocco has been published internationally in journals and edited volumes. Her work has been supported by several Fulbright grants, as well as grants and fellowships from Open Society Institute and Lund University (Sweden).

Rawan W. Ibrahim is an assistant professor at the Department of Social Work in the German Jordanian University. Her specialization lies in the field of child protection and alternative care. Her career began in residential care for severely abused children in Jordan. With the aim of supporting the Jordanian government to deinstitutionalize children, Ibrahim was the director and coinvestigator of a multiyear UNICEF-funded project in collaboration with Columbia University where the first regional foster program was established. Rawan continues to consult for the UNICEF Jordan Country Office, as well as other local and international organizations such as in northern Iraq, Indonesia, and Morocco on areas along the continuum of alternative care. In addition to deinstitutionalizing children, her interests include preparation and postcare support of youth transitioning from substitute care to adulthood and implementation science in developing economy contexts.

Ibrahim has been a member of the International Research Network on Transitions to Adulthood from Care (INTRAC) since 2006 and is a member of the International Advisory Board at the Institute for Inspiring Children's Future in the University of Strathclyde. She completed her PhD at the School of Social Work in the University of East Anglia (Norwich, UK).

Rania Jawad is an assistant professor in the Department of English Language and Literature at Birzeit University. She writes on cultural and performance politics in the Arab world with a particular focus on Palestine. Her publications include: "'Aren't We Human?' Normalizing Palestinian Performances," "Staging Resistance in Bil'in: The Performance of Violence in a Palestinian Village," "Trajectories of Travel: Augusto Boal's Liberatory Theatre Practice in Palestine," and "Barbara Harlow and the Necessity of 'Renewed Histories of the Future.'" She was a fellow of the Institute of Advanced Studies' Summer Program in Social Science from 2015 to 2017.

Suad Joseph is distinguished research professor of anthropology and gender, sexuality, and women's studies at the University of California, Davis. Her research has focused on her native Lebanon; on the politicization of religion; on women in local communities; on women, family and state; and on questions of self, citizenship, and rights. Her current research is a long-term longitudinal study on how children in a village of Lebanon learn their notions of rights, responsibilities, and citizenship in the aftermath of the Civil War and on their transnational families who have moved to the United States and Canada. She is founding director of the Middle East/South Asia Studies Program, UC Davis. She is founder and director of the Arab Families Working Group (AFWG), a group of 16 scholars undertaking comparative, interdisciplinary research on Arab families in Palestine, Lebanon, Egypt, and the United States. She is founder of the Association for Middle East Women's Studies (AMEWS) and cofounder of AMEW's Journal of Middle East Women's Studies (JMEWS) published by Duke University Press. She is also founder and facilitator (since 2001) of the American University of Beirut, the American University in Cairo, the Lebanese American University, the University of California and Birzeit University Consortium, and American University of Sharjah (UCDAR). She served as the president of the Middle East Studies Association of North America, 2010–11. She is founding and general editor of the Encyclopedia of Women and Islamic Cultures. Her edited books include: *Arab Family Studies: Critical Reviews* (2018); *Women and Islamic Cultures: Disciplinary Paradigms and Approaches* (2013); *Gender and Citizenship in the Middle East* (2000); and *Intimate Selving in Arab Families* (1999). Her coedited books include: *Building Citizenship in Lebanon* (1999); *Women and Citizenship in Lebanon* (1999) and *Women and Power in the Middle East* (2001); and *Muslim-Christian Conflicts: Economic, Political, and Social Origins* (1978). She has published over 100 articles and won many awards and prizes including the UC Davis Undergraduate Teaching and Research Award (2014, $45,000) and the Middle East Studies Association Jere L. Bachrach Life Time Service Award.

Samar Kassis is a researcher, coordinator, and an instructor at the Institute of Women Studies at Birzeit University, Palestine. Kassis received her bachelor's degree in English Literature from Birzeit University in 2001, and a diploma in Project Management from EMIDEAST Ramallah, Palestine. In 2006 she completed an advance training course on SPSS and quantitative data analysis at the Institute of Community and Public Health at BZU. She earned her master's degree in gender and development in 2014 from Birzeit University.

From 2009 until September 2013, she was a research assistant and part of a mental health unit team in the Institute of Community and Public Health at Birzeit University, Palestine. Kassis had conducted and was part of a research on Palestinian youth and traumatic experiences. The project was entitled "Youth as a strategy," which was in collaboration with North Community Based Rehabilitation Program. In addition, she conducted research on child abuse and neglect in Palestine, mortality patterns in West Bank, fertility in Palestine, birth control programs in health governmental sectors, political violence, Palestinian adolescent, political prisoners and ex-political prisoners and their families in Palestine, and gender representation in visual culture. Currently, she studies Palestinian female ex-political prisoners who had been released after Oslo Accords and the concept of resistance in the Palestinian context.

Ilham Makki Hammadi holds a PhD in anthropology from the Saint Joseph University, Beirut, Lebanon, and her thesis discusses the impact of Al Hawza Schools on Islamic women's lives. She earned her master's degree in anthropology in 2010 from the College of Arts, University of Baghdad, with the thesis topic "The political culture of Iraqi parliament's female members." She is a researcher, activist, and trainer on issues of women's rights and gender (SGBV). She is a member of the Iraqi Women's Network and the Iraqi Al-Amal Association, coordinator and supervisor of many activities and programs on the protection of women during and after conflicts, as well as programs involving women in the peace-building process. She is a teacher in the Iraqi Ministry of Education.

Lena Meari is an assistant professor of cultural anthropology at the Department of Social and Behavioral Sciences and the Institute of Women's Studies at Birzeit University, Palestine. She has special interest in the geopolitics of knowledge production; subject formation in colonial contexts; decolonizing methodologies; critical feminist theory; and revolutionary movements. Her publications include "*Sumud*: A Palestinian Philosophy of Confrontation in Colonial Prisons," "Re-signifying 'Sexual' Colonial Power Techniques: The Experiences of Palestinian Women Political Prisoners," "Colonial Dispossession, Developmental Discourses, and Humanitarian solidarity in 'Area C': The Case of the Palestinian Yanun Village," and the coedited book "Rethinking Gender in Revolutions and Resistance: Lessons from the Arab World."

Reeham Mourad is an independent urban researcher and feminist based in Cairo, Egypt. She studied architectural engineering at Cairo University. She holds double master's degrees in integrated urbanism and sustainable design (IUSD) from the University of Stuttgart and Ain Shams University where she was a Deutscher Akademischer Austauschdienst (DAAD) scholarship holder between 2014 and 2016. Her master's thesis deals with the ethnography of social relations, women's perceptions of safety, gender and class dynamics, gentrification, and contemporary art centers in two working-class neighborhoods in historic Cairo. Her experiences include ten years of working between different spectrums like architecture firms, urban studies, anthropological and feminist research where she was able to engage with local stakeholders, governmental institutions, NGOs, academics, universities, and independent research platforms. Reeham was a fellow in the New Paradigm Factory (NPF) Program by the Arab Council for the Social Sciences (ACSS) in the theme of the 2019–20 Cycle; Gendered Resistance with research titled "Spaces of Resistance: Women Maneuvering the Sha'bi Notions of El-Khalifa Neighborhood."

Sarah Shaer is a PhD student in the anthropology program at the University of Chicago. Prior to joining the University of Chicago, Sarah was a principal researcher at the Mohammed bin Rashid School of Government where she led the social policy research agenda and focused on issues related to gender and youth inclusion.

Zeina Zaatari currently works as the director of the Arab American Cultural Center and is adjunct faculty in anthropology at the University of Illinois at Chicago. Previously, she worked as research director at Political Research Associates (2017–18) and as the regional director for the MENA Program at Global Fund for Women (2004–12) where she managed a diverse grantmaking program to support women's and trans movements in the Middle East and North Africa. Zeina earned her PhD in cultural anthropology with an emphasis in feminist theory from the University of California at Davis. Zeina's research focuses on subjectivity and social movements, particularly feminist and queer. She is currently researching heteronormativity in Lebanon, looking at the interplay of family, citizenship, and access to adulthood. Her most recent publications include a chapter on "Sexual Rights Movement: Middle East and North Africa" in *Sexualities in the Middle East*, edited by John Michael Ryan and Helen Rizzo (forthcoming), "Lebanon" in *Arab Family Studies: Critical Reviews*, edited by Suad Joseph (2018), "Social Movements and Revolution" in *A Companion to the Anthropology of the Middle East*, edited by Soraya Altorki (2015), and "Desirable Masculinity/Femininity and Nostalgia of the 'Anti-Modernity': Bab el-Hara Television Series as a Site of Production" in *Sexuality and Culture* (2014). Additionally, she has authored several commissioned research publications including: "Unpacking Gender: The Humanitarian Response to the Syrian Refugee Crisis in Jordan" (2014). In 2020, she published an article titled "Sarah Hegazy and the Struggle for Freedom" in *Middle East Report Online*. She is coediting with Suad Joseph the *Handbook of Women in the Middle East* (expected 2022). Zeina serves as the associate editor for the Middle East and Africa (northern and sub-Saharan) for the Encyclopedia of Women and Islamic Cultures. She is a trainer and mentor for The Muslim Women in the Media Training Institute, and a cofounder and member of the Training to Engaged Research Group. She served for six years as secretary of the Board of the Association for Women's Rights in Development, is a member of the International Advisory Board for Astraea Lesbian Foundation for Justice, and is a cofounder and an elected adviser for the MENA Coalition of Women Human Rights Defenders. More info on publications at: https://uic.academia.edu/ZeinaZaatari.

ACKNOWLEDGMENTS

This book and the project that produced it is foremost indebted to the Foundation to Promote Open Society (FPOS), Amman, Jordan. FPOS funded the project for the Training to Transformative Gender Research (TTGR) from 2015 to 2019. The four years of funding supported the Transformative Gender Research Group (TERG) to work with two cohorts of graduate students and early career scholars to train them in critical proposal writing, research methods, data analysis, and writing and publishing. Each cohort received two years of training (four seminars each) and funding to carry out seed research project (see Chapter 2 for detailed discussion of TERG). The first cohort met during 2015–16 and the second cohort during 2017–19. Our colleague, Nadine Naber, joined TERG as one of the trainers for the second cohort. This volume is drawn from the work we (Suad Joseph, Lena Meari, Zeina Zaatari) carried out, with our first cohort, during 2015–16. Lina Abou-Habib and Islah Jad joined us partly in that training. In FPOS, we are grateful to Hanan Rabbani who guided us through the FPOS grant for the first cohort. She left FPOS shortly after and for the remaining period our program officer has been Lama Al Khateeb who, along with her staff Marina Awad, guided us through the rest of the first and through the second grant. Al Khateeb met with us on many occasions. She and Awad attended some of the training sessions for the Fellows. She was an enthusiastic supporter throughout the years of the program.

We are most grateful to Collective for Research and Training on Development—Action (CRTD.A), Beirut, Lebanon, for housing the grant from FPOS for us. Lina Abou-Habib, the director, joined us in the training but was not able to continue beyond a short engagement in the first seminar. Abou-Habib's staff Nabiha Jamal managed the finances and Nisrine Naaman managed the logistics of planning the hotels, traveling, catering, and the like. They were an outstanding team that facilitated the work flawlessly from 2015 to 2016, during the first cohort.

We would also like to acknowledge the Arab Council for the Social Sciences (ACSS), Beirut, Lebanon. While ACSS was not involved with TERG during the first cohort from which this book developed, they partnered with us for the second cohort. Their director, Seteney Shami, was visionary in working with us as a team partner. Her staff, Moushira Elgeziri, Najwa Tohme, Hiba Hammoud, and Issam Khoury, stepped up with grace and generosity for the 2017–19 cohort.

While much of the finances were handled through CRTD.A during the first cohort (and ACSS during the second cohort), some of the grant finances were handled through the University of California, Davis. Here Suad Joseph is particularly indebted to grant manager Yoke Dellenback. Dellenback impeccably managed every aspect of the grant, even assisting in tracking funds not housed at UCD.

The Suad Joseph Lab student assistants were intricately involved in preparation of materials for the seminars, designing and maintaining the website (https://sjoseph.ucdavis.edu/training-engaged-gender-research-groups), helping to prepare binders, and tracking the TTGR Fellows over the four years of the TERG project. Graduate student researchers Shawn Miller, Austin Cross, Nahrain Rasho, Mash'alle Olomi, Halle Casey, Zuzana Turowska, Aleksandra Taranov, Kelly Gove, Elizabeth Witcher, Timothy Buensalido, and Megan Klasic oversaw the many projects in the Joseph Lab and helped organize the work of the many undergraduate student assistants. They also helped in preparing binders for the seminars and reports to funders. IT staff David Nin, James Zeng, Sailesh Patnala, Nicholas Reynolds, Yong Chong, Randy Murphy, and Eeheet Hayer designed and managed the TERG and proposal writing webpages. Undergraduate student assistants Kimia Akbari, Cassie Teegardin, Layla Mustafa, and Elise Boyle gave support in preparing material for the website and for the seminars.

1 INTRODUCTION: KNOWLEDGE PRODUCTION ON WOMEN AND GENDER IN THE ARAB REGION: LOCAL CONTEXTS

Suad Joseph, Lena Meari, and Zeina Zaatari

This volume approaches knowledge production on women and gender in the Arab region through a critical examination of local fieldwork experiences carried out by women field researchers. Taking the specificities of fieldwork and the personal/political challenges faced by women researchers in the Arab region as points of departure, the volume reflects upon the structural conditions that shape the lives of the people in the Arab region today, and the ways in which knowledge about women's lives and gendered relations is produced within these structural conditions. In spite of the ethnic, cultural, and religious heterogeneity of the Arab region, its people had faced many shared structural, global, and local conditions that impacted their lives. The structural conditions, both global and local, revealed in the various chapters of the volume include imperialism; settler colonialism; neoliberalization of economies, institutions, and subjectivities; racial capitalism; securitization; and embedded patriarchal ideologies and structures. While the impact of these structural conditions varies country by country (as each chapter lays out), the constellation and conjunctures of these structural conditions are constitutive of the field and the personal/political challenges in the research conducted by the contributors to the volume. These conditions impacted different women's lives differently, as will be clear in reading the particular experiences and contexts in each chapter.

The volume assesses the implications of the economic, social, geographical, historical, and cultural dynamics for the field experience itself, and how these structural conditions are revealed through the specificities of field experience. It focuses on how the fieldwork experience is shaped by the historical period inhabited by the people, the country contexts, the nature of the state and regional social and political transformations, as well as global dynamics. The main contribution of this book lies in analyzing the fieldwork experience to better understand the politics of knowledge production by linking the research experience to the sociopolitical context, the place, and the time in which the researchers conducted their research.

Feminist researchers, particularly those from or of origins in the Arab region, have long been critical of orientalist and colonialist knowledge produced about the region. They have, for decades, critiqued narratives predicated upon assumptions, rooted in Eurocentric/orientalist epistemologies, that essentialize Arab/Muslim culture(s) and religion(s) and their impact on the position of women. Within orientalist and colonialist frameworks, factors such as political economies or imperialist geopolitics that shape women's experiences have been ignored (El Said et al. 2015). Hoda Elsadda (2004) argued that an analysis of the sociopolitical status of Arab women requires reading against the grain of biased assumptions and dismissive strategies of othering, marginalization, and prejudice. This, according to Elsadda, should be done through contextualizing and historicizing any statistical data on Arab women.

In "Anthropology's Orient," Lila Abu-Lughod (1990) indicates that writing about women and gender up to the 1960s had been plagued by the empirical gaze with a positivist-functionalist lens. The 1950s and 1960s, Deniz Kandiyoti (1996) observed, brought to the fore a focus on modernization theory with its linear trajectory. As critiques of modernization theory in the late 1970s surfaced, feminist researchers raised questions about economic liberalization's disempowerment of women and the inequities produced by local patriarchies. Kandiyoti argued for the necessity of internal critique of gendered power in Middle Eastern societies. She observed that studies influenced by Said's *Orientalism* (1978) tended to adopt binary thinking of East/West and focus more on issues of representation rather than social analysis of local institutions and dynamics. Driven by a desire to counter the dominant orientalist representation of Muslim and Arab women, researchers focused on representation and documentation, and the result was a retreat from theorization and consideration of a number of factors.

The 1970s and 1980s ushered in a period of more ethnographically based studies that aimed to counter the stereotype. Lila Abu-Lughod (2001) questioned the extent to which these studies escaped liberal values foundational to knowledge production produced in and for the West. Scholarship from the late 1980s, according to Abu-Lughod (1990), began to focus on agency, deconstruction of the notion of sex-segregated societies or public/private divide, and consideration of ideology, meaning, and power in relationships. Women's agency in the Arab world, though, was mostly treated as an indication and reflection of liberal/feminist desires (Mahmood 2004).

Deeb and Winegar's (2012) review of anthropological research on the Middle East also identified important contributions in the theorizing of agency and power relations. Marnia Lazreg (2014) examined the effects of the application of poststructuralist Foucauldian theoretical approach on studies of Middle Eastern women and gender with respect to the reveiling trend. She explored the epistemic transformation of the explanation of this trend into its justification. She provided an example of a historicized application of Michel Foucault's conception of power. Writing in 2012, Maya Mikdashi articulated "dos and don'ts" in the study of gender in the Middle East. Her categorization shed light on some of the questions that continue to plague the study of gender in the Arab region. Those "dos" include focusing on analysis rather than description, avoiding cultural and religious explanations, understanding subjectivities as complex and intersectional rather than unidimensional, and considering context and power dynamics in any study. Anaheed Al-Hardan (2014) examined the power relations inherent in imperialism and colonialism as they unfolded at all stages of a recent research project on Palestinian refugees that was conceptualized and initiated in the Western academy. She highlights the role that colonial epistemologies have played and continue to play in research projects and knowledge production of the region and the training and disciplining within academic institutions. "Upholding colonizing research epistemologies designed for researching 'others' through various informal, material, and discursive practices of power in the academy is possible because the academy is implicated in the historical and contemporary coloniality of power/knowledge" (Al-Hardan 2014, 64).

In a roundtable conversation on teaching gender and women's studies in the Middle East, Dina El Khawaga (Alfares et al. 2020) highlighted the degree to which many gender studies research centers and scholars in the Middle East tend to "resort to depoliticizing the study of gender and linking it to issues acceptable by the regime in power to mitigate adverse political contexts." This avoidance of entanglements with power structures includes focusing on narrow aspects of women's rights, on the era of modernization and enlightenment, and on women's role in social protection programs. This kind of work, El Khawaga acknowledged, is constrained by tremendous prohibitions, such as repressive regimes (authors in this volume report this as well) and lack of resources for research institutions (The Asfari Institute 2019). In an essay titled "How We Should Not Study Gender in the Arab World," Joseph Massad (2009) outlined three main approaches for studying gender in the Arab region: culturalism, comparativism, and assimilationism. Massad calls for constructing concepts and methodologies emerging from the local context and studying the local economic, social, geographical, historical, and cultural factors as dynamics that produce/are being produced by structural conditions.

The authors in this volume document how the sociopolitical conditions of imperialism, settler colonialism, racial capitalism, neoliberalism, and securitization have shaped the materiality of their own daily lives, the lives of their interlocutors, and the practices of the field research. Authors in this volume became attentive to the voices, language, and local modes of being of their interlocutors, recognizing that doing so required rethinking their research questions or theories or methods. The particularities and details of the fieldwork experience, the relationships built during the research process, the attentiveness to the voices and practices of the participants in the research, and the emotional effects the participants elicited in the researchers offer the possibility for the contributors to this volume to theorize from the local context.

The personal narrations of fieldwork experiences are accompanied by reflections, analytical interpretations, and critical insights into the broader contexts of the states in which research was conducted. The contributors engage with how feminist theories and methodologies affected their research decisions and relationships with the participants of their research. Instead of essentializing the field, the contributors to this volume reflect on what the field is and how they are positioned in the field. What does being in the field mean to them, and how was the field constituted by local and global structural conditions? The reflections include questions on the subjectivity of the researcher. They examine negotiation between the self, the location, the subject of the research, and the structural conditions that shape the research experience. They consider how they experienced and engaged with gender, class, nationality, and motherhood as shaped by local contexts. What sorts of relationships did they form? What kind of emotions did they engage, and how did these relationships and emotions shape the researcher and their ability to produce knowledge? How did they engage with the ethical responsibility toward the participants of the research? How did the structural conditions of the Arab region, under global capitalism, manifest themselves in their research?

Studying Our Own

As with the authors in this volume, we, the editors, have struggled with questions regarding the politics of producing knowledge about our regions, our communities, and ourselves. We have considered what our field is and how we are positioned in relation to it, the power structures reflected in our research questions and field experiences. We debated among ourselves what it means to be training the next generation of scholars knowing what we know about the politics of knowledge production.

As a Palestinian researcher, I, Lena Meari, have engaged with epistemological, methodological, and political considerations regarding knowledge production in the Palestinian settler-colonial context. Two of my previous research projects are particularly relevant to the issues that interest this volume. The first is my MA research project, conducted with Palestinian refugees from the village of al-Birweh. I collected and analyzed refugees' narratives on the economic and cultural modes of life, the constructed gender roles and dynamics they inhabited in their original village, and the transformations experienced following the destruction of the village by the Zionist forces in 1948. Throughout the research, I encountered epistemological questions regarding my positionality as an academic woman belonging to the third generation of a Palestinian refugee family from al-Birweh village. I had grown up in a different material reality from my Palestinian old men and women interlocutors for whom the feminist theoretical questions I posed were strange. I grappled with the power relations constitutive of the research process and the problematics of representation throughout the writing phase. I engaged with the intertwinement of theory and politics in the context of conducting research with Palestinian refugees to whom I belong, and with whom I share the struggle for the right of return to the village from which we were displaced by the violent power of the continuing Zionist settler-colonial project (Meari 2010). The research journey elicited my interest in decolonial materialist feminist epistemology and its ethical-political commitments.

My PhD dissertation research project examined *sumud* as a Palestinian philosophy of confrontation in colonial prisons. Among the various aspects explored in the research was the reconstruction of sexuality and the sexed body within the dynamics of colonial domination and anticolonial resistance in Palestine as reflected in the interrogation encounter that constitutes a unique epistemic space associated with security measures, underground activity, and secrecy. Assuming that epistemological positions intertwine with ontological assumptions and political sensibilities, I approached the interrogation from the viewpoint of resistance, aiming to engage with the processes of liberatory knowledge production and anticolonial politics (Meari 2015). I engaged with questions such as: How might I capture "revolutionary becoming?" What feminist theoretical frames and methodological tools are capable of capturing the destabilization of the sexed body and the resignification of sexuality within the broader context of anticolonial resistance? What kind of evidence might I look for in my conversations with Palestinian women strugglers? What are the ramifications of the forms of relationships that emerged out of my engagement with Palestinian women-in-*sumud*? All these epistemological and methodological issues are constitutive of knowledge production and its political implications in the Palestinian settler-colonial context.

As a feminist researcher from South Lebanon, specifically the city of Saida, I, Zeina Zaatari, was concerned with the lack of substantive knowledge produced about and from the margin of Lebanese society—the South and its women. I had grown up in Saida. I was, however, educated in Western academic institutions (the American University of Beirut and later in the United States) and was working toward my PhD in the United States. I came from an educated lower-middle-class, nonreligious, nontraditional family (my mother worked as a teacher, got married in her late thirties, and supported her family financially). My positionality led me to an interest in understanding activist women's subjectivities and choices—how and why these women make the choices to join political parties, form foundations, raise their children, and understand their motherhood. I gathered the life histories of six women, one of whom was my mother, and another two who were among her close friends. They were leftist women (who had joined political parties, organized on the ground including demonstrations, and were arrested) to whom I had access and who had transgressed many norms of their time, leading to conflicts with their families and society. My interest in their subjectivities stemmed from my bewilderment at their total erasure from the political, historical, and academic record of Lebanon. It also stemmed from a feminist commitment to understanding how we become certain kinds of political beings in the world, how we engage with power relations in our societies, and how we are constituted by and constitute structures of power and practice. While these women were familiar to me, I wanted to ensure my research spoke to the multiplicity of experiences. To complicate the narrative around subjectivity, I interviewed women who identified as Islamists and those who saw themselves as contributing charitably to society (Zaatari 2006). It was the Islamist women's stories that academics and others in the West wanted to hear and rarely those of the self-described secularists. This was a constant reminder that even with the careful choices and considerations we make in terms of the knowledge we produce, the way that knowledge is received may continue to be largely impacted by global and structural power dynamics and historical representations.

Years later, as my research shifted and I spent time interviewing queer folks (primarily women, genderqueer, and trans men), a community I self-identify with, old questions persisted, as new ones arose. I remained interested in subjectivity and the shaping of subjectivities against and alongside the heteronormative norm and despite hegemonic heteronormativity. But I was also interested in how this community comes to adulthood in a society that largely correlates adulthood with marriage and parenthood. My identity and years of engaging with the community provided me with access and a level of trust of a shared experience. Nevertheless, there were differences that were unavoidable. I lived in the United States. I enjoyed a level of comfort from an accepting and loving family that did not generate the kinds of risks or anxiety that some of my interlocutors experienced. I had to grapple with questions of safety of my interlocutors and how and where to share information I gathered. I continue to struggle between the responsibility of carrying and holding those stories and my and their interest in making their stories public, and the worry of causing harm by publishing. I suggest not only physical harm for individuals who may not be out to their families or in society at large but also epistemological harm, the harm of naming or superimposing identities and labels, of framing knowledge within a binary politicized worldview and taxonomy (Zaatari, forthcoming).

I, Suad Joseph, came up in a politically and culturally transformative global period and in a family transformed by that special time and space. I was born in Lebanon and migrated to the United States with my very working-class, devoutly Christian family as a child. The family rose, through education, into the middle and some even upper middle classes in the unusual time of the 1950s and 1960s in the United States. Aware of how chance/luck/timing/place had made my family story possible and concerned by contradictions between faith and practice of Christian churches, I committed to understanding the politics of the working class and the connections between class and religion. The accident of being a student at Columbia University during the 1968 student/community strikes was the political awakening that propelled me to study the politicization of religion in a working-class community of Greater Beirut for my doctoral research. Coming from a Marxist training, I was not a feminist when I went to do fieldwork in 1971. The second wave of feminism was sweeping academia when I returned from fieldwork and when I realized that I had interviewed mainly women in my sample of over one hundred working-class households of Camp Trad, Borj Hammoud. These women, their stories, and the field turned me into a feminist. Returning multiple times and continuing my relationships with key families there for 50 years (Joseph 2021a), I saw myself in them. I saw my possible life story, had my family not migrated. The recognition, the familiarity, the ease of immersion left me with a constant struggle to create the critical distance needed for analysis and diminished my capacity to see some of the power and even cultural differences between us. I found myself violating many rules of fieldwork of the time, as I engaged neighbors around various causes, helped them vis-à-vis the Lebanese government, and intervened in family matters. I had convictions and commitments about the political uses of religion and the political manipulations of ideologies in relation to the working class that drove some of these interventions. Reflections on my positionality, power dynamics, local politics, and personal relations were a reckoning that came later (Joseph 1988, 1990, 1993, 1995, 1996). That reckoning triggered profound changes in my research, including a rethinking of my view of the intersections of religion and class, especially in the context of the Lebanese Civil War and the rapid rise of Islamist movements. The reckoning with my intense, intimate, and very familiar relationships with my Camp Trad neighbors inspired new understanding of subjectivity and the self in the context of power, structure, and the state and nudged me into understanding ways in which knowledge production is always relational and always political.

Shifting from urban to rural research, after I became a parent, I began a long-term project on the politics of child socialization for citizenship in the aftermath of the Lebanese Civil War in 1994. I elected to do research in the village in which I was born. With my eight-year-old daughter, I entered the village as "one of them," welcomed back as a *mughtaribi* (native who migrated). The intimacy was intensified by the family relations embedded in the study, complicating my stance against the increased politicization of religion in Lebanon generally and in this Christian village in particular. In this relatively well-educated village, neighbors insisted on debating questions of gender, property, citizenship, globalization, and polarization of the populace in the aftermath of the Civil War. The state, especially the notion of the state, the law, colonialism, imperialism, politics, power, religion, positionality, selfhood—and differing philosophies of child rearing—was continually exposed, contested, engaged, and debated among my interlocutors in this place of my roots (Joseph 2021b, 2021c).

The Arab Region and the Conditionalities of Global Capitalism

The Arab region is a cauldron of wars, upheaval, dislocation, and everyday resistance, resilience, and survival. These conditions are impacting the material and social fabric of life and often escalating riches for a few and impoverishment for many. Sophisticated technologies are narrowly distributed and advanced modernities circulate among a pittance of cosmopolitan elites, while unabated and unaddressed environmental disasters escalate. Repressive regimes consolidate powers as popular uprising after uprising chases after visions of freedoms and social justice. Global political alignments produce conditions that benefit from political repression and economic exploitation of laboring men and women who work daily just to make it through to the next day. The burden of survival is increasingly being borne by women under the burdens of capitalist/patriarchal social orders (Darwish 2019; Mir 2019; Petras et al. 2013; Veltmeyer and Petras 2001). At the same time, uprisings abound in the region and people on the ground are organizing and sometimes creating alternatives at the small level. How did the region come to these structural conditions and material realities?

The cauldron is a recipe cooked up in the capitals of Western countries, regional regimes, benefiting local elites (politicians, religious leadership, and business elites), and racial and financial capital over the past several centuries. Economic and political reorganization has been taking place throughout the region, enforced through multipronged colonial and neocolonial strategies. From the period of the eighteenth and nineteenth centuries' Ottoman Empire, European countries undermined local industries and trade, extracting preferential treatment for their industries. The Sykes–Picot secret agreement of 1916 still "haunts the Middle East" (Wright 2016). The agreement, cooked up by French and British colonial regimes, with the consent of Italy and the Russian Empire, prepared for cutting the Ottoman Empire into the French and British subject states that was implemented after World War I. It mapped out artificial states, created boundaries where none had existed in order to invent, invest, and prop up regimes that could be subordinated to the will of European mandates. This set the stage for the creation of the state of Israel as a settler-colonial project in the center of the Arab region. Sykes–Picot and its aftermath were not about nation-building or establishing democratic governance. They were about control of trade routes, power, markets, labor, and resource extraction. These colonial, neocolonial, racial capitalist, and imperialist drivers have continued in different forms into the contemporary period (Dabashi 2012).

Settler colonialism in Algeria and Palestine promulgated further coercions (Fanon 1994; Khalidi 2017). Rentier economies, oil, and other mineral extractions by Western corporations and forced reorganization of agriculture throughout the region, from the nineteenth and twentieth centuries, left millions landless, jobless, and often homeless. By the twentieth century, many of the dislocated poured into the cities to create rings of slums and urban poverty. Urban population rose from close to 20 percent in 1960, to 50 percent in the early 1990s, and over 60 percent by 2020 (UN-Habitat 2020). Millions migrated from the region, spawning global diasporic communities, often facilitated by colonial policies structured to populate other colonies with productive labor. Postindependence regional states, with debt accruing to neocolonial Western powers, fell prey to financial restructuring and fiscal starvation, servicing loans to the International Monetary Fund and Western and international banks. The American and European military and industrial complex drove arms sales throughout the region. Regional militaries routinely trained in the United States and Europe (including USSR/Russia). Regional intelligence agencies coordinated activities with their donor countries.

Protests and resistance to authoritarian rule have been an ongoing political reality in the region (Bayat 2010; Evans and Phillips 2008; Khalidi 2017), though routinely squashed. Freedom of speech, the press, labor, business, and even movement were constrained by ever-more-sophisticated imported technologies of surveillance, control, and incarceration (Rezk 2017). Persecution of opposition leaders and torture techniques circulated throughout the region, schooled by masters of interrogation and intimidation in military training programs gifted by donor countries (Aboueldahab 2017).

For decades the United States, Russia/USSR, Israel, France, England, and other countries have propped up authoritarian regimes in the region (Posusney and Angrist 2005; Pratt 2006). The American and British governments directed the coup in Iran in 1953, engineered by the American CIA officer, Kermit Roosevelt. These same powers were involved in all sides of the Lebanese Civil War from 1975 to 1990, which led to the killing of 200,000 people, displacing 1 million—a quarter of the population (El-Husseini 2012; Fisk 2002)—and producing profound and enduring class and gender effects (Elmorally 2017). Israeli invasions, attacks, and a prolonged occupation in the South of the country crushed much of the Lebanese economy and its people. The Syrian army, initially invited by the Lebanese government in 1975, exerted political influence in the affairs of the country for decades even after the withdrawal of its troops from Lebanon in 2005. Western states propped up both sides of the Iran/Iraq war (1980–89), leaving a legacy of 1 million killed, 1.5 million wounded, and 2 million refugees (Walker 2016). The 11 September 2001 attack on the United States offered an opportunity for the George W. Bush Plan to be launched. It was an effort to break up Middle Eastern countries, create enough chaos and disruption to foster regime change, and control oil production in the region (Beauchamp 2015). The Bush War on Terror (including the war on Afghanistan 2001 and on Iraq 2003) left the region in disarray, with escalated or newly invented sectarian conflicts, intensified internal disruptions, and weakened governments. The war in Iraq in particular was a watershed moment for neocolonial and neoliberal strategic interventions to restructure the Arab region. Resistance to colonial interventions in the region as well as uprisings against social injustice, nevertheless, have been consistent and multifaceted.

The 2011 Arab popular uprisings caught the world by surprise. The repressions, supported by both regional and global powers, that followed were not surprising. The massive uprising in Lebanon in 2019 gave hope once again to progressive reform in the region, only to be starved by corrupted political leaders, collapsed banks, the global novel coronavirus pandemic, and the 4 August 2020 Beirut port explosion. Lebanon is regarded as one of the worst financial collapses of a country since the nineteenth century (World Bank 2021). In tandem, Israel's expansion of its settler project; its attacks on Gaza in 2000, 2004, 2005, 2006, 2008–09, 2014, 2021, and virtually every year; and its successive building of illegal settlements dispossessing Palestinians of their lands have escalated the economic, social, and political strangulation of the Palestinians. International responses have ignored the regional/global dynamics that produce and sustain these conditions. They offer humanitarian aid as the bridge to developmentalism—the neoliberal template for solutions.

Flawed and inadequate in their own terms, humanitarianism and neoliberal developmentalism have presumed that the individual is the generator of economic action, ignoring the centuries-old history of intervention by the very capitals orchestrating humanitarian aid. The continued fighting into the second decade of the twenty-first century in Iraq, Syria, Libya, and Yemen is not civil war, and the continued war against the Palestinian people is not a struggle between two nations, it is rather an expansion of a settler-colonial project. These violent incursions into the region are contemporary manifestations of global capital, global markets, and global powers capturing regional resources. They mutually constitute regional authoritarian, patriarchal, oligarchic regimes that serve the select few and impoverish millions. Those incursions have had deadly material consequences.

Realities, Conditionalities, and Knowledge Production

There Are No Civil Wars under Global Capitalism

The cauldron of wars in the Arab region, for decades, has taken a heavy toll in human life. Total violent death toll in Iraq since the American invasion in 2003 is estimated at anywhere between 500,000 (Bump 2018) and 2.4 million (Benjamin and Davis 2018). The "coalition of the willing" against Iraq, led by the United States, including the United Kingdom, Australia, and Poland, enlisted 48 countries (mostly small countries that offered nominal assistance).

In the Syrian crisis since 2011, about 5.6 million people have left Syria; over 6.6 million have become refugees in their own country; 2.98 million are in besieged areas (UNHCR 2018); and over 585,000 have been killed (Syrian Observatory for Human Rights 2020). It is a conflict driven by regional and global armaments, soldiers, money, and international and regional political designs. In Yemen since 2011, around 250,000 have been killed in what the United Nations has called the worst humanitarian disaster globally (Amnesty International 2015). The war on Yemen is driven by Saudi Arabia, supported by the United States and the United Kingdom.

Records of the United Nations Relief and Works Agency (UNRWA) reported in 2019 that the total number of Palestinian refugees was around 5.6 million, 28.4 percent of whom live in 58 camps (ten in Jordan, nine in Syria, twelve in Lebanon, 19 in the West Bank, and eight in the Gaza Strip). Estimates, however, indicated that the number of refugees is much higher, since many of them are not registered. The number of Palestinians killed since the Nakba in 1948 has reached one hundred thousand. There have been more than 1 million cases of Palestinian political detentions in Israel since 1967. The settler-colonial project to control Palestinian land and substitute Palestinians by settlers is continuing violently. More than 2,000 were killed in 2014 during the Israeli attack on Gaza. The proportion of Israeli settlers to Palestinian population in the West Bank is about 23 settlers per 100 Palestinians. It is the highest in Jerusalem Governorate, where there are 70 settlers per 100 Palestinians (PCBS 2020). Most governments of the world consider these Israeli settlements on Palestinian land as illegal. The strategy of slow death, strangulation, and territorial theft is no less brutal for its being strategically stretched over decades, supported actively by the United States and by the silence or meek admonitions of some other states.

The Carnegie Endowment reports that "of the 60 million displaced people worldwide, close to 40 percent originate from the Arab region, mainly Syria and Palestine" (Carnegie Endowment 2018). The wars, displacements, and material have wrought havoc in the Arab region in the past decades—layered upon centuries of colonial extraction and repression. States in the Arab region, supported usually by Western partners, have shored up their machinery of control and repression. Human rights violations, suppression of the press, and intrusions into the production of knowledge are often met with external silence, despite the frequent internal resistance. The 2008, the 2011, and the 2019 revolts and uprisings in the region manifest a population growing increasingly restless. Among these has been a strong women's movement and women's active engagement in every uprising from Tunisia, to Egypt, to Bahrain, to Lebanon (Hafez 2019; Stephan and Charrad 2020).

Wealth Disparities, Labor, and Education in the Arab Region

The Middle East in general (and the Arab region in particular) has the highest income inequality in the world. Alvaredo, Assouad, and Piketty (2018) found that the top 10 percent of income earners in the Middle East garner 64 percent of the region's income. In Western Europe, the top 10 percent garner 37 percent, in the United States it is 47 percent, while in Brazil it is 55 percent, and in South Africa it is 62 percent (Alvaredo et al. 2018). In another striking calculation, the authors found that the Arab Gulf countries, which account for only 15 percent of the population of the Middle East, garnered almost 50 percent of the total income of that region. The labor force in these Gulf countries includes up to 65 to 90 percent foreign workers (Qatar having the highest percentage), largely poorly paid, poorly housed, and uninsured, with no job security.

Rami G. Khouri (2019) estimates that 250 million of the 400 million people in the Arab region are poor or vulnerable—that is almost two-thirds of the total population. This makes the Arab region the world's most unequal region. Khouri predicts that this level of mass poverty at one generational level will continue in the same families for a number of generations—with living standards continuing to decline.

The Middle East and North African populations will double between 2000 and 2050. Half of the region's countries will have population increases of 50 percent or more between 2015 and 2050. Some countries (Iraq, Sudan, and Palestine) will double their population during that period (UNICEF 2019). The Arab Development Portal (2019) indicates that the Arab region has the third highest adolescent birth rate in the world. The same report finds that the Arab region has the highest youth unemployment rate in the world, averaging 26 percent. The world average youth unemployment is 12 percent (2019). Nader Kabbani (2019) reports that unemployment among youth in the Middle East and North Africa has been the highest in the world for over a quarter of a century. Youth unemployment in the region reached a high point of 30 percent in 2017, pushing them into "waithood"—waiting for jobs, marriage, homeownership, and adulthood. Unemployment among young women in the Arab region, according to UNICEF, is 39 percent—the highest in the world. Their low labor force participation (UNICEF 2019) is reinforced by modern patriarchies, upheld by authoritarian regimes, and propped up by global capitalism.

UNICEF (2019) reported that 37 percent of the youth in the Middle East and North Africa live in fragile and conflict-ridden states; 15 million school-age children are out of school (11 percent of primary schoolgirls and 9 percent of primary schoolboys; 18 percent of secondary schoolgirls, and 12 percent of secondary schoolboys). This is striking as the population of the MENA region will double before 2050 by tens of millions (an increase of 60 million in Egypt alone). Those 24 years and younger are already 50 percent of the population and will increase.

These structural conditions are linked to histories and recent iterations of colonialism, neocolonialism, imperialism, global capitalism, and the ongoing interventions of global powers in Arab regional affairs, with the complicity and cooperation of local autocrats. Many of these structural conditions are not unique to the Arab region but shared globally under the reach of racial capitalism.

These conditions structure the "field" in which the scholars in this volume have carried out their research. While this introduction focuses on the global histories of these conditionalities, the chapters to come examine the specific ways in which local conditions and structures are always in conversation with the global. Geopolitical power dynamics, global capital, and imperialism interact with local patriarchies, state formations, corruption, religious practices, authoritarian systems of governance, and the like on the ground. Authors in the chapters to come take on the specificities of the locales and address the ways these structures impact their field sites and their experiences. The connections between global and local conditionalities are central to understanding the production of knowledge on women and gender in the Arab region.

Fieldwork in Precarity

Under such conditions, what does it mean to carry out engaged gender research? What are the politics of engaged gender research? More precisely, what are the experiences of women carrying out field research in their native countries, with an eye toward a more just tomorrow? Material conditions created by colonialism, imperialism, capitalism, neoliberalism, and patriarchy are reproduced in new forms and structures. They set the stage for inequalities across the region, including gender inequalities. The social totality of the conditions under which people live and the power structures led and fed by colonialism, imperialism, and global capitalism create conditions of structural inequality in the region. They also shape the conditions under which knowledge is produced, circulated, and consumed.

The authors of an edited special issue of the *Contemporary Levant* journal titled "Ethnography as Knowledge in the Arab Region" (2017) offer a template for situating knowledge production under such local structural conditions. They focus attention on the affective elements and the embodiment of knowledge. They make the sensory, embodied, and emotive aspects of fieldwork relevant to knowledge production. The authors use "the term 'overbearing' to characterize the weight of seemingly unmoving and non-negotiable circumstances and forces" (Kanafani and Sawaf 2017, 4).

This "overbearing" context is evident in the various ways in which the authors of the politics of engaged gender research in this volume constantly navigate and negotiate their fieldwork experience. These authors devise new strategies to address specific circumstances and circumvent existing theoretical and ideological frameworks that hinder their ability to produce knowledge as they see it. Their work challenges dominant discourses including those within well-defined academic and research institutions in the region.

Engaged research recognizes that few phenomena are isolated and unchanging. It focuses on the interconnectedness of local/regional/global contexts, the fluidity of factors, the constructedness of categories of analysis, the intersectionality of those constructed categories, and the power of human agency. Engaged research recognizes the reality that the Arab region is a nexus of global interventions and transformations, many of which are not exclusive to the Arab region. It contextualizes the present within the conditionalities inherited from that history. It accounts for a century of wars on the region; violent and coercive extraction of the region's resources and labor; massive migrations and movements of peoples; imposed political boundaries, regimes, and financial restructuring; external support for authoritarian, totalitarian, dictatorial, or military regimes or kingdoms; internally corrupt political classes; and global development goals that often function to reproduce structural inequalities. It examines and connects histories of resistance and human agencies to current practices, beliefs, and challenges to these structural powers.

Engaged gender research is feminist research that critically analyzes the historical, political, economic, and social contexts of the research topic with commitment for socioeconomic justice. Engaged gender research is feminist research that lays the foundation for a more just tomorrow. Engaged gender research questions the presumptions of Arab exceptionalism (Harik 2006), challenges liberal feminisms (Abu-Lughod 2013), and critiques neoliberal developmentalism (CDS 2015). The presumptions of those approaches frame the Arab region as developmentally "delayed," caught in centuries-old religious, political, gender, and cultural dynamics. Such arguments for the exceptionalism of the Arab region typically target gender relations and women's status as prime evidence (or the cause) of the region's nonsynchronicity with "modernity" (Malak and Salem 2015). The authors of this volume argue that the conditionalities of the Arab region are relatively historically new, modern conditions generated from global as well as regional factors and, at times, stabilized for the global and regional benefits of corporate capitalist and political interests. They bring critical feminist methodologies to bear on local structural conditions.

Researching Women and Gender in the Arab Region: Feminist Methodologies

Feminist ethnographic methodologies connect the global to the local. Such approaches ask questions about women's positionality and location in the structures, activities, ideas, and events. They consider how gender is defined locally and how it is acted on and reproduced. They pay attention to how power runs through understandings of gender and gender relations and the question of agency. Feminist ethnographers reflect on their own positionality in relation to the different stages of knowledge production, from conceptualizing research questions, to the subjects of research, to specific methods, and to analysis and representation.

Feminist approaches for studying the Arab region, particularly in the twentieth century, have been dominated by liberal feminism that focuses on the appearances of gender inequalities and ignores the structural basis within which these and other inequalities exist and are shaped. The hegemony of liberal feminist frameworks has been driven by international funding agencies and by positivist academic trainings that singled out cultural factors as the primary determinant of Arab women's life conditions and gender inequalities. The focus on the liberal women's rights approach set aside the examination of the gender implications of socioeconomic and political structures. More importantly it ignored the contributions of critical feminist epistemology.

Since the 1980s, critical feminist perspectives have rejected the objectivist positivist stance and the dichotomy it creates between the knower and the known. Critical feminism has developed approaches for paying attention to the positionality of the researcher and the importance of reflexivity throughout the research process. Standpoint theory asserts that subjects occupy certain social positions and are located in particular time and place that constitute their particular perspective as the object of study (Haraway 1988; Hartsock 1983, 1985). For Hartsock, a standpoint is "achieved rather than obvious, a mediated rather than immediate understanding" (1985, 132). Hartsock adopts Marx's historical materialist approach based on mapping out the structural conditions at the level of the mode of production—the circumstances under which people meet their daily needs for food, clothing, and shelter. Like many other Marxist feminists, Hartsock criticizes Marxists' applications of the method of historical materialism for privileging the standpoint of the worker and ignoring the most fundamental site of production, those places where the satisfaction of people's needs is directly produced, particularly the domestic setting. She argues that in wage work as well as in the home, women's work keeps them involved in a world of directly meeting needs "in concrete, many-qualitied, changing material processes" (1985, 235). Himani Bannerji (2016), like Hartsock, adopts a Marxist historical materialism and examines the relation between capitalism and violence against women by addressing the methods that expose the connection between social relations and ideologies. She asserts that "what constitutes 'proof' in any social inquiry cannot be based on objectivist positivist stance" (Bannerji 2016, 7).

Rachel Sharp argues that "ethnography reinforces ontological and epistemological social atomism: the atoms of social life are individuals; their beliefs, intentions, assumptions, and actions form both the starting point of, and dictate the explanatory procedures for, grasping social reality" (1982, 49). This "methodological individualism … leads to the neglect of other dimensions of social reality, and the assumption is sometimes made that only individuals really exist; they construct their own reality" (Sharp 1982, 49). Structured patterns of social relations preexist the individual and generate specific forms of social consciousness. She calls for going beyond the observable realities and categorical separations such as the analytical and ontological separation between politics and economics. She calls attention to knowledge of the structure of social totalities that are present but phenomenally absent from the surface structure of the everyday life (Sharp 1982). Ethnography is a political practice that requires knowledge of the fissures, ruptures, and contradictions in capitalism's mode of appearance that can guide political work. "Social forms and structures are reproduced or transformed through human agency," thus "concrete individuals can move beyond the world of appearances and discover their human creativity through working to produce a world in which essence and appearance are at one" (Sharp 1982, 60–61). The above feminist methodological approaches are rich with potential for approaching gender engaged research with critical eyes.

The current volume aims to bypass the assumptions and limitations of liberal feminism, by recognizing that fieldwork is highly sensitive to the political environment in which research is conducted. Engaged gender research is a politically charged research arena. When the fieldworker is a native of the society—and a native woman—political sensibilities intensify for the fieldworker and for the field site. She is potentially able to uncover the structural conditions under the everyday appearance. This volume addresses the politics of engaged gender research from the direct experiences of women scholars carrying out such research in their native countries. The authors deploy various methodologies to capture the oppression of women that is systematic and structurally rooted in global and local conditions of capitalism, colonialism, neoliberalism, patriarchy, and racism.

Researchers in the Field: Complexity and Negotiation

The process of knowledge production has always been a political project deeply connected to power struggles in a society. While the founding of anthropology and anthropological field methods is tied to colonialism, anthropologists began questioning this legacy in the 1970s and worked to establish principles of research. The American Anthropological Association drafted codes of ethics or what was then called Principles of Professional Responsibility (1971) as a result of deeply problematic practices by anthropologists and their involvement in US foreign policy (Hill 1987). The current code of ethics (AAA 2012) continues to be debated, though still guiding generations of anthropologists. While not all of the researchers in this volume are anthropologists, most utilize feminist ethnography fieldwork methodologies that has its roots in anthropology.

The 1980s and 1990s birthed reflexive anthropology as an attempt to consider the implications of the anthropologist's positioning on the knowledge being produced (Robertson 2002). The book *Arab Women in the Field: Studying Your Own Society*, coedited by Soraya Altorki and Camillia El-Solh (1988), was a reflection of that moment. The editors explain that "production of knowledge and the validity of its content are intimately connected with the social position of its producer" (1988, 3). Borrowing from Dwyer (1982), the editors explain that the producer is not only an individual but also a set of cultural and social interests basically connected to structural power relations within and among the worlds the researcher and the subjects inhabit. Authors in the book *Arab Women in the Field* (including one of this volume's editors) grapple with various challenges to conducting research in their own societies, looking at questions of gender and indigeneity as well as being insiders or outsiders. They raise concerns about the process of knowledge production, about the researcher's experience within the field and privileging the sensory, emotive, and analytical or internal dialogue of the researcher.

Frameworks in the Field

Research questions on women and gender in the Arab region, as discussed above, often originate from culturalist and orientalist approaches, focusing on culture as the primary determinant of gender dynamics. Authors in this volume reconsider these approaches from within the field experiences. Driven by the hegemonic framework of women's rights, Souad Eddouada initially went into the field with the aim of studying an "unprecedented partnership" among Moroccan urban women's rights feminists and rural land rights activists (*sulāliyāt*). Given that she had first met the land rights activists inside the offices of various urban feminist NGOs, she assumed that her project would document the terms of the urban–rural partnership and the collaboration among the different activist groups. Further fieldwork revealed tensions, disputes, and power dynamics that kept affirming the need to change the scope of her research. She shifted from a focus on the collaboration and partnership to a study exploring the perspective of *sulāliyāt* outside of that urban–rural partnership. Eddouada's attentiveness to her research participants' narratives led her to question the liberal framework of "women's rights" and its predominant focus on gender discrimination. She writes, "the range of themes that stand out in particular in *sulāliyāt* narratives are the privatization and commodification of communal land, the corruption and lack of transparency surrounding economic and political alliances, and the abuse of power—especially in the rural and semi-urban margins of the country" (52). The liberal framework that focuses on gender discrimination as separate from class and racial discrimination affects the depoliticization of gender research in the Arab region. Sara Ababneh reflects on this process, describing her chapter in this volume as a chapter "about the struggles of doing research while attempting to say no to depoliticized gender and the search for what a more radical form of gender studies which takes seriously intersectionality and communal struggles against structural oppression, could look like" (120). Rania Jawad looks at how "political and ethical commitment shape[d] how researchers prioritize what is highlighted in one's context of knowledge production" (88) by reflecting on her own research experience and how she became more aware of her positionality and framing as the research project unfolded.

Insider/Outsider Positionality and Relationships in the Field

Researchers in this volume see and grapple with some of the issues raised by the reflexive turn in anthropology. They reflect on their identities as evolving and relational as opposed to what Robertson has called "ready to wear" products of an identity politics that has been endemic to American universities (Robertson 2002, 788). Robertson questions the assumption that "positionality" is a condition of reflexivity. One problem is the way identity becomes instrumentalized either as an assumed connection point with those one is researching or as a gate opener into the subjects of research. Another problem manifests when researchers assume they can reduce processes of identification and relationality to a couple of paragraphs in the methodology section that states one's identity vis-à-vis the subjects of the research, rather than grappling with how identity and relationality impact the knowledge being produced.

The authors in this volume address the ways their identities were perceived and negotiated and how they reflected on the process of identification throughout their research projects. As Robertson (2002) reaffirms, these interactions are laden with power but not necessarily based on preconceived assumptions about identity politics. All those involved are changed by research interactions in varying ways. Researchers in this book deconstruct the notion that they occupy predetermined insider or outsider positionalities. Similar to Al-Hardan, they question the presumed dichotomy of insider/outsider as "it ignores the political agency of actors in the community" (2014, 65) in which research is carried out and "overlooks the ways in which they position the researcher as an insider and as an outsider, and how this positioning takes place within the context of the coloniality of the overarching historical and political parameters of the numerous encounters that come to constitute our research" (Al-Hardan 2014, 65). Our authors show instead how these are often negotiated and renegotiated in the context of fieldwork. In her chapter Sarah Shaer reflects on the questions around identity and relationship in the field experience. She posits "the fieldwork encounter as familiar rather than strange and the ways in which [her] personal investments and histories, some of which [she] shared with [her] interlocutors, came to shape on what it meant for [her] to be 'in the field'" (189–90). Rather than assuming that being Jordanian will mean easier access and trust to Jordanian activists, or being Sunni Iraqi means harder access to Shi'a Iraqi women, the contributors to this volume explore how these social identities are constructed and how they shift in the field based in relationality, larger geopolitical dynamics, and the strategies used to maneuver.

Ilham Makki Hammadi considers looking like an outsider when conducting fieldwork with Shi'a women even though she is an indigenous researcher. The current political and historical dynamics in Iraq made her interest in producing this knowledge dubious and mistrusted. At the same time, she recounts various examples where these assumed identifications broke down and where expressing sympathy or building on commonality provided her with rich information and deeper trust. Kholoud al-Ajarma examines how her identities shaped her fieldwork experiences and how her fieldwork experiences transformed her identities and affects. She attempted to chart how she translates, or even adapts, her state of being and multiple identities within different field sites, in Palestine, Chile, Morocco, and Saudi Arabia. She is acutely aware of the differences between how she understood herself and how some of her identities or aspects of her identities were being received in a specific field site location. The perception of her identity and her ability to continue to perform it in the ways expected created openings or closures for her experiences in the field. While being Palestinian in Chile and Morocco enabled opening experiences and sentiments of immediate solidarity, it generated questioning for Al-Ajarma around her own identity and emotional burdens.

The webs of relationships that the researchers were involved in figured heavily in their ability to access their field site and be trusted by those they interviewed. Ababneh mentioned her close ties to two activist leaders whom she knew previously from work on Palestine that mediated her access to other activists. One of them set up meetings and on several occasions actually accompanied Ababneh to the field. "By not only introducing me to them, but also accompanying me to the interviews, Nadim gave me access not just to the trust of many participants but also to interviews that I could not have conducted on my own" (126). While Ababneh herself is Jordanian, these two activist friends are Palestinian Jordanian—a distinction with a difference in Jordan. It was these Palestinian activists who helped her gain access to Jordanian *Hirak* (labor movement) members and not necessarily her common identity with the *Hirak* activists. It is those relations rather than a perception of a static and prefigured identity formation that allowed for these exchanges and the richness of the data that she was able to gather.

Sociopolitical dynamics influence understandings of the personal and professional and how one is situated while conducting fieldwork. Rawan Ibrahim found that her experience as a Western-educated binational female has been shaped by a complex web of interrelated contextual layers. These involved both cultural context and the political and practice dynamics in the child welfare system and intersected with a number of personal and professional factors. Ibrahim speaks about the challenges she faced as a Palestinian Jordanian and Christian woman looking into a particularly sensitive topic: that of unmarried women in Jordan. She found that the critical elements of the Jordanian culture that affected her fieldwork experience were patriarchy and tribalism. Men dominated decision-making positions and were leery of a single outspoken woman and tribal affiliation provided more access. As such, she had to place more focus on her professional relationships with NGOs that she had so meticulously cultivated and think and rethink what she said and how she dressed to ensure she was taken seriously.

Discussions or claims about affects, emotions, and one's "personal" life circumstances are usually hushed or considered too reflective, particularly for women. In the efforts to ensure that women are taken seriously as researchers, discussions about personal lives are often considered inappropriate or distracting. Challenges one faced were considered personal or a specific case. They were rarely articulated among the list of challenges researchers faced in the field. Ababneh writes, "My experiences with the General Intelligence Department (GID), coupled with what happened to my friend whose children the GID had threatened, also made me realize that I was more vulnerable as a woman doing this type of research, not only in my individual capacity as a woman but precisely in my social capacity as a mother and wife" (132). Because women in Jordan do not pass their nationality to their foreign husbands and their children, Ababneh was hyperaware of the increased vulnerability this condition placed on her and her ability to conduct research about an activist movement that was rising up against the government and its policies. It was her gendered positionality, reflected in her own personal circumstance, that was a limitation and that also illuminated underlying structural and legal threats to research.

For Rania Jawad, motherhood intertwined with other structural conditions. She reflects on the constellation of settler-colonial constraints, neoliberalization of higher education, and the labor of parenting as constitutive of her field research in the place where she lived and worked. They were also parts of her life to experience and navigate. The interweaving of structural factors and her daily lived experience shaped how she conducted research and how she understood her research context "as a site of collective experiences, changing terrains, multiple labors, and affinities."

Ababneh and Jawad both speak to their motherhood as an important aspect of the fieldwork. Pregnancy was a bodily impediment at times as they both felt tired and exhausted from the physical labor required of them for their full participation and participant observation in their field. For Ababneh, it also generated fear. She writes, "I found that I was far less willing to take risks than I would have liked to take. At any sign of potential violence (during protests) I left the scene quickly. I was constantly checking where thugs were and whether their stones would reach me" (121). On the other hand, other researchers found that their single and motherless status made them at times illegible and at times an obstacle to relatability (Al-Ajarma, Ibrahim, Makki Hammadi).

Politics and Ethics of Doing Research and Questions of Accountability

Addressing issues of accountability in conducting research is laden with ethical dilemmas and questions. For whom and to whom is one accountable? How can accountability be achieved? The first principle of the Anthropology Code of Ethics that focuses on doing no harm emphasizes the importance of making an assessment as to whether the overall research or various aspects of it may impose some form of harm onto the individual participants in the research. While accountability is not only about harm, thinking of harm in the broadest of terms can be useful in thinking through some of these issues. Field researchers are urged to understand that this obligation supersedes the pursuit of knowledge.

Other scholars explore the ethical dilemmas that stem from the identity or positionality of the researcher. They examine ethical dilemmas emerging from larger structural factors that play a significant role in what constitutes a research topic or question to begin with, who is a research subject (interlocutors, informants), what methodological and epistemological frameworks are used, and the nature of the knowledge produced and who consumes/engages with/benefits from it.

Given the routinized notion of crisis that Ghassan Hage (2012) describes as the constantly shifting political context, researchers have to contest this terrain and constantly make calculated assessment of the conditions of life of research participants. "Where conflict and war situations are increasingly perceived as states in their own right rather than as transitional towards something else. As such they necessitate an alter-politics that comes from a space outside the existing unproductive and endless oppositions" (Hage 2012, 294–95). This recognition has further complicated ethical dilemmas, power relations, and accountability in knowledge production processes. Researchers' assessments are in constant dynamic flux, an "alter-politics" that looks at the situation in the field, their own investments (focus of their research and goals), and the knowledge that will be produced and shared.

In her chapter, Samar Kassis reflects on her personal experiences as a Palestinian woman researcher conducting anthropological research with Palestinian women ex-political prisoners who spent long sentences in Israeli colonial prisons. She focuses on their relationships and the ethical responsibilities toward the stories of these women and their experiences. Through her participation in sit-ins, she engaged with the women ex-political prisoners and their families on a personal level. Sitting under the tents where the protests were taking place situated her within an environment in which her relationships with these women were built on a mutual felt solidarity and trust under a colonial condition. She writes,

> A bond was built that far exceeded what I, as a researcher, could have created with these women. I became personally invested and attached to this community of women and to the Palestinian struggle as viewed from their position. My research made me committed to all aspects of the Palestinian prisoners' issues and causes, as well as with the women and their families personally. (108)

While conducting research, scholars need to consider the topic and population of their research and the degree to which these are entangled with the dominant power structures. Conducting research necessitates constant maneuvers and decisions around permits, access, confidentiality/anonymity, managing fear and raises the question of how these decisions are made. Is it possible to do any kind of risk assessment without the inclusion of research participants?

Safety concerns for researchers increases in conditions of ongoing war, occupation, and colonization. Jawad's ability to reach her research subjects to conduct interviews, to participate in conferences to speak about her research findings, or to attend the theatrical productions she was hoping to focus on was severely limited by the Israeli occupation and its various monitoring and surveilling strategies. Similarly, Kassis speaks to the brutality and inhumanity of life under the Israeli occupation that affects all Palestinians and ultimately shapes the research field in profound ways. She reckons with the impact of "the violent murders of Palestinians by Israeli soldiers at checkpoints, the constant arrests of Palestinians at roadblocks and from their homes, the demolition of Palestinian houses, the oppression that occurs in Israeli prison and interrogation centers, as well as all the types of extensive forms of humiliation and acts of injustice perpetrated against the indigenous Palestinian communities" (103). These ongoing daily realities also build on historical personal and collective aggression that impacts on the scholar's ability to conduct research and produce knowledge. Kassis brings a case in point—her two brothers had been jailed and tortured in Israeli prisons. She observes how "the deep intimacy with their cause and their sacrifice was not something [she] could leave in the space of the fieldwork" (103).

Doing fieldwork in a pottery village in Egypt that underwent a process of gentrification since 2008, Reeham Mourad speaks of her feelings of insecurity in the current conditions in Cairo. She writes, "Sometimes I felt insecure because of the different levels of the scrutiny spatially manifested on my way to the pottery village. My insecurities do not only come from the sense that the street is under constant surveillance, but also from my awareness of my being 'a stranger' in the context" (74). Saja Al Zoubi's research was severely limited in Syria as a result of the ongoing civil war. Working in rural communities interviewing women, she found herself facing dangerous situations regularly. She needed to hire local drivers who knew how to navigate the terrain. There were bombings at unexpected moments. She escaped local guest houses, finding out later that they had been bombed to pieces. Ilham Makki Hammadi had to navigate conducting research in a country ravished with occupation and a supposedly "postwar" context in Iraq. The Iraqi landscape has been hostile to researchers. Local researchers have borne the brunt of heightened conflicts on perceived identities that have been energized and propped up by the US-led occupation. Makki Hammadi speaks to the challenges she faced as a Sunni Iraqi woman researching Shi'a women who were studying in the Hawza. In many instances, Hawza officials gave her implicit and explicit threats regarding what she would publish.

Sexism in the Field

Several of the researchers speak explicitly to challenges in being taken seriously as researchers that stemmed from sexism. They experienced this not only in the field but also in the professional/collegial experience, from fellow researchers or professors. Al-Ajarma recalls an offhand comment made by a male academic about how her place should be in the kitchen, if she found Foucault difficult to understand. She reviews how some of these experiences in the field contradicted with her positioning of herself as an independent woman. Al-Ajarma may have adopted an understanding of independence prefigured in the neoliberal rational subject that is separate from familial or gender-based relationships or those that assume being independent means being able to do things on one's own. However, her autonomy may not circumvent structures of patriarchy inherent in these societies. As she traveled to Mecca, she found she had to ask her father to join her, as local regulations necessitated the presence of a male guardian for a woman under 45 years of age. She added, "Such encounters within a patriarchal structure profoundly conflicted with my understanding of my identity as an independent woman and, I must add, the restrictions on my mobility was part of my encounter with this patriarchal structure, resulting in inner tensions" (210).

While Al-Ajarma was invested in an image of herself as an independent woman, Ababneh reflected and questioned these assumptions about selfhood. Ababneh's father insisted on attending any meeting between her and the GID, inserting the personal in the professional. Ababneh writes, "It was this relational capacity (a member of a family) that my father sought to underline, and that I did not try to dispute, understanding that being seen as an 'individual' was far less advantageous for my case." While still operating within the patriarchal logic of the state and society, Ababneh recognized the potential for bargaining that may provide her with more spaces to maneuver around her research. In the end, her father's presence at the GID did not prevent her from being subject to a deeper line of questioning about her research. It is possible to think that it may have buffered what could have been an even harsher experience had she been seen as an "independent" woman.

Al Zoubi shares struggles with sexism in the field, particularly from her male coworkers or supervisors that tended to limit her ability to do her work or to forge alliances. "Do not waste your time and get married," Al Zoubi's professor advised her when she was preparing for her MA program in 2006. She also recalls frequent managers who created obstacles in front of female researchers or who would treat them as younger and unexperienced, devaluing the work they do and their authority.

Sexism is also connected to the devaluing of feminism and feminist methodologies. Al Zoubi's field of home economics was deemed as an unnecessary and irrelevant study given that it primarily focused on women and their experiences. On the other hand, it was seen as potentially dangerous as it disrupted "Arab family principles." Makki Hammadi's emphasis on feminist methodologies in her fieldwork experience was rejected by her professors while she was working on her PhD. She was warned not to challenge long-held cannons about the importance of quantitative research methods.

Ethical Dilemmas in the Field

Ababneh's chapter interrogates the role of fear in her fieldwork and the kinds of knowledge she wanted to produce. For Ababneh, the question of what she publishes and what kind of knowledge she produces arose early on in the course of doing fieldwork and in the form of questions or questioning by her interlocutors. Her encounter with the GID made her even more cognizant of the potential dangers of the interviews she was conducting. She refers to offering her interviewees the use of pseudonyms. They refused to use pseudonyms. Ababneh was still worried that perhaps they were miscalculating the potential dangers. Ababneh reflected on the risk of infantilizing her research participants—treating them as incapable of making their own decision regarding the risk to their lives. Engaging in conversations with the activists gave her a space to flush out these concerns and, in the end, respect the wishes of her interlocutors.

Jeffrey Sluka (2012) argues that it is possible to manage danger and to look toward research participants for strategies. "After all, for the research participants, these dangers are part and parcel of their 'normal' or everyday life which they have had no choice but to learn to adapt to" (Sluka 2012, 321). In this volume, Ababneh writes,

> I finally reached a conclusion while speaking to Mahdi al-Saafeen, one of the youth activists I interviewed extensively. Al-Saafeen argued that I needed to respect the agency of my participants. He continued that they were adults who knew the risks they were taking. I needed to respect their decision and not assume that I was more aware of their interest than they were themselves.

Thinking about the process of knowledge production as a collective rather than an individual process, Ababneh made the choice of including their names to give credit to their ideas and analysis in developing her arguments and analysis.

Speak with Whom? Publish What?

Sherine Hamdy (2017) raises questions about public anthropology, interrogating what kinds of publics an ethnographer engages. Within the context of political repression, wars, heavy bureaucracy, and tremendous economic upheaval, what risks does public ethnography entail and what possibilities are there for engaging with various publics? Hamdy explores the challenges of translation across divided audiences and the dilemmas that researchers face in producing knowledge in a deeply charged geopolitical context. Hamdy speaks of the ethnographer's illegitimacy, which can stem from many places, including the celebration of hard and positivist science and technology and dismissal of perceived softer fields of humanities and social sciences, the perception of the researchers' positionality in the field vis-à-vis the "subjects" of their study, and the investment that many researchers place on working with marginalized communities and speaking truth to power. Much of this gets negotiated in the field in terms of access and relationship—these perceptions open and close doors constantly. However, the knowledge produced through engaging publics also presents challenges that require constant navigation. These issues affected several of the researchers in this volume.

Hamdy's access to research subjects (patients) was restricted by doctors. The doctors seemed under the shadow of their middle- to upper-class performance of respectability politics and in many instances internalized colonialism (feeling ashamed that the patients, often poor and uneducated, would "represent" Egypt negatively). She received similar rebuke from Egyptian academics who also attacked her for tarnishing Egypt's reputation. She found that she had to not only present her arguments but also speak about what she is not arguing. She writes,

> My work argues against the received wisdom in the United States, Canada, Western Europe, and Australia that Islam is a religion that necessarily breeds authoritarianism, intolerance, misogyny, and violence and against the dominant view in Egypt that only the educated middle and upper classes can speak, lest the uneducated, illiterate, marginalized, peasant, or urban poor shame the nation, or all Arabs, or all Muslims. (Hamdy 2017, 294)

The tumultuous situation in Iraq like in other countries of the region gave Makki Hammadi, in this volume, pause to consider the implications of what she may publish. This was of concern in relation to her own safety and in relation to the safety of the women she interviewed. It raised questions about the kinds of knowledge she was invested in producing about a community that is perceived negatively and with suspicion in the region. Some level of censorship often translates to self-censorship. Often government offices require review to approve or censor publications. There may be political repercussions for publishing. Makki Hammadi, who was employed by the Ministry of Education, and Al Zoubi, who worked for a governmental research center, worried about their jobs, their ability to continue doing research and produce knowledge, and their access to opportunities for their own ongoing professional development.

Ababneh had to negotiate expectations by her interlocutors about what she would be willing to publish, her own fears and worries for herself as well as them, and the ethics of producing knowledge. She did undergo an hour and a half interrogation at the GID to assess whether she posed any threat. The conversation was not conducted under duress. Nonetheless, the experience instilled in Ababneh a stronger sense of being surveilled and followed. As the activists of the *Hirak* continued to fight, they asked her whether she would be able or willing to publish all that they said to her. "We are not adhering to any red lines (*khutut hamra'*), will you adhere to any?" (129) Ababneh knew that she was not "willing to go as far as they had gone." Nonetheless, she was called for an interview about her research by the director of the GID (the secret police).

The Politics of Engaged Gender Research

Each scholar in this volume has faced the structural conditions bequeathed by global histories and local dynamics. Each has made choices about fieldwork relationalities. Each has confronted how to protect their interlocutors and what data can be published. Each has taken account of power, class, gender, and technologies of surveillance and control. Each has wrestled with her own positionality in her native "field." Each has reflected on the responsibilities for the production of knowledge under the conditions they inherited and the possibilities for knowledge production for future generations. It is with the eye toward tomorrow that they reckon with today and push the boundaries of what is known, what is knowable, and what needs to be known. It is this unrelenting engagement, this commitment, this refusal to not know what can be known. It is the insistence on the rigorous attention to the local in the context of its histories that invents spaces for innovative knowledge that is productive of possible futures. It is the insistent centering of the questions of gender and agency within the structural conditions of power, of history, of locality, of globality that will remake our understandings of the past and present and open pathways for different kinds of futures.

Bibliography

AAA (American Anthropological Association). 1971. "Past AAA Statement on Ethics: Principles of Professional Responsibility." https://www.americananthro.org/ParticipateAndAdvocate/Content.aspx?ItemNumber=1656.

AAA (American Anthropological Association). 2012. "AAA Statement on Ethics: Principles of Professional Responsibility." https://www.americananthro.org/LearnAndTeach/Content.aspx?ItemNumber=22869&navItemNumber=652.

Aboueldahab, Noha. 2017. *Transitional Justice and the Prosecution of Political Leaders in the Arab Region: A Comparative Study of Egypt, Libya, Tunisia, and Yemen.* London: Bloomsbury.

Abu-Lughod, Lila. 1990. "Anthropology's Orient: The Boundaries of Theory on the Arab World." In *Theory, Politics, and the Arab World: Critical Responses*, edited by Hisham Sharabi, 81–132. London: Routledge.

Abu-Lughod, Lila. 2001. "Orientalism and Middle East Feminist Studies." *Feminist Studies* 27 (1): 101–13.

Abu-Lughod, Lila. 2013. *Do Muslim Women Need Saving*? Cambridge, MA: Harvard University Press.

Alfares, Dalal, Dina El Khawaga, Hanane Darhour, Islah Jad, and Nermin Allam. 2020. "Teaching Gender and Women's Studies in the Middle East." *Al-Fanar Media: Covering Education, Research and Culture*, 20 October 2020. https://www.al-fanarmedia.org/2020/10/teaching-gender-womens-studies-in-the-middle-east/, accessed 16 December 2021.

Al-Hardan, Anaheed. 2014. "Decolonizing Research on Palestinians: Towards Critical Epistemologies and Research Practices." *Qualitative Inquiry* 20 (1): 61–71.

Altorki, Soraya, and Camillia Fawzi El-Solh. 1988. *Arab Women in the Field: Studying Your Own Society*. Syracuse, NY: Syracuse University Press.

Alvaredo, Facundo, Lydia Assouad, and Thomas Piketty. 2018. "Inequality in the Middle East." *Vox EU*, 13 August 2018. https://voxeu.org/article/inequality-middle-east, accessed 16 December 2021.

Amnesty International. 2015 "Yemen War: No End in Sight." https://www.amnesty.org/en/latest/news/2015/09/yemen-the-forgotten-war/, accessed 16 December 2021.

Arab Development Portal. 2019. *Youth in the Arab Region*. New York: United Nations Development Programme.

Bannerji, Himani. 2016. "Patriarchy in the Era of Neoliberalism: The Case of India." *Social Scientist* 44, nos. 3/4 (March–April): 3–27.

Bayat, Asef. 2010. *Life as Politics: How Ordinary People Change the Middle East*. Stanford, CA: Stanford University Press.

Beauchamp, Zach. 2015. "Yes, Bush Helped Create ISIS—and Set Up the Middle East for a Generation of Chaos." *Vox*, 2 June 2015. https://www.vox.com/2015/6/2/8703059/bush-isis-middle-east, accessed 16 December 2021.

Benjamin, Medea, and Nicolas Davies. 2018. "The Staggering Death Toll in Iraq." *Salon*, 19 March 2018. https://www.salon.com/2018/03/19/the-staggering-death-toll-in-iraq_partner/, accessed 16 December 2021.

Bump, Philip. 2018. "15 Years after the Iraq War Began, the Death Toll Is Still Murky." *Washington Post*, 20 March 2018. https://www.washingtonpost.com/news/politics/wp/2018/03/20/15-years-after-it-began-the-death-toll-from-the-iraq-war-is-still-murky/, accessed 16 December 2021.

Carnegie Endowment. 2018. "Refugee Crises in the Arab World." https://carnegieendowment.org/2018/10/18/refugee-crises-in-arab-world-pub-77522, accessed 16 December 2021.

"Casualties of Mideast Wars." *Los Angeles Times*, 28 February 1991. https://www.latimes.com/archives/la-xpm-1991-03-08-mn-2592-story.html, accessed 16 December 2021.

CDS (Center for Development Studies). 2015. *Critical Readings of Development under Colonialism: Towards a Political Economy for Liberation in the Occupied Palestinian Territories*. Birzeit, Palestine: CDS.

Dabashi, Hamid. 2012. *The Arab Spring: The End of Postcolonialism*. London: Zed Books.

Darwish, Mahmoud. 2019. *Palestine as Metaphor*. Northampton, MA: Interlink Books.

Deeb, Lara, and Jessica Winegar. 2012. "Anthropologies of Arab-Majority Societies." *Annual Review of Anthropology* 41: 537–58.

Dwyer, Kevin. 1982. *Moroccan Dialogues: Anthropology in Question*. Baltimore, MD: John Hopkins Press.

El-Husseini, Rola. 2012. *Pax Syriana: Elite Politics in Post War Lebanon*. Syracuse, NY: Syracuse University Press.

Elmorally, Reham. 2017. *Gender Dynamics during and after the Lebanese Civil War, 1975–1990. A Marxist Feminist Perspective*. Norderstedt, Germany: Grin.

Elsadda, Hoda. 2004. "Women in the Arab World: Reading against the Grain of Culturalism." *Internationale Politik und Gesellschaft* 4: 41–53.

El Said, Maha, Lena Meari, and Nicola Pratt. 2015. *Rethinking Gender in Revolutions and Resistance: Lessons from the Arab World*. London: Zed Books.

Evans, Martin, and John Phillips. 2008. *Algeria: Anger of the Dispossessed*. New Haven, CT: Yale University Press.

Fanon, Franz. 1994. *A Dying Colonialism*. New York: Grove Press.

Fisk, Robert. 2002. *Pity the Nation: The Abduction of Lebanon*. New York: Nation Books.

Hafez, Sherine. 2019. *Women of the Midan: The Untold Stories of Egypt's Revolutionaries*. Bloomington: Indiana University Press.

Hage, Ghassan. 2012. "Critical Anthropological Thought and the Radical Political Imaginary Today." *Critique of Anthropology* 32 (3): 285–308.

Hamdy, Sherine. 2017. "How Publics Shape Ethnographers: Translating across Divided Audiences." In *If Truth Be Told: The Politics of Public Ethnography*, edited by Didier Fassin, 287–309. Durham, NC: Duke University Press.

Haraway, Donna. 1988. "Situated Knowledges: The Science Question in Feminism and the Privilege of Partial Perspective." *Feminist Studies* 14, no. 3 (Autumn): 575–99.

Harik, Iliya. 2006. "Democracy, 'Arab Exceptionalism,' and Social Science." *Middle East Journal* 60, no. 4 (Autumn): 664–84.

Hartsock, Nancy. 1983. "The Feminist Standpoint: Developing the Ground for a Specifically Feminist Historical Materialism." In *Discovering Reality*, edited by S. Harding and M. B. Hintikka, 283–310. Springer, Dordrecht, Holland: Springer.

Hartsock, Nancy. 1985. *Money, Sex, and Power: Toward a Feminist Historical Materialism*. Boston, MA: Northeastern.

Hill, James N. 1987. "The Committee on Ethics: Past, Present, and Future." In *Handbook on Ethical Issues in Anthropology*, edited by Joan Cassell and Sue-Ellen Jacobs. American Anthropological Association. https://www.americananthro.org/LearnAndTeach/Content.aspx?ItemNumber=12911&RDtoken=19713&userID=5089&navItemNumber=731.

Joseph, Suad. 1988. "Feminization, Familism, Self and Politics: Research as a Mughtaribi." In *Arab Women in the Field: Studying Your Own Society*, edited by Soraya Altorki and Camillia F. Solh, 25–47. Syracuse, NY: Syracuse University Press.

Joseph, Suad. 1990. "Working the Law: A Lebanese Working Class Case." In *The Politics of Law in the Middle East*, edited by Daisy Dwyer, 143–60. South Hadley, MA: J.F. Bergin.

Joseph, Suad. 1993. "Fieldwork and Psychosocial Dynamics of Personhood." *Frontiers* 13 (3): 9–32.

Joseph, Suad. 1995. "Selfhood and Ethnographic Writing." *Bahithat* 2 (Fall): 141–53.

Joseph, Suad. 1996. "Relationality and Ethnographic Subjectivity: Key Informants and Construction of Personhood in Fieldwork." In *Feminist Dilemmas in Fieldwork*, edited by Diane Wolf, 107–21. Boulder, CO: Westview Press.

Joseph, Suad. 2021a. "Brothers and Sisters, Husbands and Wives: Love, Power, and Being an In-law." In *Brothers and Sisters: Sibling Relationships across the Life Course*, edited by Ann Buchanan and Anna Rotkirch, 105–21. Switzerland: Palgrave Macmillan.

Joseph, Suad. 2021b. "Cooking in the Cauldron: Middle East Studies: 1966–2020." Zoom Video, 1:14:12. 19 November 2020. youtube.com/watch?v=uRdwN-p4Uv8&feature=youtu.be.

Joseph, Suad. 2021c. "God, Workers, Women, and Self: Convergences, Accidents, and Other Uncertainties in Half a Century of Fieldwork in Lebanon." *Ethnologie Francaise* 52 (2): 383–92.

Kabbani, Nader. 2019. *Youth Employment in the Middle East and North Africa: Revisiting and Reframing the Challenge*. Doha, Qatar: Brookings Doha Center.

Kanafani, Samar, and Zina Sawaf. 2017. "Introduction: Being, Doing and Knowing in the Field: Reflections on Ethnographic Practice in the Arab Region." *Contemporary Levant* 2, no. 1 (May): 3–11.

Kandiyoti, Deniz. 1996. "Contemporary Feminist Scholarship and Middle East Studies." In *Gendering the Middle East: Emerging Perspectives*, edited by Deniz Kandiyoti, 1–28. Syracuse, NY: Syracuse University Press.

Khalidi, Rashid. 2017. *The Hundred Years' War on Palestine: A History of Settler Colonialism and Resistance 1917–2017*. New York: Metropolitan Books. Henry Holt.

Khouri, Rami. 2019. "How Poverty and Inequality Are Devastating the Middle East." *Carnegie Corporation of New York*, 12 September 2019. https://www.carnegie.org/topics/topic-articles/arab-region-transitions/why-mass-poverty-so-dangerous-middle-east/.

Lazreg, Marnia. 2014. "Post-structuralist Theory and Women in the Middle East: Going in Circles?" In *Arab Feminisms: Gender and Equality in the Middle East*, edited by Jean Said Makdisi, Noha Bayoumi, and Rafif Rida Sidawi, 344–54. London: I.B. Tauris.

Mahmood, Saba. 2004. *Politics of Piety: The Islamic Revival and the Feminist Subject*. Princeton, NJ: Princeton University Press.

Malak, Karim, and Sara Salem. 2015. "Reorientalizing the Middle East: The Power Agenda Setting Post-Arab Uprisings." *Middle East: Topics and Arguments* 4: 93–109.

Meari, Lena. 2010. "The Roles of Palestinian Peasant Women: The Case of al-Birweh Village, 1930-1960." In *Displaced at Home: Ethnicity and Gender among Palestinians in Israel*, edited by Rhoda Ann Kannaneh and Isis Nusair, 119–32. Albany: State University of New York Press.

Meari, Lena. 2015. "Re-signifying Sexual Colonial Power Techniques: The Experiences of Palestinian Women Political Prisoners." In *Rethinking Gender in Revolutions and Resistance: Lessons from the Arab World*, edited by Maha El Said, Lena Meari, and Nicola Pratt, 59–85. London: Zed Books.

Mikdashi, Maya. 2012. "How Not to Study Gender in the Middle East." *Jadaliyya*, 21 March 2012. https://www.jadaliyya.com/Details/25434, accessed 16 December 2021.

Mir, Salam. 2019. "Colonialism, Postcolonialism, Globalization, and Arab Culture." *Arab Studies Quarterly* 41, no. 1 (Winter): 33–58.

PCBS (Palestinian Central Bureau of Statistics). 2020. "Dr. Ola Awad, Reviews the Conditions of the Palestinian People via Statistical Figures and Findings, on the 72nd Annual Commemoration of the Palestinian Nakba." http://www.pcbs.gov.ps/site/512/default.aspx?lang=en&ItemID=3734.

Posusney, Marsh Pripstein, and Michele Penner Angrist, eds. 2005. *Authoritarianism in the Middle East: Regimes and Resistance*. Boulder, CO: Lynne Rienner.

Petras, James F., Henry Veltmeyer, and Humberto Marquez. 2013. *Imperialism and Capitalism in the Twenty-First Century: A System in Crisis*. New York: Routledge.

Pratt, Nicola. 2006. *Democracy and Authoritarianism in the Arab World*. Boulder, CO: Lynne Rienner.

Rezk, Dina. 2017. *The Arab World and Western Intelligence: Analysing the Middle East, 1956–1981*. Edinburgh: Edinburgh University Press.

Robertson, Jennifer. 2002. "Reflexivity Redux: A Pithy Polemic on 'Positionality.'" *Anthropological Quarterly* 75 (4): 785–92.

Said, Edward. 1978. *Orientalism*. New York: Vintage Books, A Division of Random House.

Sharp, Rachel. 1982. "Self-Contained Ethnography or a Science of Phenomenal Forms and Inner Relations." *Journal of Education* 164, no. 1 (Winter): 48–63.

Sluka, Jeffrey. 2012. *Ethnographic Fieldwork: An Anthropological Reader*. Hoboken, NJ: Wiley-Blackwell.

Stephan, Rita, and Mounira M. Charrad, eds. 2020. *Women Rising: In and Beyond the Arab Spring*. New York: New York University Press.

Syrian Observatory for Human Rights. 2020. "Nearly 585,000 people Have Been Killed since the Beginning of the Syrian Revolution." https://www.syriahr.com/en/152189/?__cf_chl_jschl_tk__=pmd_vFNBHaDEyICmnr1jJU9g6hFhn.fvrk.J7Re5pFPqKgc-1630539309-0-gqNtZGzNAeWjcnBszQh9.

UN-Habitat (United Nations-Habitat). 2020. *The State of Arab Cities 2020: Financing Sustainable Urbanization in the Arab Region (Executive Summary)*. United Nations Publications.

UNHCR (United Nations High Commission for Refugees). 2018. "Syria Emergency." https://www.unhcr.org/en-us/syria-emergency.html, accessed 16 December 2021.

UNICEF (United Nations Children's Fund). 2019. *MENA Generation 2030*. New York: UNICEF.

Veltmeyer, Henry, and James F. Petras. 2001. *Globalization Unmasked: Imperialism in the 21st Century*. London: Zed Books.

Walker, John. 2016. "New Borders, Old Enemies, The Iran-Iraq War." *Warfare History Network* (blog). https://warfarehistorynetwork.com/2016/11/03/new-borders-old-enemies-the-iran-iraq-war/, accessed 16 December 2021.

World Bank. 2021. "Lebanon Sinking into One of the Most Severe Global Crises Episodes, amidst Deliberate Inaction." Press release, 1 June 2021. https://www.worldbank.org/en/news/press-release/2021/05/01/lebanon-sinking-into-one-of-the-most-severe-global-crises-episodes, accessed 16 December 2021.

Wright, Robin. 2016. "How the Curse of Sykes-Picot Still Haunts the Middle East." *New Yorker*, 30 April 2016. https://www.newyorker.com/news/news-desk/how-the-curse-of-sykes-picot-still-haunts-the-middle-east, accessed 16 December 2021.

Zaatari, Zeina. 2006. "The Culture of Motherhood: An Avenue for Women's Civil Participation in South Lebanon." *Journal of Middle East Women's Studies* 2 (1): 33–64.

Zaatari, Zeina. Forthcoming. "Sexual Rights Movement: Middle East and North Africa," In *Sexualities in the Contemporary Middle East*, edited by J. Michael Ryan and Helen Rizzo. Syracuse, NY: Syracuse University Press.

Arabic Bibliography

معهد الاصفري للمجتمع المدني والمواطنة. 2019. رصد وتوثيق تجارب الدراسات الجندرية في الجامعات والمراكز البحثية العربية. حلقات نقاشية إقليمية. يونيو/حزيران.

(Ma'had al-asfari lil-mujtama' al-madani wa al-muwatana. 2019. *Rasid wa tawthiq tajarib al-dirasat al-jandariyya fi al-jami'at wa al-marakiz al-bahthiyya al-'arabiyya. Halaqaat niqashiyya 'iqlimiyya. Uniyu/ hizayran*. http://www.activearabvoices.org/uploads/8/0/8/4/80849840/women_and_gender_-_v.2.2_-_digital__1_.pdf) (The Asfari Institute for Civil Society and Citizenship. 2019. Monitoring and Documenting the Experiences of Gender Studies at Arab Universities and Research Centers. *Regional Discussion Sessions*, June 2019. http://www.activearabvoices.org/uploads/8/0/8/4/80849840/women_and_gender_-_v.2.2_-_digital__1_.pdf), accessed 16 December 2021.

مسعد، جوزيف. 2009. كيف يجب ألا ندرس النوع الإجتماعي (الجندر) في العالم العربي. مجلة الآداب 57 (8–7): 26-20.

(Massad, Joseph. 2009. "*kayfa yajibu ala nadrus an-naw' al-'ijtima'ii (al-jandar) fi al-'alam al-'arabi.*" *Majalat al-'adab* 57 (7–8): 20–26.) (Massad, Joseph. 2009. "How We Should Not Study Gender in the Arab World." *al-Adab Journal* 57 (7–8): 20-6.)

2 THE POLITICS OF TRAINING FOR ENGAGED GENDER RESEARCH

Suad Joseph

The overwhelming majority of research about the Arab region that is published, circulated, and regularly cited has been produced by Western scholars. Increasingly over the past several decades, Arab scholars in the Arab region and in the diaspora have produced prodigious amounts of research on the Arab region, which is published, circulated, and regularly cited. Overwhelmingly, still, theorization about the Arab region builds on Western-based theories, and Arab scholars producing highly recognized research receive their theoretical and methodological training and advanced degrees in Europe or the United States. AlThe research of these highly productive recognized Arab scholars is published in journals or by publishing houses in Europe or the United States—in Western languages. Indeed, scholarly recognition in Arab and Middle East studies is still, in a variety of its meanings, Western based (see Joseph 2020a; Lockman 2016; Mitchell 2018; Said 1978 for histories of Middle East studies).

To motivate, mentor, and train early career scholars to carry out rigorous research from which they could build their own theoretical frameworks to understand their own countries drives the project that came to be called Training for Engaged Gender Research (TERG) (https://sjoseph.ucdavis.edu/training-engaged-gender-research-groups). The concern that led to the founding of TERG is that Arab scholars have relied on theories about their societies built from outside their societies. Decolonizing theory is an ongoing project throughout the Arab region and the globe (de Sousa Santos 2007; Hoppe and Nicholls 2010; Mbembe 2015; Ralph 2020). Decolonization does not necessarily entail rejection of theories and methods originating outside the region (Mignolo and Walsh 2018, 3). It calls for localization, contextualization, and historicization (de Sousa Santos 2018) of research in/of the region. As Edward Said noted decades ago, theory travels, and as it travels, it becomes something beyond what it was (Said 1982). In addition to training that is already available in the region and regardless of the power and productiveness of imported/adapted theories, the skills to carry out rigorous research and develop rigorous theory need to be further nurtured within the Arab region.

Training for Engaged Research Group (TERG) emerged from the long-standing commitment of its trainers to mentor early career scholars in general and those from the Arab region in particular.[1] The beginnings of TERG were seeded in the Arab Families Working Group (AFWG). Both TERG and AFWG were founded by Suad Joseph (Joseph 2020a). AFWG was founded in 2001. The 16 scholars of AFWG (Lamis Abu Nahleh, Ibrahim Elnur, Hoda Elsadda, Omnia El Shakry, Barbara Ibrahim, Penny Johnson, Islah Jad, Suad Joseph, Ray Jureidini, Mona Khalaf, Eileen Kuttab, Jihad Makhoul, Annelies Moors, Nadine Naber, Martina Rieker, and Zeina Zaatari) were based overwhelmingly in Egypt, Lebanon, and Palestine. AFWG met two to three times a year (mainly in Egypt, Lebanon, or Palestine). The scholars engaged in collaborative, interdisciplinary, and comparative research on Arab families and youth. AFWG was purposefully diversified by age, gender, generation, and disciplinary training. It engaged in outreach activities with civil society organizations, government organizations, the media, and the larger community of scholars (Joseph, and Rieker 2010). It produced a number of publications, limited circulation products, and other materials (https://sjoseph.ucdavis.edu/arab-families-working-group). The archives of AFWG are housed in the library of the American University in Cairo.

Originally conceptualized as an exclusively collaborative research project, AFWG, alongside its research, began, in 2008, to attach workshops to its own meetings to train early career scholars in proposal writing and research design. The goal was to mentor the next generation of researchers working on Arab families and youth. For this work, AFWG was funded by Ford Foundation, Cairo, and the International Development Research Center, Ottawa. (AFWG had been earlier funded also by the Population Council, Cairo; UNICEF, Cairo; American University in Cairo; and the University of California, Davis.) By 2010–12, AFWG started focusing almost exclusively on training early career scholars. IDRC funding ended, but Ford funding continued.

After ten years of AFWG's training of early career Arab social science scholars in proposal writing and research design and with Ford funding nearing its end, Joseph formed a group to focus explicitly on training early career scholars in rigorous research on gender. That group included Joseph, Zeina Zaatari, Lena Meari in the first cycle to be joined in the second cycle by Nadine Naber (and for a brief time Lina Abou-Habib and Islah Jad participated in the first cycle). Joseph, Zaatari, and Naber had all been active members of AFWG and actively engaged for a decade in the training and mentoring of early career scholars through AFWG.

Zaatari, Naber, and Meari had all been graduate students of Joseph and had been trained in Joseph's annually taught seminar on proposal writing and research design at the University of California, Davis.

As Ford Foundation funding was nearing its end, Joseph turned to the Foundation to Promote Open Society (FPOS) Amman, Jordan, and secured two rounds of funding (2016–17, 2018–19) to train early career Arab scholars. Each round lasted for two years. The new group eventually called itself "Training for Engaged Research Group." TERG launched in 2015 (https://sjoseph.ucdavis.edu/training-engaged-gender-research-groups).

TERG Training Vision

The driving goal of TERG (and AFWG in its second decade) was to provide fine-grained training in critical thinking and critical analysis for early career scholars (fellows of the program) to carry out rigorous research and build rigorous theory about their own societies. Teaching proposal writing and research design is a pedagogical tool to achieve multifaceted outcomes. Good research proposals demand a clear answerable question; a provisional commitment to a plausible answer; a thorough understanding of what research has already been carried out on the question; an analysis of the contributions and limitations of extant research; a coherent argument that the research proposed will produce better answers to the question; and a strong rationale as to why this research should be carried out on behalf of science and the social good. The organizing questions are: What is your question? What is your preliminary answer to the question? How have others answered the question? What is missing in the way others have answered the question? Why is your answer a better answer to the question? Why should we answer the question?

A good research proposal is a logical argument on behalf of a plausible idea — the preliminary answer to the question posed. Developing a good research proposal requires training in developing foundational concepts, training in interrogating the assumptions built into the concepts, and training in deriving the logically necessary anticipated outcomes of the concepts and the assumptions built into the concepts. Training to develop research proposals is training in conceptual thinking, logicality, argumentation, and ultimately in theory-building that produces projections (propositions, hypotheses) that can be empirically tested. Underlying the argument in logic is probabilistic thinking—the recognition that theory is productive if it is generative of real-life understandings that must be scrutinized and stand the test of the lived world (Joseph n.d.).

Throughout the training seminars, TERG interrogated "categorical thinking" (Joseph 2020b). Categorical thinking, the process by which we collect diverse events, situations, people, and things into groups, is inherent in language, embedded in every sentence uttered. It is the functional mandate of categorical thinking to elide differences and to treat members of a category as if they all possess all the characteristics that define the category. Categorical thinking readily subsidizes hierarchy and oppositionality. The recognition and critique of the uses of categorical thinking to promote racism, sexism, classism, and all forms of inequality-making is essential to critical thinking (Joseph n.d.). The deployment of categorical thinking is, however, found in both progressive and regressive politics (Spivak 1988, 2008).

TERG worked to train fellows to interrogate categorical thinking by decoding the assumptions built into foundational categories of social science research. Foundational concepts questioned included notions of the "self," "family," "kinship," "class," "gender," "masculinity," "femininity," "race," "religion," "ethnicity," "tribe," "state," "equality," "social justice," "rights," "human rights," "citizenship," "ethics." Many more were investigated and discussed for their appropriateness to Arab societies. Frequently, the reckoning led to the recognition that many foundational social science concepts had built in assumptions that were raced, classed, gendered, and culturally Western (Joseph 1994, 1997, 1999, 2000, 2018). Often, those assumptions carried historically informed biases that were either irrelevant to the Arab region or misconstrued or distorted realities on the ground in the Arab region.

TERG training invited fellows to embrace doubt and uncertainty. Scientific doubt and uncertainty, we suggested, opens scholars to continually interrogate the basis of their own beliefs and their own conceptual investments. Doubt leads to genuine questions, genuine curiosity, and reasoned uncertainty about plausible answers to answerable questions. Good science is willing to self-correct or to be corrected by the more rigorous research of others. Good scholarship requires scholars to be open to changing their minds should research findings warrant reconsideration. Good scholarship, we guided our fellows, is not wedded to its own thinking but committed to the appropriateness of the approach and the outcomes based on rigor and transparency. Good scholarship, we contended, befriends doubt and uncertainty as the constant companions of curiosity and inquiry (Joseph n.d.).

TERG engaged the fellows around the hierarchal relationships often generated in the fieldwork condition (Joseph n.d.). Engaged research requires reckoning with power. Power inequality is often implicit and at times explicit in the relationship between researchers and their interlocutors. The researcher is often subjected to power differentials in relation to local authorities or the state in which they are doing research. This is particularly so in an area of the world that is characterized by authoritarian regimes, frequent surveillance, and suppression of the press/media and scholarship. How the researcher addresses, adapts, resists, and responds to power are critical to the research process and research outcomes (see introduction to this volume).

Of special importance in TERG training were discussions concerning carrying out research under conditions of violence, political upheaval, conflict, or in regimes where researchers may be monitored closely by state agencies. What kind of research can be carried out under such circumstances? What risks are reasonable or unreasonable? What can researchers publish/disseminate from data collected under such conditions (see introduction to this volume).

TERG engaged fellows in conversations around feminist fieldwork. What constitutes feminist fieldwork (see introduction to this volume)? What constitutes feminist methods? What constitutes feminist ethics in the field? What constitutes feminist research questions? What constitutes feminist theory? What constitutes feminist relations to power in fieldwork (see introduction to this volume). How does one center-stage gender in research design and methods? How does the fieldworker recognize intersectionality and gender within intersectional relations/conditions?

TERG seminars paid special attention to Human Subjects Protocols. While institutional review boards (IRBs) that review proposals for their adherence to Human Subjects Protocols are common in many (not all) American and European universities, they are more unevenly found in regional Arab universities. How does the research protect their interlocutors? How is confidentiality respected during data gathering? When is it better to not publish/disseminate, even if data is obtained with the consent/recognition of consequences of the interlocutors?

Ongoing discussions considered the meaning of "engagement" and what it meant for the fellows in relationship to their work and their specific countries. All the fellows were from the Arab region, citizens of and residents in the Arab region. All came to the training programs with commitments to research projects. The projects invariably had key social problems as their subjects. The social problems identified invariably produced inequality, disenfranchisement, social disengagement, and were costly to the subjects of research and to their societies on multiple levels. The fellows took on such projects as part of their own commitments to their societies. AFWG and TERG did not direct them to these commitments. They came to AFWG and TERG because they were already committed. AFWG and TERG amplified, trained, and offered tools to channel the commitments already embraced by these emerging scholars.

Toward this end, TERG encouraged dialogic engagement and collective commentaries on the work of each fellow. At every seminar, the fellows were organized in different groups that read and listened to each other's work. With a mentor at each table, they worked together to critique, give feedback, and strengthen each other's proposals or methods or analysis or writing. We encouraged them to continue working together beyond the seminars. We set up Facebook pages for their continued connection. A number of them organized in-person or online writing/discussion groups to maintain the momentum of the collective engagement in between seminars. That work paralleled the ongoing one-on-one mentoring between fellows and their mentors that sustained the engagement between seminars. The spirit was one of collaboration and collective input for the collective good. Many of the fellows continue to work together and to be connected with each other and/or the AFWG/TERG scholars, years after the seminars, as they built and continue to build communities for the production of socially engaged knowledge.

All TERG trainers, Meari (2014, 2015a, 2015b, 2017), Naber (2009, 2012, 2016, 2018), and Zaatari (2014, forthcoming), and Joseph (n.d.) engaged the fellows in discussions of the social good. To what end is research conducted? What are the researchers' obligations to the communities with whom they engage to carry out the research? Who owns the research? Who are the beneficiaries of the research? How does the research return to the communities from which "data" is extracted? What are the political constraints under which research is conducted? How does research untether itself from hegemonic frameworks? TERG fellows were invariably highly committed to the communities with whom they worked and the countries in which they were not only researchers but also engaged citizens.

TERG Training Program

With FPOS funding, TERG organized two rounds of two-year training seminars for groups of up to 25 early career scholars from the Arab region. The training was called Training to Transformative Engaged Gender Research (TTEGR). In the first cycle, TERG partnered with the Collective for Research and Training on Development-Action (CRTD.A) (https://crtda.org.lb/), Beirut, Lebanon, under the leadership of Lina Abou-Habib. In the second cycle, TERG partnered with the Arab Council for the Social Sciences (ACSS) (http://www.theacss.org/), Beirut, Lebanon, under the directorship of Seteney Shami.

The TERG program was designed to spend six months training fellows in proposal writing, six months on data collection, six months on data analysis, and six months on writing (2016–17, 2018–19). Each fellow of the program was given a modest seed grant (US $5,000) to carry out a research project during the training seminar in their home countries. Each fellow was assigned one of the trainers as a personal mentor to work with them continuously on their assignments. In the second year of each of the two-year cycles, the mentors were changed so that each fellow had an opportunity to work with different styles of training. In parallel, four in-person, three-day seminars were held in Amman, Jordan. Lectures on critical topics were offered. For example: doing fieldwork under conditions of war, violence, and state surveillance; ethics of research; ethics of research funding; ethics of representation; diverse methodologies such as feminist approaches to participant observation, discourse analysis, content analysis, interviews, focus groups, oral histories, note-taking, surveys, media analysis, archival analysis and documents; human subjects protocols; and writing and publishing strategies. Special attention was given to working with the subjects of violence, sexual colonial violence, intimate violence, and sexual harassment and how not to study gender-based violence. Throughout the seminar, attention was paid to the conditionalities of power, whether it was based in global, state, gender, race, class, or other matrices. Throughout the seminar, the intersectionality of power, global conditions, state, gender, race, class, and other matrices was center-staged.

This book emerges from the work of the first cohort of early career scholars in the TTERG. The cohort jelled quickly. The chemistry among and between the fellows and the trainers was electric. The research carried out by these early career Arab scholars was pioneering and cutting edge. We wanted to capture that spirit. We wanted to publish that spirit. We wanted other emerging scholars in gender research to be challenged, motivated, inspired by the spirit of this cohort of early career scholars. The second cohort was equally compelling. TERG did not pursue publishing with the second cohort as many had already engaged in their own publishing careers.

The Politics of Funding

Funding research always has a politics. The priorities of funding agencies, the changing personnel of foundations, and the constant challenges of the political environment that the funders themselves inhabit affect what they are willing/able to fund and how they manage their relationships with the scholars they fund. Both AFWG and TERG had to address these constant uncertainties. A change in government in the country of one funder led to an exodus of program officers who had been enthusiastic about our work. Changes in administrative leadership in several funding agencies led to internal strategic planning and critical shifts in their funding priorities. Increased surveillance and government supervision in another country led one funder to suspend the work they had funded with our program, although allowing us to complete the final year, with modifications.

From 2008 to 2019, for both the AFWG and the TERG, funding was a constantly negotiated issue. With all the funders (AFWG also had funding from the Population Council, Cairo; UNICEF, Cairo; the Social Research Center at the American University in Cairo; University of California, Davis) AFWG and TERG had excellent program officers in all the foundations and excellent relations with the program officers. As AFWG funding stretched over two decades and TERG funding stretched for over half a decade, we found that program officers changed; presidents of foundations changed; and policies, programs, and mission objectives changed. Between IDRC, Ottawa; the Ford Foundation, Cairo; and the FPOS, Amman, there were over a dozen different program officers with whom AFWG and TERG worked. In several instances, program officers moved from one foundation to another. We remained in contact with these program officers and our project earned funding from them in their new foundation. For each of these foundations, national presidents or executives, regional directors, and program officers changed multiple times. In-house programs, policies, and mission objectives changed in each of the foundations during two decades of funding. AFWG and TERG learned to adapt to these changes.

As Suad Joseph was the proposal writer/fundraiser for both AFWG and TERG, she was constantly reaching out to understand foundation dynamics, to decipher changing foundation priorities, to translate/adapt AFWG and TERG vision to the changing priorities, and to build and expand relationships with program officers. Building good relations with program officers often translated across foundations, and program officers from different foundations shared information with each other or as program officers moved from one foundation to another. This intense work, combined with the unrelenting requirement for reports to funders, managing budgets across half a dozen institutions, and constantly working to identify additional funding possibilities, meant that, for international collaborative projects, it seemed as if the time taken with these funding activities sometimes was almost as much as the time devoted to the work of the project. It would have been difficult for a junior scholar. Recognition of these political realities contributed, in part, to the recruitment, in both AFWG and TERG, of an intergenerational collaborative team, with the senior person taking responsibility for fundraising.

Given that foundations generally do not accept unsolicited applications, the frequency of changes within foundations required constant communication and engagement with program officers to sustain the relevance of our work to their mission objectives. It meant adapting our work to accommodate organizational shifts, resulting in adjustments in the work. For example, when Canadian national elections ushered in a more conservative government at the end of the first decade of the twenty-first century, IDRC adjusted its approach to funding. They had been the largest funder for AFWG prior to 2012. The program officers who had supported the AFWG program left IDRC, some because they were uncomfortable with some of the changes at IDRC. While IDRC continued to fund AFWG for a while, AFWG had to accommodate changing foundation authorities and work styles. Eventually, IDRC discontinued funding AFWG. We had to look elsewhere for funding.

Differences in foundation goals affected our training program. In the Cairo program, Ford asked AFWG to change groups that we were training every six months or every year. Ford's goal was to reach many early career scholars as possible. The FPOS, on the other hand, accepted TERG's wish to do more in-depth training with fewer emerging scholars. It was unprecedented in the Arab region to have a non-university research training institute last two years. The result of this difference in foundation goals was that in the Cairo, Ford-funded AFWG program, a number of the fellows returned and took the seminar multiple times and one even signed up for the TERG program. They wanted to learn more than they managed to absorb in the short program. None of the Amman-based FPOS-funded TERG fellows repeated the seminar. With that program, we trained fewer scholars, but more in-depth.

At times, internal strategic planning in foundations led to changes for funding priorities. The Ford Foundation, Cairo, ended the gender program that had funded AFWG. However, Ford had been enthusiastic about AFWG generally. A chance meeting with the Ford program officer in higher education resulted in conversations on how to adjust AFWG's work to fit with the higher education program. The research component of AFWG focusing on families and youth did not fit within the funding mandate of the higher education program. However, AFWG's training and mentoring program fit well with the mandate of Ford's higher education program. Ford then funded only AFWG's training and mentoring program. Though AFWG was funded for close to a decade under the higher education program at Ford, some AFWG members were less interested in this new focus, preferring the research focus. The shift in Ford led to changes in AFWG.

Additional shifts in Ford affected who AFWG could serve. Directives from the New York Ford headquarters refocused the Egypt regional office to become more country focused. As a result, AFWG was asked to focus on training Egyptian early career scholars exclusively. For a few years we were permitted to include a small contingent of Lebanese and Palestinian fellows. Later we were allowed to include only Egyptian fellows.

At times, shifts in country government environments for funding agencies affected our training program. In the very last year of Ford AFWG funding, 2018, the Egyptian government required all NGOs to reapply for their licenses. During the application process, the foundations were not allowed to work in Egypt or with Egyptians. As a result, AFWG was allowed to include any regional Arab early career scholar, except Egyptians, and hold the seminar only outside Egypt.

Knowing that funding was always contingent, we were always looking for additional funders for our work. Foreseeing that Ford funding might be near ending, Joseph, in 2013, engaged with the FPOS around the project of mentoring regional early career scholars. After three years of discussions, the first round of funding became available in 2016. Shortly after that the regional director of FPOS changed. The program officer changed several times. By the time of the second round of funding (2018), FPOS had shifted the focus of the program under which TERG was funded to gendered violence in public spaces. TERG accommodated by issuing its call to mentor regional early career scholars who focused on gendered violence in public spaces. Though TERG's interests are far broader than gender violence, it turned out to be a focus of many regional scholars who desired training. Such negotiations and shifts are common with projects relying on foundation funding. There is nothing specific to AFWG or TERG about this.

To maintain its mission to train emerging scholars in the Arab region, AFWG, and later TERG, needed to adapt as foundations shifted their funding priorities. Throughout these shifts in the funding agencies, however, both AFWG and TERG were entirely free and independent in the specific lectures, readings, content, and methods of training. It is common to find differences in the goals of the funder and the goals of scholars. Adaptation is a common approach. The key for us was that we never did anything that was not already under the umbrella of our own mission. We looked for points of convergence between our projects and the funders' goals. The conversation to find those convergences was an exercise in productive politics.

The Politics of Training

While the general themes of the training, the duration, and the constituents we recruited were at times shaped by the funding foundation, we were entirely free in the actual curriculum and training. Conversations with fellows were broad-ranging, covering a large landscape of social, ethical, theoretical, political, moral, academic, and personal life-concerns. We regularly offered lectures, readings, and discussions on historicizing and contextualizing the subjects and subject matter of research, and presenting examples and templates for the historical construction of the region. We taught theory building and decolonizing theory. Our programs included lectures and discussions of the ethics of doing fieldwork under conditions of violence, government censorship and surveillance of research, and protection of interlocutors.

Ethical concerns led to the discussion of human subjects protocols. Human subject protocols are followed by some but not all universities in the Arab region. We found that some European universities do not follow human subjects protocols as well. For many of the AFWG and TERG fellows, Human Subjects Protocols was a new idea. The discussions engaged the fellows in addressing ethics not as a technical requirement of fieldwork but as a foundational approach to ethical considerations of research, specific to the conditionalities of their locations and contexts. What research is done, how it is done, who does it, who is included or excluded, how research subjects are protected, how data is analyzed, what is published and disseminated, how/where/by whom it is published and disseminated—an endless series of questions lived under the umbrella of the politics of training for engaged research.

Neither the trainers nor the fellows shied away from discussing controversial political issues in AFWG or TERG. Rather we engaged, contextualized, and historicized them. At one point, in one seminar, in Cairo, a couple of suited-up men entered our seminar room, sat in the back, and remained in the seminar for some time. We never knew the identity of the men, but speculation among some led to concerns about surveillance and security in Egypt at the time. In Amman, our advance team had to obtain security clearance and government permits to carry out our seminars. For one seminar, our advance team arrived at the hotel to find that for some reason, there was no permit to carry out the seminar in that hotel. Quick work on the part of the advance team located another site to carry out the seminar. We never knew why the hotel had not been able to obtain the permit. Some of our fellows told us they had to be careful about how they reported to their universities or employers of the work they were doing in the training seminars. Some confided that they did not report the training at all, fearing repercussions. Others faced security challenges in order to carry out the research they had envisioned as part of the training.

Training, as with all education, is always carried out in a political setting with political constraints and political realities. While the AFWG and TERG training may seem straightforward in some locations it is not so in all locations. Knowledge production always engages a political process. The challenges we experienced of funding, security approvals, encouraging early career scholars to engage with critical thinking reflect the reality that knowledge production is a political process. For some of our AFWG and TERG fellows, the training was undoing what they had been trained to do as researchers, or how they were trained to think conceptually, or what they considered to be theory or methods. For some, the training was unsettling the status quo of their society or even life. It was not surprising that the training was experienced by some as threatening to the status quo. Recognizing the politics of training required understanding the politics of knowledge production and the skills to identify the power relations that inhabit all social conditionalities, including the gendered, classed, and raced intersections of power relations. Seeing power relations in their own societies and integrating power analysis into their research questions and data collection and analysis transformed the approaches of many of the TERG fellows. For some, the training reinforced directions they were already moving toward and gave them tools they had been seeking. We managed, under these circumstances, to nevertheless deliver training that was engaged and committed.

In the TERG curriculum, the fellows were offered four in-person seminars (three days each) over the course of the two years. The first seminar focused on proposal writing, with the following six months spent devoted to working with each fellow on their proposals. The second seminar focused on data collection. Each fellow was given a small grant to carry out the research planned in their proposals. The second six months, each fellow was mentored regularly as they gathered data, submitted data, reviewed the relevance of the data to the project goals—in a variety of projects and variety of fieldwork conditions. The third seminar focused on data analysis. Specific attention focused on what constitutes data and how data becomes evidence in the context of a logical argument. The third six months entailed analyzing the data in relationship to the argument in the proposal. Recognition of how data transforms into evidence and how evidence reshapes arguments were addressed. The fourth and final seminar focused on writing for publication. Different platforms, venues, outlets in different languages, disciplines, and regions of the world were examined and evaluated. The fellows had the remaining time to complete their project and submit to publications. Many did and many successfully used these projects as applications for doctoral programs, applications for jobs/positions, or in their merit/tenure packages.

In every aspect of the TERG program we set out to teach skills of critical thinking and critical analysis. Foundationally, we were committed to empowering and building confidence based on rigorous skills enhancement. Mentoring meant working one-on-one with fellows. Fellows were required to turn in regular work to their assigned mentors. Mentors worked with them on their specific projects throughout the duration of the projects. Fellows in the TERG program had the opportunity to work with two different mentors over the course of the two years, in addition to having access to all the mentors during the four seminars. These relationships were modeled on nonhierarchical engagement, dialogic teaching, and recognition that the starting place is always wherever the fellow is. Many of these relationships, forged in the intensity of training, have endured as personal and professional relationships in life-pathways.

The passion of the fellows was paralleled by the passion of the mentors. For the mentors, there was a commitment to train the next generation of knowledge producers for the Arab region. All of the TERG mentors are of Arab origin. AFWG was a cross-section of Arab, European, and Arab-American mentors, the majority of whom lived in the Arab region. To a person, the AFWG and TERG mentors saw the Arab region not simply as a location for their work. Rather, the Arab region, to the mentors, is a site of multilayered experiences and commitments that have been and are life-long. Bound by work, kinship, friendship, culture, and history, the well-being of the people of the Arab region is a commitment of the heart and soul.

The fellows came with passions of their own. Almost all the fellows indicated that they had not had access to the AFWG or TERG kind of training at their home institutions. A number indicated that the training was transformative for them, offering them a critical edge. Many fellows went abroad for further education. Some remained abroad. The majority stayed in the Arab region. Many of the fellows became academics; others went into government agencies; others in civil society organizations. Many fellows have remained in touch with their mentors, sharing their career developments. Many have remained connected with other AFWG or TERG seminar fellows. Whatever their career paths, all took away with them some of the skills, some of the critical thinking, some of the theory building, some of the historicizing, the contextualizing, the localizing, and decolonizing the politics of knowledge production on behalf of their own region. They took with them the relationships, the commitments, the passion, and the will to build knowledge for the social good for their own countries. That endures.

Note

1   Suad Joseph has taught proposal writing and research design at the University of California, Davis, for 40 years. She developed the graduate seminar required of all anthropology PhD students for the Anthropology Department in the late 1970s/early 1980s and taught it exclusively for around 30 years. She annually offers a condensed version of this seminar at the invitation of the UC Davis vice provost for Academic Affairs for new and advanced faculty. She has offered this seminar to faculty and students in departments from humanities, social sciences, math, and physical sciences at UC Davis, UC Berkeley, State University of New York, Cortland, American University of Beirut, American University in Cairo, Lebanese American University, Birzeit University, Cairo University, Zayed University, University of Zurich, the UN Economic and Social Commission of West Asia, Middle East Studies Association of North American, and a number of government and nongovernment organizations in a number of Middle East countries. She has served on the review panels of a number of governmental and nongovernmental funding agencies. Over the course of two decades, Joseph, through AFWG and TERG as well as on her own, has trained perhaps one thousand or more early career and advanced scholars in proposal writing and research design in the Arab region. See http://sjoseph.ucdavis.edu/ for multiple pages on proposal writing, research design, and various collaborative, interdisciplinary projects. TERG trainers Lena Meari, Zeina Zaatari, and Nadine Naber all received their training at UC Davis, in anthropology, under the mentorship of Joseph. They were all trained in research methods and design. Each, at their own universities and institutions and through their advocacy work, continued to mentor and train early career scholars. Lena Meari mentors Palestinian students at Birzeit University in research methods and design. Zeina Zaatari mentors students at the University of Illinois, Chicago where she serves as director of the Arab American Cultural Center. Nadine Naber, in addition to mentoring at the University of Illinois, Chicago, has founded her own consulting firm to train social justice researchers: https://nadinenaber.com/.

Bibliography

de Sousa Santos, Boaventura, ed. 2007. *Another Knowledge Is Possible: Beyond Northern Epistemologies*. London: Verso.
de Sousa Santos, Boaventura. 2018. *The End of the Cognitive Empire: The Coming of Age of Epistemologies of the South*. Durham, NC: Duke University Press.
Hoppe, Elizabeth A., and Tracey Nicholls, eds. 2010. *Fanon and Decolonization of Philosophy*. Lanham, MD: Lexington (Rowman and Littlefield).

Joseph, Suad. 1994. "Problematizing Gender and Relational Rights: Experiences from Lebanon." *Social Politics* 1, no. 3 (Fall): 271–85.

Joseph, Suad. 1997. "The Public/Private: The Imagined Boundary in the Imagined Nation/State/Community: The Lebanese Case." *Feminist Review* 57 (Autumn): 73–92.

Joseph, Suad, ed. 1999. *Intimate Selving in Arab Families: Gender, Self, and Identity*. Syracuse, NY: Syracuse University Press.

Joseph, Suad, ed. 2000. *Gender and Citizenship in the Middle East*. Syracuse, NY: Syracuse University Press.

Joseph, Suad, ed. 2018. *Arab Family Studies: Critical Reviews*. Syracuse, NY: Syracuse University Press.

Joseph, Suad. 2020a. "Cooking in the Cauldron: Middle East Studies 1966–2020." Zoom Video, 1:41:12. 19 November 2020. https://www.facebook.com/Jadaliyya/videos/446795856303515.

Joseph, Suad. 2020b. "Brothers and Sisters, Husbands and Wives: Love, Power, and Being an In-Law." In *Brothers and Sisters*, edited by A. Buchanan and A. Rotkirch, 105–21. London: Palgrave Macmillan.

Joseph, Suad. N.d. Lectures on Proposal Writing and Research Design. Unpublished.

Joseph, Suad, and Martina Rieker. 2010. "Introduction: Rethinking Arab Family Projects." *Framings: Rethinking Arab Family Projects*, volume I, Arab Families Working Group.

Lockman, Zachary. 2016. *Field Notes: The Making of Middle East Studies in the United States*. Stanford, CA: Stanford University Press.

Mbembe, Achille. 2015. "Decolonizing Knowledge and the Question the Archive." https://wiser.wits.ac.za/system/files/Achille%20Mbembe%20-%20Decolonizing%20Knowledge%20and%20the%20Question%20of%20the%20Archive.pdf, accessed 16 December 2021.

Meari, Lena. 2014. "Sumud: A Palestinian Philosophy of Confrontation in Colonial Prisons." *South Atlantic Quarterly* 113 (3): 547–78.

Meari, Lena. 2015a. "Reconsidering Trauma: Towards a Palestinian Community Psychology." *Journal of Community Psychology* 43 (1): 76–86.

Meari, Lena. 2015b. "Re-signifying the 'Sexual' Colonial Power Techniques: The Experiences of Palestinian Women Political Prisoners." In *Rethinking Gender in Revolutions and Resistance*, edited by Maha El-Said, Lena Meari, and Nicola Pratt, 59–85. Lessons from the Arab World. London: Zed Books.

Meari, Lena. 2017. "Colonial Dispossession, Developmental Discourses, and Human Solidarity in 'Area C': The Case of the Palestinian Yanun Village." *Community Development Journal* 52 (3): 506–23.

Mignolo, Walter D., and Catherine E. Walsh. 2018. *On Decoloniality: Concepts, Analytics, Praxis*. Durham, NC: Duke University Press.

Mitchell, Timothy. 2018. "The Middle East in the Past and Future of Social Science." *Columbia Blogs* (blog). https://blogs.cuit.columbia.edu/tm2421/files/2018/01/Szanton-ed-Middle-East-in-Soc-Sc'i.pdf.

Naber, Nadine. 2009. "Transnational Families under Siege: Lebanese in Dearborn, Mic;higan, and the 2006 War on Lebanon." *Journal of Middle East Women's Studies* 5 (3): 145–74.

Naber, Nadine. 2012. *Arab America: Gender, Cultural Politics, and Activism*. New York: New York University Press.

Naber, Nadine. 2016. "A Call for Consistency: Palestinian Resistance and Radical US Women of Color." In *The Color of Violence: The INCITE! Anthology*. Durham, NC: Duke University Press.

Naber, Nadine. 2018. "Towards the Sun." In *Towards the Sun*, edited by Nadine Naber and the Arab American Action Network, 23–25. Washington, DC: Tadween Publishing, A subsidiary of the Arab Studies Institute..

Naber, Nadine, and Amaney Jamal, eds. 2008. *Race and Arab Americans Before and After 9/11: From Invisible Citizens to Visible Subjects*. Syracuse, NY: Syracuse University Press.

Ralph, Laurence. 2020. *The Torture Letters: Reckoning with Police Violence*. Chicago: University of Chicago Press.

Said, Edward. 1978. *Orientalism*. New York Pantheon Books.

Said, Edward. 1982. "Traveling Theory." In *The World, the Text, and the Critic*, 226–47. Cambridge, MA: Harvard University Press.

Spivak, Gayatri Chakravorty. 1988. "Can the Subaltern Speak?" In *Marxism and the Interpretation of Culture*, edited by Cary Nelson and Lawrence Grossberg, 271–313. Basingstoke, UK: Macmillan.

Spivak, Gayatri Chakravorty. 2008. *Other Asias*. Malden, MA: Blackwell.

Zaatari, Zeina. 2014. "Desirable Masculinity/Femininity and Nostalgia of the 'Anti-Modernity:' Bab el-Hara Television Series as a Site of Production." *Sexuality and Culture* 19: 16–36.

Zaatari, Zeina. Forthcoming. "Sexual Rights Movement: Middle East and North Africa." In *Sexualities in the Middle East*, edited by John Michael Ryan and Helen Rizzo. Syracuse, NY: Syracuse University Press.

PART 1

MAGHREB (NORTH AFRICA)

3 DOING FIELDWORK WITH WOMEN LAND RIGHTS ACTIVISTS IN MOROCCO: POWER RELATIONSHIPS WITHIN FEMINISM AND ITS DISCURSIVE FRAMEWORK OF RIGHT

Souad Eddouada

Introduction: My Research Project and Positionality

The recent feminization of the protest movement around land rights in Morocco—known publicly under the name السلاليات (*sulāliyāt*)[1]—has been the subject of coverage by various local and international media, most of which has addressed the issue in terms of the rural, uneducated, and vulnerable women who sought, and got, support from their human rights and women's rights "partners." The support provided by these urban center–based women's rights activists included free access to workshops and classes, as well as education and knowledge about human rights, feminism, and the protest culture and its norms. For example, the more established urban center–based human rights and women's rights NGOs offered trainings on how to write—and chant—slogans that address the struggles these women have had with their brothers and male family members over access to communal lands privatization "benefits." Meanwhile, السلاليات (*sulāliyāt*) training workshops centered mainly on increasing knowledge about legal changes and the codification of gender equality and parity in both the 2004 Family Code and the 2011 constitutional reforms. Thus, according to the women's human rights organizations involved, the path the السلاليات (*sulāliyāt*) need to take involves tapping into their country's "highest ideals," as inscribed in the constitution, and mobilizing other women who share similar family grievances. However, most women's rights activists—including the Association Démocratique des Femmes du Maroc (ADFM) and the Federation de la Ligue Démocratique des Femmes du Maroc (FLDDF)—have formulated السلاليات (*sulāliyāt*) issues in terms of gender discrimination. A considerable number of the السلاليات (*sulāliyāt*), whom I interviewed and got to know closely, highlighted not just discrimination but the intersection of gender discrimination with the other local political and economic systems that produce the inequality that women often share with men. In fact, the range of themes that stand out in particular in السلاليات (*sulāliyāt*) narratives are the privatization and commodification of communal land, the corruption and lack of transparency surrounding economic and political alliances, and the abuse of power—especially in the rural and semiurban margins of the country.

I have been a student of Moroccan feminist social movements since 1998. While I was a graduate student in English studies, I inadvertently started working for a women's rights NGO in Rabat. The NGO was the leader of the feminist groups lobbying for changes to the Family Code, a movement that started in the early 1990s with the One Million Signature campaign that gathered signatures in favor of family code reforms. As an NGO employee, I had the chance to witness most of the networking and coordination meetings that took place at the NGO offices. At the meetings, the main topic of discussion was how to unify the feminist groups around one common feminist memorandum that would be addressed to the newly appointed socialist prime minister. Indeed, the politics of the end of the 1990s were mainly characterized by the strong presence of reform on the state's agenda and the validations for change put forth by civil society activists. In that context, it was up to feminists to unify their claims and present their common grievances and demands for reform to the person in the role newly designed and appointed by the king: a socialist activist who was getting ready to lead the state's transition to justice and democracy. As I watched the divisions, disputes, and competition for leadership among feminists during those long coordination meetings, I thought a lot about the challenges that feminist ideals must confront before any possible grassroots intervention on behalf of what is usually framed as "women's rights" can come to fruition.

I have always admired feminist critical studies of regimes of truth in rights discourses (Abu-Lughod 2009; Jad 2003; Joseph 1994; Scott 1996), because they have helped me make sense of the unease I have felt since I was first exposed to women's rights activism as a graduate student and an employee at women's rights NGO in Rabat. Watching the dynamics among the activists—the competition over leadership, the internal power dynamics defining who could speak and whose voices remained unheard—I felt a silent resentment that built up over time. Those feelings were revived when I heard the السلاليات (sulāliyāt) stories, in which the women rejected being patronized and being told what to do by their "women's rights educators." I identified with the السلاليات (sulāliyāt) not only because I share their working-class and rural origins but also because their stories gave meaning and shape to the alienation I have always felt around women's rights conferences, seminars, and other meetings about how women can gain access to the rights that men already have (Mackinnon 1998, 296). I see the ways in which these institutional responses have attempted to address these issues without questioning the very system that produces the inequality at the heart of the matter.

This chapter is a reflection on the new context for doing fieldwork on gender in Morocco post-Arab uprising and post–gender-based reforms, and on methodologies that can adequately respond to that context. Given this context and my own ambivalent experiences with women's rights activism as a graduate student, I participated in a training course in engaged research methodologies, in which the research is driven by lessons from the field, and I developed a research question based on those approaches. This new context has revealed an interesting reconfiguration of the terms of the debate—and its players—around what constitutes and frames the "women question" in Morocco. Representations of the women question—as advocacy for and/or opposition to gender equality, as women's rights versus the Islamist agenda, or as modern versus traditional values—have been challenged by the eruption of bottom-up, female-led street protests in rural areas and in the suburbs of urban centers. These eruptions are redefining the conversation about women, exposing power relations within feminism and its discursive framework of rights and laying bare the gap that I have just mentioned, between the inequalities that are ostensibly being addressed through activism led by long-standing NGOs, and the system that continues to reproduce those inequalities. In each case, the changes that are emerging operate within their leaders' specific local socioeconomic situations, and the political issues at play are largely structured by the intersection of socioeconomic inequalities and political authoritarianism.

Feminism and Difference, or Women as a Regime of Truth

Reading and learning more about feminist critiques of the women's rights framework helped me come to terms with the constraints of those frameworks and, in turn, question the idea that feminist representations of women necessarily lead to liberation. Islah Jad's article on "NGO-ization of the Arab Women's Movement" is a case in point. Jad discusses the limitations for NGOs in some Arab countries, which stem mainly from their dependence on international aid for short-term projects that serve an externally imposed agenda. Her piece questions the equation of the very existence of NGOs with social change (Jad 2003). She also points to the challenge inflicted by the class divide between poor and middle-class women, arguing that assumptions about their similar needs and interests may undermine the commitment to equality (Jad 2003). In a similar vein, and from an anthropological perspective, Abu-Lughod raises concerns about class and educational privileges that can be divisive, including instances in which organizations use their religious knowledge to claim local intervention on behalf of women and women's rights. Abu-Lughod worked with women in rural Egypt and Palestine, and she juxtaposes the complexity of their lives with the "legalistic rights framework and its incommensurability with everyday lives" (Abu-Lughod 2009).

The possibility of learning about research tools that I could use to deploy both my experience and the readings of critical feminist activism in the Middle East and North Africa (MENA) region was a gift that came from my participation in the two-year-long seminar in Training for Engaged Transformative Gender Research, a program organized and run by Dr. Suad Joseph in collaboration with Dr. Lena Meari and Dr. Zeina Zaatari. The training offered a golden opportunity for me to learn about some key anthropological research tools and then practice them by studying a topic of interest to me (throughout the chapter I will refer to the insights gained from the mentors of the training course). I wanted to work on a topic that involved ordinary women living outside urban centers; I chose, therefore, to study the land rights activists known as the السلاليات (sulāliyāt). Little did I know that the السلاليات (sulāliyāt) would not only teach me about their struggle over collective land but also shine a light on my old experiences with feminist activism, pushing me to revisit them and to examine more closely my ambivalence about feminist activism in my country. Indeed, some of the NGOs who led the debates over changes to the Family Code three decades prior had become partners to the السلاليات (sulāliyāt) in their struggle for equal land rights and shares.

During the workshop I learned a lot not only about rigorous field work but also about engaged research. Engaged research means that despite the researcher's need to have a research plan, the researcher needs to remain open to and mindful of the lessons coming from the field (Joseph 2015). It also means a constant reflection on, and review of, the assumptions behind the research categories. Maintaining this alert attitude offers both the researcher and the researched the possibility of building up a rapport that addresses rather than denies the power relationship involved in any researcher/researched experience (Meari 2015). Over the two years of the seminar, it was exciting to meet with women from almost every Arab-Muslim country. For me, learning about the commonalities and differences between my country and the other countries in the region highlighted the specificity of my work with the السلاليات (*sulāliyāt*). The alliance between السلاليات (*sulāliyāt*) women and the urban NGOs is definitely the first example of a partnership between established urban NGOs and rural women. I developed a research question designed to delve into the specificities of the السلاليات (*sulāliyāt*) women's conditions and investigate what put them at the forefront of collective land privatization protests;[2] this question then guided the road map for my fieldwork. In addition to the specific case of the السلاليات (*sulāliyāt*), I was interested in the partnership between veteran feminists and this growing rural female protest movement more broadly.

Both the training and the السلاليات (*sulāliyāt*) topic offered the experience a fresh start, that of a beginner where everything is new even when it sounds familiar. I went to the field without much knowledge about collective land issues generally or about other studies done on collective land in Morocco. That lack of knowledge was the reason for so many of my moments of confusion and uncertainty, but it also helped me realize the extent to which السلاليات (*sulāliyāt*) are the owners of valuable knowledge, and thus, it helped me to see and value the knowledge that comes from daily life experience. Moreover, listening to the urban activists and the السلاليات (*sulāliyāt*) juxtaposed feminist discourse with grassroots activism (i.e., the work of the السلاليات (*sulāliyāt*)). That fact helped me navigate twists and turns during my fieldwork, as I shifted my research from the partnership itself to the gap and the incommensurability between feminist and human rights discourses, and السلاليات (*sulāliyāt*) experiences and actions. Focusing on this incommensurability gradually exposed the extent to which the rights framework can become a regime of truth that reveals the power dynamics between the feminist and human rights activists and the grassroots that they imagine they represent: the السلاليات (*sulāliyāt*).

السلاليات (*Sulāliyāt*) involvement with their communities' struggle against expropriation, along with their ability to stand against corruption and abuse of power, shows the social justice nature of the women's struggle and demonstrates the extent to which the "concept of woman has lost its analytical credibility" (Alcoff and Potter 1993, 3). That latter point is in line with recent reconfigurations around the "women question" that I mentioned at the outset, and indeed the nature of the women's fight is evidence that "gender as a category of analysis cannot be abstracted from a particular context while other factors are held stable ... gender cannot be adequately perceived-except as a component of complex interrelationships with other systems of identification and hierarchy" (Alcoff and Potter 1993, 3). While the السلاليات (*sulāliyāt*) recognize that they are discriminated against because of their gender, they do not see gender as the only factor in their oppression. Yet the urban activists operate within a framework that does not see the land expropriation, the corruption and abuse of power, and the neoliberalization of the economy as a women's or feminist issue.

I initially went into the field with the aim of studying an "unprecedented partnership" among urban feminists, human rights activists, and rural land rights activists. Given that I had first met the land rights activists inside the offices of various urban NGOs, I assumed that my project would document the terms of the urban–rural partnership and the collaboration among the different activist groups. However, further fieldwork revealed tensions, disputes, and power dynamics that kept affirming the need to change the scope of my research from a focus on the aforementioned collaboration and partnership to a study exploring the perspective of السلاليات (sulāliyāt) outside of that urban–rural partnership.

Being open to making those changes was an approach I had explored in the Engaged Transformative Gender Research training and workshops, which emphasized a number of research premises including, but not limited to, commitment to the field (Joseph 2015). From the very beginning, the workshop's focus on the need for research driven by relevant empirical questions rather than preconceived assumptions about research subjects set the tone for responding to and interacting with lessons from the field. The workshops also drew attention to knowledge as a construct, a point that requires the researcher to question the assumptions behind established research categories, concepts, and assertions. Understanding the assumptions behind these concepts (Joseph 2015) is a necessary phase in ethical and field-committed research. Rather than proceeding from a commissioned research agenda that is very often derived from essentialist assumptions about the culture to be studied, engaged research questions—rather than assumes—the capacity of those concepts to speak for the field. In this sense, the dominance of preconceived concepts loses some of its grip on the field, leaving room for the research participants to show the relevancy of their complex and concrete lives. The popularity of topics such as domestic violence and honor killings, for example, reveals deep-seated assumptions about the intrinsic violence of Arab-Muslim culture. Moreover, the MENA region's dependence on international research funding creates and perpetuates fixed assumptions about an entire region. For example, research funding goes mostly to gender-based domestic violence. Such an industry then produces knowledge that glosses over colonial violence, economic violence, and neoliberal policies; violence, instead, is reduced to a patriarchal, oriental man's violence toward his wife and the structure of the psychology of an oriental man, who is assumed to be a violent man (Meari 2015). In contrast, an engaged research agenda addresses the gap between the field and the researcher, rather than obscuring it. Sharlene Hesse-Biber similarly makes this point about feminist praxis: "To engage in feminist theory and praxis means to challenge knowledge that excludes, while seeming to include" (Hesse-Biber 2007, 1).

It should be noted that feminist knowledge building constitutes one of the cornerstones of the partnership between the urban feminists and the land rights activists, and yet that practice insufficiently addresses the gap between the "educators" and those being educated. The experience of observing the outcomes of both this urban–rural partnership and the "feminist socialization process" was a fascinating part of my fieldwork learning experience, as I got to speak with السلاليات (*sulāliyāt*) about their perceptions of the terms used to represent them in national and international women's rights forums. These conversations exposed from the very beginning the power structures of the rights-based framework, in the sense that the conversations juxtaposed the dichotomy between "teachings or teachers" and "recipient or beneficiaries" that characterizes the rights framework.

In fact, engaging with the power relationships between the researcher and the researched by looking at knowledge as it emanates from positions of power and privilege is another key aspect of committed research. The research agenda needs to address the power relationship between the researcher and the researched. Changing the name of the research participants does not do much and is insufficient. Even for the most sensitive researcher, the power relationship cannot be transcended, since the researcher will analyze the life, ideas, and behavior of the researched and produce a text representing the researched; as Lena Meari points out, "we cannot go beyond but can only learn how to deal with power relationship" (Meari 2015). Even if the researched and researcher come from the same class and nationality, the power relationship cannot be transcended. The power relationship takes various forms depending on the race, class, gender, and colonial history of the people being researched. In a similar vein, there is no such a thing as an abstract researcher; the power relationship can be subject to change because it is not fixed. Additionally, those who work with marginalized, vulnerable populations need to be aware of the risk of constructing those groups as victims and the researcher as the agent who will save these vulnerable populations. Victims are unable to act, and in fact, it is quite valuable for researchers to find strategies that not only look at power structures but for sources to counter power. Instead of relying on the dichotomy of victim or hero, one can be both victim and hero (Meari 2015).

Although the perspective of the السلاليات (*sulāliyāt*) is embedded within the intersections of gender and class, ethnicity, and structural economic and political violence, the movement is nevertheless managing to challenge the rights framework championed by urban feminists. As noted at the outset, their stories complicate debates about the meaning of "women's rights activism" because gender discrimination proves to be too narrow (Rignall 2019, 3) and too small a category to describe their struggle. Working with land rights activists as an engaged researcher has shown me that the neoliberal age—and the state's appropriation of human and women's rights rhetoric—has made it so that female land rights activism can only survive and grow outside the agenda of the very feminist activists who led the gender-based reforms of the last three decades. In what follows, I reflect further on the shifts and twists that characterized my fieldwork experience and on how responding to the lessons from the field—as part of my engaged research approach—necessitated the need to account for an emerging female leadership that operates not only outside the urban centers but also beyond the "universal" abstract and apolitical language of feminism with regard to female autonomy and gender equality. My decision to account for السلاليات (*sulāliyāt*) leadership was a strategic one, and I adopted this approach in order to draw attention to their counterpower rather than construct them as mere victims of inequality who are waiting to be saved. For this reason, I used qualitative methods, including nondirective and unstructured collective interviews, instead of the one-on-one interviews that I had initially planned, which allowed space for "the researcher and the researched to participate in structuring reality" (Altorki and El-Solh 1988, 4). My planned research methods were constantly undermined by the السلاليات (*sulāliyāt*) terms: the السلاليات (*sulāliyāt*) refused anonymity and confidentiality because they wanted to take credit for their struggle. They not only agreed to have their voice recorded, some of them asked to be videotaped, as speaking to the camera was more of an outlet for their frustrations and disillusionment.

I adapted my methods in part because I felt I had to fulfill the role of communicating their concerns to the highest authorities. Some of them addressed the king and expressed how supportive they are of his leadership. Others sought international media because their experience is that the local media is beholden to other interests. I met a journalist from the *New York Times* who was reluctant, in the beginning, to report the السلاليات (*sulāliyāt*) story because she thought that it would be too complicated to explain the issue to an American audience. Later, she decided to cover the story, and the *New York Times* piece proved to be very effective in scaring off the police (Alami 2017). The women told me that they dealt with less police harassment and fewer threats of expulsion from their houses after the article was published. Even now, they continue to post the article together with the French *Le Monde* piece on their Facebook page to remind the authorities how far they can get.

السلاليات (*Sulāliyāt*) stories of struggle against land grabbing, abuse, and economic and political power shift our focus from the patriarchal family to neoliberal and political authoritarian structures. Deeply rooted in their particular socioeconomic circumstances—including land expropriation and the displacement of indigenous peasant populations in the name of "development" and the "public common good"—السلاليات (*sulāliyāt*) women anchor their discussion of gender dynamics within the intersectional structural inequalities that are produced and reproduced through land commodification and the alliance between the open market economy and patriarchal political authoritarianism.

Fieldwork Shifts and Changes

The exploration phase of my preliminary research led me to the Azilal region, where I first met السلاليات (*sulāliyāt*) women in the offices of the FLDDF, a leading women's rights NGO tied to universal and international feminism. As was the case with other urban associations, such as the ADFM, FLDDF positioned itself both as a partner and mediator between the السلاليات (*sulāliyāt*) and researchers, journalists, and even government officials. I was advised to speak to the urban association's leaders before meeting the السلاليات (*sulāliyāt*), so I first conducted semistructured interviews with the leaders of FLDDF. During the interviews and meetings I had at FLDDF's offices, the leaders pointed to the fact that the women's mobilization in Azilal mainly started after reports about women's protests in Kenitra region showed that women had managed to achieve recognition, not only receiving a share of the land benefits but also being appointed as official tribe delegates, in some cases. Upon learning that fact, I then had to shift my fieldwork to Kenitra in order to learn more about the protest movement there.

Despite needing to relocate my fieldwork, the research question I came up with during the Transformative Engaged Gender Research training—about the specificities of the السلاليات (*sulāliyāt*) women's conditions that led to their involvement in the protest movement around collective lands privatization—proved to be a very useful entry to the field. The question allowed me to look at the commonalities, differences, conflicts, and disputes over divergent interests and helped me to avoid homogenizing the movement; the question also revealed new issues in terms of how the territory, so to speak, had been divided between women's rights activists and the السلاليات (*sulāliyāt*). In fact, compared to Azilal, the division in Kenitra embodied a sharper divide between the territory of women's and human rights and السلاليات (*sulāliyāt*) territory. The urban activists were clear about who was allowed to "benefit" from their support and visibility in both local and national media. For example, most of the meetings and protests are reported by the main public television, and only the السلاليات (*sulāliyāt*) affiliated with the urban NGO are invited to speak—and then only about their struggles with their brothers and with the dominant "masculine mentality" in their village, which prevents their access to their land "benefits." Because I was initially interested in the "partnership" between urban feminists and السلاليات (*sulāliyāt*) women, I went to the field with the aim of learning about the perspective of feminist and human rights activists toward السلاليات (*sulāliyāt*) women. I was interested in how feminist and human rights discourses had shifted to accommodate new issues, such as those specifically related to السلاليات (*sulāliyāt*) concerns.

The first meetings and interviews at the FLDDF elucidated some of the terms of the urban–rural partnership, but it also highlighted the power dynamics that shaped the relationship between the السلاليات (*sulāliyāt*) and the LDDF (Berriane 2016). The urban feminists positioned themselves not only as educators providing guidance about the path to maximum gains within the state's framework of apolitical, "development"-oriented guidelines but also as guardians speaking in the name of, and instead of, the السلاليات (*sulāliyāt*), seeking not to undermine entrenched political power but instead to look for ways to fit within the spaces offered by the "performance of human rights" (Slyomovics 2005, 9).

For example, while telling the story of the partnership between the السلاليات (sulāliyāt) and the FLDDF, Latifa, one of the leaders of FLDDF in Beni Mellal, explained how important it was for the السلاليات (sulāliyāt) to learn to navigate within networks where political and economic power are interwoven and, therefore, are active participants who feed the aforementioned performance of human rights. In that sense, an alignment with the state's support for local development initiatives can be a space within which السلاليات (sulāliyāt) can safely operate. This is why Latifa thought that attaching "development" to the name of the first السلاليات (sulāliyāt) association in Beni Mellal could constitute a smart move; as she said, "having development in the name of the association would give more chances for the association to be granted the authorities' license because it would sound less political." For Latifa, "السلاليات (sulāliyāt)'s objective is to learn the language and the vocabulary of rights and start referencing the constitution that guarantees gender parity" (Latifa, pers. comm., January 2016). What Latifa is describing here—the depoliticization and forced conversion of السلاليات (sulāliyāt) experiences of expropriation into an apolitical rights framework that can be conveyed through local and international forums—stands out the first notable aspect of the gap but also, and perhaps more importantly, of the incommensurability between the السلاليات (sulāliyāt) and the terms in which they are represented (Abu Lughod 2009).

As I have already noted, my first meeting with السلاليات (sulāliyāt) proved to be quite challenging and disruptive to "my research plans." Instead of the one-on-one interview I had planned, I had a group of land rights activists show up to the meeting and turn the interview into a focus group of their own. In Kenitra, family members of the السلاليات (sulāliyāt) women joined the meeting, and one father commented constantly on what the السلالية (sulaliya) said. In this case, I embraced the approaches I had learned through my engaged research trainings, holding onto empathy, and opting to leave aside my rigorous research methods and plans. That decision helped me bond with the السلاليات (sulāliyāt) and laid the groundwork for a relationship of trust that allowed me the possibility of going beyond mere interview and opening space for their genuine and transparent conversation about power and powerlessness. Watching the السلالية (sulaliya) tell their stories about the complexity of their everyday struggles against the expropriation of their land offered me a new perspective, one that had been unknown to me until then. Moreover, the knowledge this perspective provided was too concrete and detailed to be subsumed into predetermined categories and concepts, and it was difficult for me to fully capture and convert what I learned into writing. In truth, despite the assumption that "indigenous field-workers are believed to be able to avoid the problem of culture shock or anomie" (Altorki and El-Solh 1988, 8), that they are expected to be less likely to experience "cultural fatigue"—namely, the strain of being a stranger in an unfamiliar cultural setting and the demands that places on their role as researcher (Altorki and El-Solh 1988, 8)—I did experience "cultural fatigue." The fieldwork tested my limited attention span and my capacity to listen to stories. I felt anxious that I might not be able to translate meaningfully. I felt that my interviewees expected me to be part of the solution to their problem, which further increased the initial feelings of anxiety and helplessness I had experienced.

My lack of awareness of "the wider implications of the social reality" (Altorki and El-Solh 1988, 8) of the collective land issue constituted both a handicap and an advantage. My lack of formal knowledge helped me open up to the السلاليات (sulāliyāt) experiences, which put me in the position of being a silent observer and a woman, more than a researcher (Joseph 1988). The السلاليات (sulāliyāt) stories were both new and familiar. Narratives about ancestral and identity-based connections with the land recalled my own family stories about land disputes and the dominant arbitrariness of who gets and can claim a share of the land. Speaking to the السلاليات (sulāliyāt) revived memories of stories from generations of women in my family, who told of their alienation in both the villages they had come from and the urban spaces where they later moved. I could identify with the السلاليات (sulāliyāt) stories because of my working-class and rural origins, but while I could have conversations with the urban feminists because of my education and research interests, I could not relate to them personally as I did with the السلاليات (sulāliyāt).

In fact, my underlying discomfort with the elite feminists involved with the rights framework was brought to surface by the السلاليات (sulāliyāt) stories about how they have had to struggle not only for their land but also for the very terms of their representation. One of my first glimpses of the power dynamics between the السلاليات (sulāliyāt) and the feminist groups came while listening to Aya's story about how difficult it was for her to negotiate between the feminist urban organization's control of the protest agenda and the women of her village, who would refuse to stand in a protest, with banners, over issues such as domestic violence and the marriage of minors, a story that, to my mind, echoes Lena Meari's aforementioned point about commissioned research ideology—that it is very often derived from essentialist assumptions that should be questioned rather than reinforced. In listening to السلاليات (sulāliyāt) stories, I tried to do the opposite, to respond to lessons from the field, rather than operate according to preconceived assumptions. I kept returning to the ways in which their narratives pointed out this incommensurability between their lived experiences and the terms they were being offered via the right framework. In turn, that experience confirmed a discomfort I have long had with the meaning of debates and conferences on "gender mainstreaming," "women's emancipation," and "liberation" for the women they have claimed to represent. The subsequent stories of the السلاليات (sulāliyāt) who left the urban NGOs because of the restrictions their membership required show the constraints of the rights framework—but their stories also showed me the ways in which the urban NGOs and their activists have created and fed another oppressive regime in the name of women's rights and gender equality. Any voice that does not provide a case against domestic violence and/or an oppressive father, husband, or brother has been diminished and silenced in order to affirm the official line, which says that loss of women's land can be attributed to the "masculine mentality"—that it is being taken away by male family members in accordance with customary local laws. By insisting that the السلاليات (sulāliyāt) only tell stories that uphold this narrative, urban feminist activists are supporting the oppressive regime and obscuring the bigger story—that land is being expropriated and people are being displaced in the name of development and the common good.

The tension between the urban activists' narrative and that of the السلاليات (sulāliyāt) constitute not only a discord but incommensurate stances on land grabbing and its consequences. I chose the السلاليات (sulāliyāt) perspective and maintained the position of the learner of their knowledge and the meanings they attach to displacement and/or eminent police evacuation, disillusionment with urban activists, progressive politics, and the judiciary. The السلاليات (sulāliyāt) I worked with did not adhere to the feminist agenda; their stories disrupted all my expectations about their appropriation of "feminist vocabulary" and I therefore had to choose whether to listen and be open to the fact they were not interested in answering my questions about how their involvement into activism transformed gender dynamics in their communities. I had to abandon my research plan and scope to the السلاليات (sulāliyāt) stories about the loss of the land, the corrupt officials and the complicity of the judiciary, the activists, some journalists, and the new land settlers' "development" projects. The السلاليات (sulāliyāt) were, in fact, pointing out how power does not only dominate and oppress but also constitute subjects (Mahmood 2005). The السلاليات (sulāliyāt) subjectivity constitute in a sense a challenge to any paradigm outside their story with land expropriation.

The contrast between feminist activism that ultimately reinforces an oppressive regime and the السلاليات (sulāliyāt) activism that resists the rights framework is illustrated in stories from two women. Saida Idrissi, a member of ADFM, another women's rights association based in Rabat, recounted a story that explains some of the strategies of urban feminist activists:

> We developed a play out of the السلاليات (sulāliyāt)'s stories that the women performed in the 2014 International Forum on Human Rights in Marrakesh. I could see the change of these women whose fear disappeared, and we could see strong women emerging, we had to work with them to work on becoming loud and then work with them to convince them that they are discriminated against, that what they are undergoing is violence because they were women. Their knowledge was only about their duties not their rights, and they were afraid to confront family members. We worked with them to question family loyalty when it contradicts their rights, when faced with discrimination. Now we realize that we gained a women's movement aware and capable of complaining and addressing the authorities ... women who act and do not wait to be assisted. (Idrissi 2015)

Listening to Saida's victorious tone as she describes her capacity, as a feminist activist, to turn a spontaneous reaction to discrimination into a "women's rights movement," I recalled Soukat's story of how, at the same human rights forum, the television cameras were turned off when she took the microphone during a session on السلاليات (*sulāliyāt*) rights to raise the story of the expropriation of her village's land, a story that resists the rights framework in Saida's story. Soukat had already refused to take part in the play because she thought that it did not represent her plight and those of her people. Looking at the same event from the perspective of these two different narratives—and especially from the perspective of Soukat's silenced voice during the human rights forum—suggests the ways in which reformist feminism, a feminism that "demands equal rights for women within existing class struggle" (hooks 2000, 101), can become an active participant in terms of seriously constraining women's agency in the context of an authoritarian state feminism. For the human rights and women's rights activists, the tragedies of land expropriation were simply an issue of the unequal division of benefits among men and women; they treated the topic as an example of the "masculine mentalities" that need to be eradicated by converting the *sulāliyāt* into feminist activists who advocate for an equal share of land that, in fact, has already been grabbed—and so is largely imagined. The difference between the two women's perspectives revealed not only the class differences but also the urban terms in which the issue has been formulated, which totally disregard the centrality of land and the meaning of its commodification for rural populations who perceive the loss of the land as a loss of *raison d'être* (reason for existence). In order to hear that difference, I had to respond to what I was actually hearing from Soukat, not to rely on established conceptions for what constitutes oppression.

The underlying discrepancy between السلاليات (*sulāliyāt*) women's narratives and the representation of their struggle with land expropriation by the ADFM and FLDDF meant, for me, that carrying on with a research project on a rural and urban partnership for gender equality would imply participation in silencing many of the السلاليات (*sulāliyāt*) I met, talked to, and gotten to know very closely. Between the urban feminists and rural السلاليات (*sulāliyāt*) women; between the work, the activism, the multiple workshops, sit-ins, and protests; between Soukat, Khadija, Aya—there was a clear incommensurability, a rupture between السلاليات (*sulāliyāt*) lived experiences and daily struggles and their representation by both the urban activists and the local and international media, which had mostly been reporting the urban feminists' expansion of Moroccan feminism to rural parts of the country. As Edward Said reminds us, "all representations are misrepresentations" (Said 1978). Studying representation on the basis of human rights or women's rights or any other ideal must be juxtaposed with stories from the grassroots. In revealing the paradoxes of feminist activism, I seek not to undermine the importance of that work but to provide a venue for a conversation from the perspective of the grassroots that define its *raison d'être* in the first place. For such a conversation to be effective, an engaged research methodology has to be followed: we must listen to and interact with the concrete details, with what is actually being said, rather than proceed based on preconceived assumptions derived from a rights framework.

The paradox of a rights-based "regime of truths" (Abu-Lughod 2009) is that it can recreate other frameworks of exclusion that can be even harder to fight than overt patriarchy because of how much silencing they entail. This fact is illustrated by Aya's experience; her encounter with the FLDDF shows how she worked to mobilize the women of her village to come protest for their land, only to find out that the protest's banners and slogans (provided by the FLDDF) were about violence against women and underage marriage. Aya had a hard time communicating the FLDDF's argument to the women of her village, who felt manipulated by the idea that their issue is a form of "economic violence" and that they are victims of their own lack of feminist consciousness. Indeed, she could not convince them because she herself does not believe that framework is appropriate for the fight against land grabbing, even if she agrees that violence against women is a form of injustice.

My encounter with the السلاليات (*sulāliyāt*) meant learning not only about their own stories but also about their perspectives toward how they get represented by their feminist and human rights activists' "sisters and brothers." While listening to them in accordance with the tenets of engaged research, I could see from the very beginning the gap between their narratives and the narratives promoted by leaders of the feminist and human rights groups. That gap became more substantial—and became a more pronounced topic of their narratives—as most of them left the urban NGOs and cut all ties with those who had introduced them to activism and advocacy for their land rights.

Conclusion

I came to the topic of the السلاليات (*sulāliyāt*) thinking that I would be studying an unprecedented alliance between elite urban veteran feminists and rural women who were seeking support for their battle against the norms of land benefits distribution. The first interviews confirmed that assumption, as they all happened within the offices of these urban women's rights or human rights associations themselves. I also observed protests where the human rights activists were there to "supervise" and provide guidance to the protestors. The urban human rights and women's rights activists had set the terms of the debate according to an effectively state-approved, rights-based framework, and so what I saw in their offices and at their protests reinforced the assumptions that had initially guided my understanding of the partnership. However, when I had the chance to interact with the السلاليات (*sulāliyāt*) women who made up the other half of the urban–rural partnership, I realized that I had to shift my approach. I relocated my fieldwork and spoke with the women in a variety of formats. By acting as an engaged researcher—that is, by allowing the accounts of the women themselves to shift the terms of my investigation—I was able to see more clearly the ways in which a rights-based framework is incommensurable with the lived experiences of the السلاليات (sulāliyāt).

In response, and in an attempt to examine knowledge as it emanates from positions of power and privilege, I then organized a study day at my university and invited some السلاليات (sulāliyāt). Both the study day I organized at Ibn Tofail University in Kenitra and the interviews with السلاليات (sulāliyāt) outside the auspices of the urban women's rights associations revealed more about the dynamics of the power relationships between the militant feminists and the السلاليات (sulāliyāt). These revelations reinforced the idea that fieldwork needs to start from the viewpoint and the concrete lives of marginalized people (Alcoff and Potter 1993, 5). Listening to السلاليات (sulāliyāt) narratives of frustration—of being patronized and alienated by militant human rights and feminist activists— reveals the many unexamined assumptions that guide formal research and suggests that research often maintains power and privilege rather than questioning it. Working with the السلاليات (sulāliyāt) also revived my own memories of experiences that I had with militant feminism while I was a graduate student, and the discomfort and biases I developed in reaction to elite reformist feminism. Even if my biases have partly informed my research since, they have also helped me to recognize السلاليات (sulāliyāt) agency outside and, apart from, formal militant feminism norms and values. My own experiences and my work with the السلاليات (sulāliyāt) have also helped me to recognize possibilities for activism outside a rights-based, legalistic framework—to avoid being crippled by abstract, fixed, and predetermined categories that may or may not be meaningful to large segment of the population and to instead remain open to insights relevant to concrete life experiences.

Notes

1 This research fieldwork was accomplished thanks to Open Society Foundation funding and the guidance provided by the Training for Engaged Transformative Gender Research workshops run by distinguished professor of gender and sexuality Suad Joseph and professors Lena Meari and Zeina Zaatari. I am indebted to Lena Meari for reading and commenting on many drafts of this chapter.
According to Moroccan economist Mohammed Said Saadi, "Sulala is the patrilineal genealogical relationship among members of an ethnic group with collective land ownership. السلاليات (sulāliyāt) are women descendants from the same Sulala or ethnic group" (Saadi 2017, 5). Additionally, Moroccan political scientist Yasmine Berriane notes: "The term 'السلاليات (sulāliyāt)' appeared in Morocco's public sphere in relation

to a women's movement that began in 2007. It refers to women who belong to communities with use rights to collectively owned land" (Saadi 2017, 351).

2   I am particularly grateful for Dr. Suad Joseph's support during this process.

Bibliography

Abu-Lughod, Lila. 2009. "Anthropology in the Territory of Rights, Islamic, Human, and Otherwise." *Proceedings of the British Academy Lectures* 167. DOI:10.5871/bacad/9780197264775.003.0008.

Alami, Aida. 2017. "In a Fight for Land, a Women's Movement Shakes Morocco." *New York Times*. https://www.nytimes.com/2017/05/07/world/africa/morocco-sulaliyyate-lands-women-inheritance.html.

Alcoff, Linda, and Elizabeth Potter. 1993. "Introduction: Feminisms Intersect Epistemology." In *Feminist Epistemologies*, edited by Linda Alcoff and Elizabeth Potter, 1–14. New York: Routledge.

Altorki, Soraya, and Camillia Fawzi El-Solh, eds. 1988. "Introduction." In *Arab Women in the Field: Studying Your Own Society*, edited by Soraya Altorki and Camillia Fawzi El-Solh, 1–24. Syracuse, NY: Syracuse University Press.

Berriane, Yasmine. 2016. "Bridging Social Divides: Leadership and the Making of an Alliance for Women's Land-Use Rights in Morocco." *Review of African Political Economy* 43 (149): 350–64.

Hesse-Biber, Sharlene N. 2007. "Feminist Research: Exploring, Interrogating and Transforming the Interconnections of Epistemology, Methodology and Method." In *Handbook of Feminist Research: Theory and Praxis*, edited by Sharlene N. Hesse-Biber, 2–27. London: Sage.

hooks, bell. 2000. *Where We Stand: Class Matters*. New York: Routledge.

Idrissi, Saida. 2015. Interview with the author in March 2015.

Jad, Islah. 2003. "The NGO-ization of Arab Women's Movements." *Al-Raida Journal* 20 (100): 38–47. https://doi.org/10.32380/alrj.v0i0.442.

Joseph, Suad. 1988. "Feminization, Familism, Self and Politics." In *Arab Women in The Field: Studying Your Own Society*, edited by Soraya Altorki and Fawzi Camillia El-Solh, 25–48. Syracuse, NY: Syracuse University Press.

Joseph, Suad. 1994. "Problematizing Gender and Relational Rights: Experiences from Lebanon." *Social Politics International Studies in Gender, State, and Society* 1, no. 3 (Fall): 271–85.

Joseph, Suad. 2015. "Overview of Components of a Research Proposal." Lecture, Training on Engaged Transformative Gender Research, Beirut, Lebanon.

Mackinnon, Catherine. 1998. "Difference and Dominance: On Sex Discrimination." In *Feminism and Politics*, edited by Anne Philips, 295–313. Oxford University Press.

Meari, Lena. 2015. "Power Relations in Field Work Research." Lecture, Training on Engaged Transformative Gender Research, Amman, Jordan.

Morsy, Soheir. 1988. "Fieldwork in My Egyptian Homeland: Toward the Demise of Anthropology's Distinctive-Other Hegemonic Tradition." In *Arab Women in the Field: Studying Your Own Society*, edited by Soraya Altorki and Camillia Fawzi El-Solh, 69–90. Syracuse, NY: Syracuse University Press.

Rignall, Karen. 2019. "Is Rurality a Form of Gender-based Violence in Morocco?" *Journal of Applied Language and Culture Studies* 2: 15–33.

Saadi, Said. 2017. "Sulalyyat Movement For Dignity and Land Rights." In *Men Defending Equal Inheritance Laws*, edited by Hakima Lebbar. Rabat: Fan-Dok.
Said, Edward. 1978. *Orientalism*. New York: Vintage Books.
Scott, Joan W. 1996. *Only Paradoxes to Offer: French Feminists and the Rights of Man*. Cambridge, MA: Harvard University Press.
Slyomovics, Susan. 2005. *The Performance of Human Rights in Morocco*. Philadelphia: University of Pennsylvania Press.

4 THE DAY I BECAME A GENTRIFIER: NARRATIVES FROM THE OUTSIDER/ INSIDER ETHNOGRAPHER IN THE FIELD

Reeham Mourad

Prologue

Back in spring 2016, I conducted a field study at the pottery village as part of my master's thesis. One of the main chapters of the thesis focused on gentrification and gender dynamics. This previous field experience provoked another set of questions forcing me to return to the pottery village again three years later in an attempt to trace gentrification and its cultural and gender implications. I went from being a monthly amateur visitor to a resident at the pottery village. My understanding of the nature of the pottery village has been reshaped from spring 2016 to spring and summer 2019 when I conducted ethnographic field research at the same location twice respectively.

The day I became a gentrifier is a deep dive into the subjective narratives of my journey at the pottery village, Kom Ghorab, old Cairo. These narratives illustrate my positionality as an ethnographer with reference to: the local community of the pottery village, the pottery village as a spatial context witnessing a wave of gentrification since 2008, and the studio I had rented for my six-month stay.[1] I position myself as an outsider and an upper-middle-class female. I had the means to pay a monthly rent that was twice the sum of what a resident potter pays per year for the usufruct.² That was the first milestone on the story of becoming a gentrifier among other creative class artists who had a connection with the village.³

I demonstrate the challenges and ethical dilemmas I was confronted with during my stay at the pottery village between December 2018 and May 2019 where I carried out an ethnographic study of a paper titled "The Production of Culture, Gentrification and Gender Implications at the Pottery Village, Kom Ghorab, Historic Cairo."⁴ I aimed at exploring the various social groups present within the urban community at the village by dealing with local potters, in addition to working-class women from Kom Ghorab, upper-middle-class women visitors, contemporary artists, and researchers who are recognized as the creative class at the pottery village.⁵

The pottery village has been witnessing a wave of cultural gentrification since the foundation of Darb 1718 in 2008.⁶ Potters have been replaced by contemporary artists who are highly visible at the pottery village with their cultural practices.⁷ These cultural practices create a wave of protection as a tactic from the working-class men in Kom Ghorab toward their wives and Darb 1718 in which local men do not allow their wives to go to the village. To this day and by comparing my two field experiences in 2016 and 2019, I demonstrate what I witnessed in the field through the flow of anthropological levels; notions of selfhood, personhood, and individuality; and the process of reconnecting, resocializing, and reexperiencing with the interlocutors. Moreover, I demonstrate how my positionality has been transformed from being an outsider researcher to an insider gentrifier. In doing so, I draw upon "gentrification" as an urban phenomenon in the pottery village, and the formulation of the pottery village as a field of social interaction and cultural production. Furthermore, this is an attempt to understand how the flow of the fieldwork is transformed according to the circumstances of the pottery village nature.

Contextualizing the Field

The pottery village is a newly built environment constructed during the millennium development plan in the period between 2000 and 2007 (Sayed 2016). The construction phase took seven years. The village consists of 30 workshop units. Every local potter/artisan has a unit. Cairo's governorate did not have a plan to relocate the potters to continue their work. Potters had to deal with the relocation on their own. During the years of construction, most of the potters/artists lost their client base. Therefore, some of the potters lost their jobs and were compelled to shift to other professions during those years of construction, leading to the loss of valuable craftsmen resulting in the deterioration of the craft. A few of the original artists and potters remained committed to the industry, in spite of losing their customers. Potters were struggling to make ends meet during these years. Many pottery artisans started working in other professions to earn their living, and as a consequence, the pottery industry has witnessed a breakdown. Potters returned to their newly built workshop units while in debt due to the accumulative usufruct they had to pay during the construction phase. They began to rent either the whole unit or part of it in order to increase their income. The right to rent the building rises from the concept of usufruct. In 2008, Darb 1718 Contemporary Art and Culture Center was founded by the contemporary artist Motaz Nasr as a focal gathering point for budding contemporary artists. Also, the 25th of January uprising caused both a boom in the landscape of local contemporary arts and an economic breakdown in the pottery industry. Darb 1718's fame has been rising ever since. Moreover, the presence of Darb 1718 has attracted various arts, cultural, and design entities like Azza Fahmy Design School to move into the pottery village.[8] On the other hand, there are only nine out of 30 potters who still maintain the industry. Due to these circumstances, gentrification was perhaps not intended; however, it has become a fact inside the pottery village. The rents have been gradually increasing parallel to the social displacement of the local potters with the contemporary upper-middle-class artists (the creative class) at the pottery village. The socioeconomic composition of the pottery village has henceforth changed and accompanied by new gender implications and dynamics.

The Field's Constituents

> A social space is always, and simultaneously, both a field of action … and a basis of action. (Lefebvre 1991, 191)

To answer such a question and to conduct the ethnographic study, I started to think about the "field" from a multidimensional perspective. In my case, the field is situated more precisely as a site constructed through the shifting entanglements of an anthropological notion of cultural areas (Gupta and Ferguson 1992, 8). The notion of cultural areas could be supplemented and manifested through the ideas of ethnicity, religion, and languages. The idea of the field is formed through constructing a space for possibilities (Gupta and Ferguson 1992, 2). The field, with all it might contain, is the imperative possibility of anthropology whether it is physical or conceptual. Not to mention that some anthropological ideas about the "field," culture areas, and geographical specializations have been transformed by anthropologists' encounters with the crude realities of decolonization (Gupta and Ferguson 1992, 10). In that sense, the pottery village, as the field, is constructed through intertwined local and imperialist cultures, accompanied by normalized yet conservative societal standards, a combination of historical narratives, and my latter social connections in 2019.[9,]

The field is a place where the transition from theory to reality takes place and vice versa. It is a testing ground for the ideas of researchers. It is the place where the anthropologist wears the lens of the flaneur and is critical about the past as well as current events while capturing the culture of the society.[10] I was trying to define the field and my relationship to it back in the spring of 2016. I struggled to position myself as an ethnographer or a feminist researcher. I was scratching the surface of exploring how ethnography would work. This propelled me to return to the pottery village.

Hunting for a Place "A First Step Again into the Pottery Village"

In November 2018, I called a friend who had rented a ground-floor studio at the pottery village back in 2017 to connect me to any potter through whom I could find a place to stay. He put me in touch with a local sculptor at the pottery village. I called him and he welcomed me to visit him in his studio. He tried to connect me to one of the workshop unit's owners that might sublet me a space at his unit.[11] I waited for the man and when he came, I began to introduce myself as a researcher who needs a studio for six months to conduct a field study. He told me that he only has one available space on the ground floor where the monthly rent was five thousand Egyptian pounds. This was not convenient for my budget. When I started to negotiate the rent, he stated that this might be the cheapest studio I could find to rent. He asked me several questions about the nature of my research, what I am going to do, and why I need to rent a studio. I explained that my research deals with the historical narratives of the pottery village ever since the start of the millennium development plan. At this point, I did not tell him about the gender-related aspects of my research since it is critical to speak of gender issues in such a conservative area. To my surprise, he mentioned that if I was a university student who was only interested in visiting the area for research purposes or art projects, he would help me like other students who come to the pottery village to work on their graduation projects. He added that since I will become part of the pottery village community as an inhabitant who will rent a studio, he cannot reveal any information about the pottery village to me because he considered me an outsider. Outsiders should depend on themselves, he explained. I agreed to smoothly end the conversation and seal the deal. The incident was always memorable to me during my fieldwork as it positioned me from the beginning of the field as an outsider.

Another artisan at the pottery village introduced me to Hesham Zean, who is the son of one of the original potters 'Amm Zean. After a brief introduction about myself, a short discussion on why I need to rent a studio at the pottery village, and negotiating the rent again, Hesham agreed to rent me a studio at his father's building unit. I became the outsider who does not belong to the pottery village's original community but the insider who came in and resided like any upper-middle-class artist, architect, or researcher in which I can assume that I slightly belonged to this community.

An Anthropological Overview

The fieldwork experience is widely discussed by anthropologists; it reveals problems such as the representation of self, communication, the interpretation of societies, and how personal relationships affect data (Ellen 1984). According to Roy Ellen (1984), social anthropology works on three levels. The first level is the declared object that makes the anthropologist constitute some ideas of the society since this object is considered as the fountainhead (Ellen 1984). The second level is the perspective of the anthropologists trying to make real statements about society by being an individual component involved in the historical time-flow and particular incidents (Ellen 1984). The third one is the relationship of the self to others that is based on a set of assumptions and predictions by the anthropologist (Ellen 1984). Accordingly, my decision to start the fieldwork with participant observation was influenced by these three levels. I began by capturing the lived experiences in the village, followed by oral history sessions to identify the object of the study represented in the historical narrative of gentrification as an urban and cultural phenomenon. The declared object in my study is gentrification that constitutes the current everyday life of the pottery village as a village for contemporary arts. This period reformulated my understanding of the historical narratives of the pottery village's development plan in which the narratives themselves produce the new cultural image of the village's society as a gentrified place. I based my initial framework on the preliminary observation to establish my departure point; where will I begin, with whom, and what issues I am going to focus on? Throughout my stay, my relationship with the interlocutors has been influenced by factors such as age, class, gender, and appearance. These factors define how the locals interact with me given that, at first glance, I am still an outsider. The relation of the self (the ethnographer and the person) to others is built and transformed through the everyday interaction with the research interlocutors in which the self is produced by the perception of others based on the above-mentioned factors. In doing so, I place a special focus on the direction in which my interaction with the research interlocutors took place and changed over six months given that the pottery village is an enculturated community as interpreted and described by the locals.[12] Therefore, I began to reflect on my journey to the field on a daily basis, exploring how to arrive at the field as an outsider given my social class status as an upper-middle-class female.

The Daily Commute

Every morning, I think of my daily ride from my home in Heliopolis to the pottery village.[13] As previously mentioned, the pottery village is located in Kom Ghorab neighborhood and nearby the Religious Complex.[14] The inhabitants of Kom Ghorab demonstrate that their area is exceptionally different. It is home to three significant religious institutions: Amr Ibn-El-Aas Mosque, The Hanging Church, and Ben Ezra Synagogue. According to the inhabitants, these institutions distinguish the area for its privacy, intimacy, and spirituality, calling for a certain level of respect in many regards. My decision on how to dress was always based on the field's circumstances. Soraya Altorki (1988) reflected on her ethnographic experience of being a Saudi Arabian woman studying her own society by stating that when she showed affirmation/conformity to the Saudi Arabian culture, it gave her more freedom to maneuver the field. Therefore, I tried to match the way I dress up to the local context standards where I was residing for six months. On my way to the field, I witnessed varying degrees of scrutiny: the building guard who closely observes the passersby, the checkpoint I go through at the metro exit, and the policemen standing at the checkpoint as well as on the metro station platform.

I have two ways of commuting to the field, the underground metro and taxi. To avoid Cairo traffic, I prefer to take the underground metro despite how messy and crowded it is as it remains the fastest means of transportation in Cairo. I ride the women-only cabin in the metro for safety reasons to avoid sexual harassment during the morning rush hours. When I arrive at my destination, the Mar-Girgis station, it is a ten-minute walk to the pottery village. During this short walk, I pass through a narrow alleyway packed with policemen who guard the Religious Complex. At the beginning of Qasr El-Sham' street, there is another electric checkpoint secured by policemen where the street is blocked by metal barriers for security purposes. The dominating presence of security forces on the streets of Cairo has been normalized since the 25th of January uprising back in 2011. To reach the pottery village, I pass by some local coffee shops where local inhabitants gaze at me. Local inhabitants in Kom Ghorab usually associate the chaos accompanied by the 25th of January uprising with a security breakdown. Therefore, they justify the presence of the police checkpoint as an essential need that protects their safety and that of visiting tourists. Sometimes I felt insecure because of the different levels of the scrutiny spatially manifested on my way to the pottery village. My insecurities do not only come from the sense that the street is under constant surveillance but also from my awareness of being "a stranger" in the context. This made me feel that I am under the spotlight until I gradually became an insider. I was afraid of being requested to be routinely checked by the policeman in the checkpoint. Although expected as part of everyday life, this did not happen. This dilemma was on my mind during my stay at the pottery village since I am still an outsider.

But arriving in the field daily does not mean that I am intimately connected to the community of the pottery village. It seemed that it is my everyday struggle and joy to comprehend the dynamics of the pottery village in order to outgrow my status as "the outsider." This status remains as a daily concern of being located in a community where displacement, identity, and the culture of differences are embodied (Gupta and Ferguson 1992). It is crucial to investigate this embodiment through the intertwined aspects of personhood, selfhood, and individuality in the process of experiencing and understanding the cultural society of the pottery village.

Portraying the Self

Poole's (2002) notion of "self" is distinctive in which the self is recognized and influenced by the world and people. The process of exploring the "self" is through thoughts, feelings, and other people's perspectives (Poole 2002). Consequently, my ethnographer's notion of self intersects with the research interlocutors to reshape the ethnographer's positionality.

Given "human beings as … living entities among many such entities in the universe, … [as] centers of being or experience, or … [as] members of society" (Harris 1989, 599), the formulation of personhood is associated with human nature, cultural forms and social forces in which he or she expresses a sort of understanding, judgment, and responsibility in a socio-moral order (Poole 2002, 842). Personhood, in the field, cannot be separated from the entitlements of particular social groups. In other words, it is defined by social interaction with others. A set of individuation processes shapes the sense of selfhood through the inward and outward-facing, and the representation of the self within the sociocultural encounters. It is inseparably connected to the perception of others about the person (Poole 2002, 843). Selfhood is a layered process in which multiple representations are organized, contextualized, and negotiated (Ewing 1990, 274). From the notions of personhood and selfhood, individuality is constructed through clutching moral values, recognizing the goals and constraints in the field in which he or she can make choices and be flexible with plans, and gathered through and embedded in lived experiences (Poole 2002, 844). Poole (2002, 845) adds to the Western perspective of individuality, which has a different kind of uniqueness apart from the sociocultural traditions. Thus, the ethnographic field experience by individuals should recognize the local understanding of personal and cultural differences. By contextualizing myself, given the above, as an outsider who is perceived by the locals as a stranger veiled but with curly bangs, I had to reconnect, resocialize, reexperience the pottery village again to understand how my personhood, selfhood, and individuality are intertwined and formulated in the presence of and interaction with the local interlocutors during the six months of the field study.

Reconnecting in the Enculturated Field

The Intertwined Outsider/Insider

There was a personal incident that took place in spring 2016 when I conducted my preliminary field research. I was walking from the metro station to the pottery village, and I noticed that the men along the street were staring at me. I did not feel comfortable back then and I asked the upper-middle-class women working at several art entities in the pottery village if they have the same feeling given that their appearance and outfits look different from those of the locals. The answer was yes. I accompanied a female from Tarek Waly's heritage center to experience this walk together and we heard catcalls. Since then, these experiences have been integrated as a legitimate source in my understanding of gender implications of cultural gentrification due to the presence of Darb 1718.

Since 2018, I have been developing an in-depth interest in feminist methodologies and feminist geography in which I am inspired by feminist geographers' work on the complex relationship between women and cities. Besides, feminist methodologies helped me get closer to the community at the pottery village in which I am clear about my positionality, methodology, interlocutors, research questions, and objectives. Therefore, I was seeking the local women with whom I am willing to work. At the beginning of the fieldwork, Hesham introduced me to Moustafa.[15] I tried to remind him that I am the girl who came in the spring of 2016. I was so glad that Moustafa remembered me since I used to meet him every day I went to the village.

The familiarity with the field resulted from how social interaction encloses and shapes sociocultural phenomena (Bruner and Bornstein 1989). It has also culminated through the interactive processes, their structure, contents, contexts, and actors in addition to how the person becomes an actor taking part in these processes to position the self through a status that excogitates social relations in a certain society (Poole 2002). Moreover, these processes require the acquisition of skills, sensitivities, and dispositions appropriate to such social participation (Poole 2002). Accordingly, I started to explore new people at the pottery village and reconnect with the people I used to know since 2016. I revisited Fayqa, a woman who manages a pottery workshop whom I had interviewed back in 2016. On the right entrance of the village, I met 'Umm Adel (mother of Adel), a woman from Kom Ghorab who sells sandwiches, cigarettes, and biscuits. I visited her to buy a sandwich among other artists who are used to dealing with her. This process inevitably entails some degree of resocialization by interacting with locals of the pottery village. In addition, I was invited for a cup of mate tea with a musician who also rents a studio at the pottery village. I was eager to explore how artists experience the enculturation of the village and how they position themselves among other outsiders/gentrifiers. Throughout the process of socialization, I went to Darb 1718's administrative office with help from Hesham to introduce myself to the staff. I took a tour with Moustafa within the pottery village and he started to introduce me, as a relocated researcher, to the local potters and artists. Sometimes, I would knock on the doors of the local potters on my own to buy local pottery products from them in order to have more conversations for my research.

As previously mentioned, I could not introduce myself back in 2016 as an ethnographer because I was not one of the pottery village's social network. I was just a daily visitor hosted at Tarek Waly center in addition to my nonfamiliarity with important anthropological concepts and methodologies. With time, I started to introduce myself as an ethnographer. This happened as a result of my accumulated knowledge and awareness of the village's sociocultural context. I also started doing oral history sessions, participant observation, and in-depth interviews to trace the historical narrative of gentrification and respectively its cultural and gender implications. Given my positionality, I was very sensitive about my academic terminologies since it is becoming a habit of mine to mix my native Egyptian Arabic dialect with some English terms. Language was one of the ethical dilemmas I had to deal with later and give attention to during my chats with the locals. This intertwined relationship with the locals of the pottery village of being an outsider who is becoming an insider remains manifested in every step I took during the field experience. Whenever I tried to make new connections, my choice of language was sometimes a barrier with certain interlocutors, while being a useful tool when attempting to connect with other artists.

Locals got used to asking me why I rented a studio. My conventional answer is that I need to record and observe the everyday life and cultural practices happening in the pottery village. Thus, my work might not be affected since I live in the village. Surprisingly, some research interlocutors working at Darb 1718 with a sociology and/or political science education were so supportive and engaged in my ethnographic research. Sometimes, I was impressed by some of the locals' perspective and understanding of my research and presence. In the beginning, I thought that being a local ethnographer relocated to the pottery village in a working-class neighborhood might be a commonly accepted matter since I am Egyptian. Nevertheless, the historical background of the ethnographic work reveals that ethnography traditionally focused on the Western gaze toward the exotic East (Gupta and Ferguson 1997). This was slightly similar to my case in which I, as an outsider, would explore how gentrification as a representation of cultural imperialism affects local inhabitants since I am seen as a well-educated researcher who studied abroad. Meanwhile, the current status of the pottery village accepts the presence of diverse groups of artists from all over the world who can display their art at Darb 1718's galleries.

Since the anthropologist's goal in the field is to illustrate the culture of a group of people in a way that makes the features of this culture seem familiar, it has been a struggle to write on the cultural difference of several social groups. Lila Abu-Lughod (2008) discussed how the knowledge produced in this regard should be differentiated between the subjectivity of the researcher and whose culture is studied. She also clarified that culture's advantages remove differences like behaviors, customs, traditions, rules, plans, recipes, instructions, or programs—culture is learned and can change (Abu-Lughod 2008, 55). Given the pottery village as an imperialist context, my research assumption, and from preliminary socialization in the field, I recognized that I carried a Western perspective and gaze with me into the local field. Sometimes I smoke cigarettes and invite male and female friends to my studio, which is not familiar in such a conservative context. Since I am still seen as an outsider who does not share the same values as those residing in such a conservative area, this required me dealing with its standards.

Apart from the village's indigenous social network, few researchers might be interested to be part of the pottery village and work with the local artisans. Despite my privileged position in the pottery village, I feel fortunate to have been one of these "few." Being an Egyptian and having gradually become aware of the use of language during my communication with local potters gave me the advantage of being able to get help both from the local potters as well as the contemporary artists. To this end, reconnecting, resocializing, and reexperiencing were important pillars in my methodology while bonding with the locals. Nevertheless, some eyes inside the pottery village wondered what I was doing there. That became apparent during my first meeting with a sculptor and a friend of his. The sculptor's friend, who has a workshop unit at the village, claimed that the knowledge I produce on the pottery village would not be helpful to him, nor the potters, or the artists since he believes in practical work rather than academic knowledge. Although this may be true, I did not react to this incident but his question triggered an ethical aspect that I did not think of. What would I contribute to the local community with my research? I could not find an answer back then. Positioning myself as the least credible member in this conversation with fear made me readjust my original research methodology to avoid some disagreements within the community of the pottery village about my presence.

When I started, the ethnographic fieldwork was divided into three phases: participant observation, oral history with local potters, and focus group discussions with local women. My preliminary focus was on tracing gentrification and capturing gender oppression.[16] Accordingly, my initial interlocutors were potters and local women. During the first phase of the field, I adopted participant observation to form my ideas about the village's society. Secondly, I started the oral history sessions in order to understand how gentrification as a phenomenon became rooted in the village over the years. Later, I had to reach out to local women to investigate if they are oppressed as I assumed.[17] Due to difficulties in the field that restricted me from gathering all women in one place, I had to replace the focus group discussions with in-depth interviews with local women to avoid any sensitive issues that might emerge. After conducting in-depth interviews, I arrived at a different perspective that contradicts my assumption about them being oppressed or prohibited from accessing the village. Local women resist being oppressed and continuously try to get exposed to the art activities in the pottery village. I quickly learned that my positionality as a researcher sometimes disorientated my research. Henceforth, I decided to put aside my biases regarding this issue to allow the interlocutors' insights to direct this specific part of my research. I learnt that I should not position myself over what is acknowledged in reality given that it was only my third month at the village. This ethical dilemma, throughout the process of socialization and learning, became a turning point in conducting the field. Under these conditions, my research question and methodology were slightly amended again. Moreover, a new question arose from this wrong assumption that included the upper-middle-class female artists working inside different art entities at the village as new interlocutors. These female artists revealed how gender interaction and dynamics took place inside the pottery village in addition to their own perspectives about the village as an enculturated field.

After the last phase of data collection and being among the pottery village society, it was already my sixth month of stay. I could no longer renew my contract to extend my stay. In the summer of 2019, I continued the fieldwork remotely. The upcoming interlocutors were upper-middle-class artists. I arranged the in-depth interviews in a Greco cafe at Maadi.[18] Although I thought it would be easy to reach out to the artists from the pottery village, the situation was not as I imagined. Being present and visible, during my six-month stay in the pottery village, gave me the credibility to easily conduct the fieldwork and gain access to the interlocutors as a trusted researcher. For this reason, my choice of upper-middle-class artists was influenced by the connections I made during my stay. I tried to reconnect again with the female artists I used to know during the field research. I managed to meet one female artist working at "Azza Fahmy Design School."

Overall, I was conscious enough with regard to my presence. I usually think about the relationship between "the self" and "the others." I often ask myself: what constitutes "me" in relation to them? My answer is that I am an outsider/insider who had an intercultural field experience. This experience has formed the paradox regarding gentrification as a phenomenon I criticize through my research and my positionality as a gentrifier in which I became.

Why the outsider/insider? This is an interconnected relationship between "the self" and "the others." Sometimes, I am the insider who resided in the pottery village not only to seek answers for my questions but also to build human connections with the locals. On the other hand, I am the gentrifier that rented a studio to spend a couple of months conducting the field research and then leave. At the end of the day, I am neither a potter nor a local. I am an outsider coming for academic purposes in the field. I am a woman with curly bangs that made the locals perceive me as a hipster or an artist among others at the village. During this stage of my work, I managed to break the barrier of being an outsider. I went outside the physical boundaries of the pottery village which I had always perceived as restrictive for certain local people. As Diane Lewis (1973) eloquently explained, "The insider, on the other hand, is accountable; s/he must remain in the community and take responsibility for her/his actions. Thus, s/he is forced through self-interest to exercise discretion" (588). I started to initiate visits to local women at their homes where I can record their life stories to test my previous assumptions and biases. I became the locus of their daily experiences during these visits in which perceiving and exchanging ideas about myself and them formulated a new form of social interaction during the field.

Conclusion

To this end, the pottery village as a field was also constructed through my intertwined lens as an outsider/insider ethnographer in how I perceive it at the beginning of my field experience, by the end of my stay, and how the pottery village is. The process of understanding the village lies between my perception and reality. From the beginning, I thought of the pottery village as an enculturated place where the process of acquiring certain characteristics and cultural practices by a social group or individuals (Poole 2002) reshaped the village's image. In other words, the current artistic image of the village is taken as reality despite the historical narratives that interpret the transformations from a village for potters to a village for contemporary arts. I previously understood that the society of the village was dominated by a certain social group enculturating the rest of local social networks as well as the village itself. In fact, the nature of the village as a place for potters, and its historical location, made the process of enculturation pour into a cohesive cultural community where the potters, sometimes, collaborate with contemporary artists and vice versa. These aspects remain significant; the pottery village produces a culture embodied in the pottery industry in addition to contemporary arts.

My accumulative understanding of the village is a subjective product of the process of socialization with the interlocutors and the transformation of my positionality. Moreover, I claim that I became enculturated throughout the field experience. I was gradually acquainted with the cultural and societal norms of the pottery village during my stay. Therefore, I as an ethnographer averted my plans several times and revisited the field based on the pottery village circumstances.

More importantly, the opportunity to conduct ethnographic fieldwork is considered a signal for ethnographers to be aware of the nature of the field, its indicators and orientations rather than studying the field separate from its social groups and historical narratives. Finally, after being enculturated by, and indulged in the pottery village community, my positionality as an outsider gradually vanished. I left my studio's door open sometimes to all of my friends at the village. I started to smoke cigarettes inside the village instead of smoking only at my closed studio. I became fearless of the potters' gazes at me as they too became used to my presence and behaviors. I also kept on releasing my curly bangs out of my gypsy head scarf. Since I became aware of these acts and began confronting them, I felt like an insider. Even when I became an insider, I remained the gentrifier.

Notes

1. Gentrification is defined (Smith and Williams 2013) as a social transformation, physical conversion, and economic change in the land and housing markets and a process of capturing injustices between social classes that is created by urban markets and policies (Glass 2010) accompanied by urban renewal of old and historic districts.
2. Usufruct is a legalized right to use property (i.e., a building) for a little amount of money paid yearly in the case of the pottery village. It has an estimated cost of 1100 Egyptian pounds. Local potters own the building, but they don't own the land. They take advantage of the building as a property.
3. Creative class is a key concept defined by Richard Florida (2012) as a class that includes people in science and engineering, architecture and design, education, arts, music, and entertainment whose economic function is to create new ideas, new technology, and new creative content. They are characterized by a modern urban lifestyle.
4. This chapter problematizes the impact of gentrification as a representation of cultural imperialism and the rising of the creative class as a social group in Darb 1718 on the everyday life of the pottery village by capturing the gendered implications of gentrification, and indicators of gender oppression resulted from cultural imperialism and other mixed gendered interaction, artists' lifestyle, and practices.
5. Social group is a concept defined by Iris Young as a collective of persons differentiated from at least one other group by cultural forms, practices, or way of life (Young 2009).
6. Darb 1718 is an Egyptian nonprofit organization founded in 2008 as an art center and gathering point for all contemporary art events in Egypt. It is located in the pottery village, Kom Ghorab, Cairo. See https://darb1718.com/darb1718/vision-mission/.
7. Cultural practices are shared perceptions of how people routinely behave in a culture. They are inferred by perceptions of common behavior of others. See Frese (2015).
8. Azza Fahmy is a jewelry designer who founded a design school at the pottery village.
9. Cultural imperialism is one of the five faces of oppression defined by Iris Young. It involves taking the culture of the ruling class and establishing it as the norm. The groups that have power in society control how the people in that society interpret and communicate. Therefore, the beliefs of that society are the most widely disseminated and express the experience, values, goals, and achievements of these groups (Young

2009). Conservative, within local communities, means that people who keep on their traditions to respect and protect each other. The youth respect the elderly. These traditions must be respected within the whole community. Also, being "Conservative" has another notion when it comes to women. Women are not allowed to freely dress outside their houses and move in public spaces and streets. They wear the black, tall outfit "Abaya" as well as veils (Sayed 2016).

10 Flaneur is a French word. Its meaning is someone who walks around not doing anything in particular but watching people and society (Cambridge English Dictionary).

11 Each unit consists of three floors: ground, first, and a rooftop. Every floor is divided into smaller spaces.

12 During the field research, local interlocutors describe the pottery village and Kom Ghorab neighborhood as they are exposed to a process of enculturation where the local inhabitants and children can experience and attend art activities and concerts. Also, children of Kom Ghorab attend music and drawing classes at Darb 1718 and take part in further street theatre performances.

13 Heliopolis is an upper-middle-class neighborhood located on the eastern side of Cairo.

14 The Religious Complex is located in Coptic Cairo. It is a historic and touristic area that contains various churches, The Synagogue (the Jewish Temple) and Amr Ibn mosque.

15 Moustafa is a man from Kom Ghorab neighborhood. He works for Darb 1718 art center. He was my key person to the local community at the pottery village in 2016.

16 Oppression is a structural concept defined by Iris Young. There are five "faces" or types of oppression: violence, exploitation, marginalization, powerlessness, and cultural imperialism. See Young (2009).

17 Oppressed groups, in the research context, are defined according to which social group (i.e., contemporary artists) is dominating the pottery village with certain cultural practices that might not allow another powerless social group (i.e., local women) to access the village due to the cultural openness of the dominating social group.

18 Maadi is an upper-middle-class neighborhood located on the Nile. It is four metro stops ahead of the pottery village.

Bibliography

Abu-Lughod, Lila. 2008. "Writing against Culture." In *The Cultural Geography Reader*, edited by Timothy S. Oakes and Patricia L. Price, 50–60. New York, NY: Routledge.

Altorki, Soraya. 1988. "At Home in the Field." In *Arab Women in the Field: Studying Your Own Society*, edited by Soraya Altorki and Camillia Fawzi El-Solh, 51–59. Syracuse, NY: Syracuse University Press.

Appell-Warren, Laura P. 2014. *Personhood: An Examination of the History and Use of an Anthropological Concept*. Lewiston, NY: Edwin Mellen Press.

Bruner, Jerome S., and Marc H. Bornstein, eds. 1989. "On Interaction." In *Interaction in Human Development*, 217–39. Hillsdale, NJ: Lawrence Erlbaum Associates.

Ellen, Roy F., ed. 1984. *Ethnographic Research: A Guide to General Conduct*. London: Academic Press.

Emerson, Robert, Rachel Fretz, and Linda Shaw. 2011. *Writing Ethnographic Fieldnotes*. Chicago: University of Chicago Press.

Ewing, Katherine P. 1990. "The Illusion of Wholeness: Culture, Self, and the Experience of Inconsistency." *Ethos* 18 (3): 251–78. DOI:10.1525/eth.1990.18.3.02a00020.

Faraday, Annabel, and Kenneth Plummer. 1979. "Doing Life Histories." *Sociological Review* 27 (4): 773–98. https://doi.org/10.1111/j.1467-954X.1979.tb00360.x.

Florida, Richard. 2012. *The Rise of the Creative Class—Revisited: Revised and Expanded*. New York: Basic Books.

Frese, Michael. 2015. "Cultural Practices, Norms, and Values." *Journal of Cross-Cultural Psychology* 46 (10): 1327–30. https://doi.org/10.1177/0022022115600267.

Glass, Ruth. 2010. "Aspects of Change." In *The Gentrification Debates: A Reader*, edited by Japonica Brown Saracino, 19–30. New York: Routledge.

Gupta, Akhil, and James Ferguson. 1992. "Beyond 'Culture': Space, Identity, and the Politics of Difference." *Cultural Anthropology* 7 (1): 6–23. DOI:10.1525/can.1992.7.1.02a00020.

Gupta, Akhil, and James Ferguson, eds. 1997. "Discipline and Practice: 'The Field' as Site, Method and Location in Anthropology." In *Anthropological Locations: Boundaries and Grounds of a Field Science*, 1–46. Berkeley: University of California Press.

Harris, Grace G. 1989. "Concepts of Individual, Self, and Person in Description and Analysis." *American Anthropologist* 91: 599–612. DOI:10.1525/aa.1989.91.3.02a00040.

Jackson, Jean E. 1990. "'I Am a Fieldnote': Fieldnotes as a Symbol of Professional Identity." In *Fieldnotes: The Makings of Anthropology*, edited by Roger Sanjek, 3–33. Ithaca, NY: Cornell University Press. https://books.google.com.eg/books?id=kjOJT739rO0C&printsec=frontcover&source=gbs_ge_summary_r&cad=0#v=onepage&q&f=false.

Lefebvre, Henri. 1991. *The Production of Space*. Translated by Donald Nicholson-Smith. Oxford: Blackwell.

Lewis, Diane. 1973. "Anthropology and Colonialism." *Current Anthropology* 14 (5): 581–602.

Poole, Fitz John Porter. 2002. "Socialization, Enculturation and the Development of Personal Identity." In *Companion Encyclopedia of Anthropology*, edited by Tim Ingold, 831–60. London: Routledge.

Sanjek, Roger, ed. 1990. *Fieldnotes: The Makings of Anthropology*. Ithaca, NY: Cornell University Press. https://books.google.com.eg/books?id=kjOJT739rO0C&printsec=frontcover&source=gbs_ge_summary_r&cad=0#v=onepage&q&f=false.

Sayed, Reeham. 2016. "Mapping the Impact of Women's Perceptual Safety on Public Space: Investigating the Relationship between Gender, Class, Cultural Centers and Social Relations in Sha'bi Districts in Cairo." *Master's Thesis*, University of Stuttgart, Germany and Ain Shams University, Cairo, Egypt. https://iusd.asu.edu.eg/wp-content/uploads/2017/08/10-Mourad.pdf.

Smith, Neil, and Peter Williams, eds. 2013. *Gentrification of the City*. New York: Routledge.

Young, Iris. M. 2009. "Five Faces of Oppression." In *Geographic Thought: A Praxis Perspective*, edited by George Henderson and Marvin Waterstone, 55–71. London: Routledge.

PART 2

MASHRIQ (ARAB EAST)

5 REFLECTIONS ON THE STRUCTURAL AND DAILY REALITIES OF FIELD RESEARCH

Rania Jawad

Very soon after the fall 2015 academic semester had started at Birzeit University in Palestine where I teach, I was debating whether to attend an upcoming three-day workshop on fieldwork ethics and research methods that was to take place in Amman, Jordan. Amman is approximately 70 kilometers from Ramallah where I live, but because of the multiple border controls—the Israelis (the settler-colonial regime), the Palestinians (the colonized whose border presence is more show than control), and the Jordanians (who do not challenge the colonial regime but rather benefit economically)—the trip takes a minimum of three hours on an exceptionally "good" day, and at least five on average in my recent experience. The multiple factors I debated formed a web that made it clear to me I would not make the workshop: I had just entered my ninth month of pregnancy and I could tangibly imagine the physical and psychological wear and tear of the colonial border crossing that involved hours of getting in and out of cars and buses and submitting my passport and body to varying colonial border checkpoints; I was on a five-day-a-week teaching schedule at the university and would need to organize makeup classes in addition to the bureaucracy of requesting permission from the university for even a short leave; my three-year-old daughter would not be making the trip with me although I knew she would prefer to; and my residency in Palestine was constantly under threat by the Israeli regime, which refuses to provide long-term residency for individuals like myself who do not carry a local ID number (al-Haq 2019).[1]

The constellation of such factors—settler-colonial constraints, neoliberalization of higher education, and the labor of parenting—became constitutive of my field research in the place where I live and work, as they were also parts of my life to experience and navigate. My decision not to undertake the trip to Amman was not based on a calculation of all the factors combined or by producing a certain hierarchy to know which to consider the most influential in my decision-making. Nor was my decision taken alone but in dialogue with those immediately affected by what I decided. The interweaving of structural factors and my daily life shaped how I conducted research and how I understood my research context as a site of collective experiences, changing terrains, multiple labors, and affinities.

The chapter is comprised of reflections on the experiences of conducting research on the ways Palestinian artistic production is mobilized by various institutional bodies as a resource for addressing gendered violence in Palestinian communities. I address three issues: (1) how academic representations of structural violence can dominate and overtake understandings of how individuals and communities experience that violence; (2) how political and ethical commitment shapes how researchers prioritize what is highlighted in one's context of knowledge production; and (3) how the interweaving of the structural and lived experience historically, socially, politically, and personally situated can become an essential prism to reflect upon research. Specifically, I focus on the labors of conducting research while living and working in a settler-colonial field, being a working mother and a university professor, alongside experiences of driving while conducting field research, the companionship of friends and colleagues, and feelings of being targeted, of complicity, and of intellectual affinities. I outline concerns I had about the ethics and politics of conducting gender research and why I projected these concerns onto my research subjects. As a result, my research focus shifted to an analysis of the reflections my research subjects had on the work they were doing.

I do not generalize my context of field research as a place or a people but consider it in terms of a wider social terrain (Nast 1994) that also includes my home, my work, and my political commitment to an anticolonial liberation struggle. The context of my field research, a construction that is also in motion undergoing changes, includes my students at the university, the colonial regime of control, my teaching and administrative work, my family and social network, my research subjects and reading public, and my sensory responses and emotions. Dorothy E. Smith's (1990) highlighting of the local and particular brings into relief my personal (family labor) and work (university labor) commitments, which are formative factors of my field research as is the settler-colonial border regime and its broader violence. During my research, certain factors shaped the trajectory of my fieldwork and became more central to my understanding of the material. At other moments, these same factors played less defining roles.

I do not define these factors via key structural categories or concerns of scholarly methods alone, such as personal positioning (gender, class, insider/outsider) or access (to language, archives, research subjects). In part, this is because I experienced them as accumulative, partial, interwoven, changing, and ongoing rather than as clear defining factors or events. My experience, moreover, stands in clear contrast to the Israeli regime's colonial policing and enforcement of restrictive categories. As I do not carry local residency status in Palestine, I have needed to apply for visas (or what is officially titled a "visitor permit") issued by Israel for over the past decade, at times as a doctoral student conducting dissertation research, as an individual visiting extended family, as a spouse married to a Palestinian resident, and as an academic employed by a Palestinian university. Recently, my application to the Israeli authorities for an extension of my visa to reside in Palestine with my husband and two children was denied on the basis that I cannot be married to a Palestinian and be employed at a Palestinian institution at the same time.

In Soraya Altorki and Camillia Fawzi El-Solh's edited volume *Arab Women in the Field*, Suad Joseph describes in her contribution the multiplicity of identities and roles she carried or took on over the years of her fieldwork in Lebanon in the 1970s. At one moment in her reflection, she describes being torn by the conflicting demands she felt and consequently putting "in eighteen- to twenty-hour days" (Joseph 1988, 28). Describing time during fieldwork in such terms appears less about time "spent in" the field than highlighting what it means to be "living in" the field with professional, personal, and political commitments. She notes how she considered time with family as personal and not professional, locating time into discrete categories and only in retrospect blurring those distinctions. Time also became a major factor in my understanding of field research where the question for me was arguably less "where is the field?" (D'Amico-Samuels 1991) than "when is the field?" With my full-time university teaching load, political commitments, and care for my two young children, I constructed discrete categories not in terms of my identity or positioning but rather with regard to how I understood research time. "When could I create time for research?" was a more difficult question to deconstruct than what and where constitutes my research.

When They Hear What We Write

As I was conducting the research for a theater project that addressed gendered violence, I had been invited to participate in a few different forums locally and regionally that brought together scholars and artists to discuss concerns, analyses, and developments in the Palestinian cultural sphere. In contrast to academic arenas where I had earlier presented my preliminary research on the theater project and which were US-based academic associations, the discussions in these forums were predominantly conducted in Arabic. Being conscious that my audience was now comprised of many of my research subjects, I became more aware of the positioning of the researched to the researchers and was interested in the artists' relationships and perceptions of those who were researching and writing about them.[2]

This became most prominently visible at a symposium on contemporary theater practices in Palestine, when a theater artist based in Hebron (in the south of the West Bank) responded to two papers that were presented one after the other on the work of a Theater that is based in Jenin refugee camp in the north of the West Bank. I had stepped out to nurse my young child and missed the majority of the two papers that were each presented by a French female researcher, but I returned to hear the artist's response. He explained sardonically that after listening to the two papers that narrated the work of the Theater through the violence of Israeli military occupation, he was now afraid to again make the trip north to Jenin and visit his friend (who was sitting to his left and was the artistic director of the Theater). The images of armed soldiers, subjugation of Palestinians, and an imposed military surveillance state detailed in the papers depicted Jenin as a site of violence, which as he insinuated any listener (regardless of where she/he is from) would fear to visit.

I and most others in the audience, the overwhelming majority of whom were Palestinian, laughed, although we felt the antipathy in his voice as he spoke. The dissonance between the two presenters' depiction of their encounter with the violence of colonial occupation and the theater artist's life in it was stark (see Lamia Moghnieh 2017). His intervention, which grew more impassioned as he spoke, was a response directed not only to their reading of what he lives but a prevalent politics of representation of Palestinian experience that privileges depictions of Israeli military occupation. The long history of the Zionist narrative covering over the historical realities of Palestine was here and now coupled with the imaging of Israeli military occupation that speaks for Palestinian life. The artist's response was thus also a critique of the documentation being produced by researchers, arguably the majority of whom come to Palestine in an act of solidarity. The documentation that researchers (myself included) produce on Palestinian theater-making contributes to an archive of representing Palestine and Palestinian life. The theater artist's intervention was a clear critique of how representations of settler-colonial violence can cover over and define Palestinian life. The structural frame of settler-colonial violence enwrapped the image of Jenin the researchers presented, and this acted as a form of violence that initiated the artist's anger. What was potentially an attempt at solidarity with Palestinian artists was directed toward a European academic audience raising questions on the ethics of writing about violence and of solidarity acts.

Writing Context

In April of 2016, I attempted to write a piece on the experience of writing from a place of colonial violence, one that addressed an everyday presence of structural violence. My purpose was to acknowledge the constitutive realities of our contexts of scholarly production that are edited out of our academic writing and particularly those realities that are not directly related to our subjects of study. I wanted to acknowledge and give space to those realities that are often formative of our ways of thinking and that simultaneously shift or disrupt our ability to write academically.

I had been writing on a moment of intellectual production in twelfth-century Andalusia and how it was narrated by various writers to put forth particular epistemological claims, which I continue to contend with today in my work on Arab cultural production. Over the time of writing this piece, the Israeli army had raided the university campus more than once in the late-night hours, one of my students had been arrested on her way to the university, and the Israeli army had escalated its targeting and murder of Palestinian youth. It was not just that the subject matter of the current analysis I was writing departed from my other writings that foregrounded settler-colonial conditions. I was overwhelmed by the mediatized and seemingly constant production of visual and textual documentation of colonial oppression circulating online. Via online media sources, I witnessed violence in streets I had passed numerous times before and I learned of these developments on similar temporal planes as those living thousands of miles away. Considering the geographic and temporal displacements between the subject matter I was writing about and the place from which I wrote, I attempted to close the gap. I wanted the site of my writing in contemporary Palestine to be visible in my text on a twelfth-century Andalusian thinker. The exercise was not about my positioning but how what I understood as my context was shaping my way of perceiving and thinking, my approach to texts, and my writing process. I wanted to bring together the immediacy of the contexts from which I was writing with the formal academic writing we are institutionally trained to produce.

The attempt to acknowledge the immediacies of my context when writing an academic text failed and became more of an intellectual exercise than a document of an everyday settler-colonial present and knowledge production. In part, this is because the material realities of my context could not be defined by the colonial conditions alone. I was also carrying a high teaching load at the university, had a number of scholarly commitments, and just had my second child. Without myself or my husband having family nearby, my body and mind were mostly preoccupied with daily (and hourly) realities of caring for our two children, in addition to teaching four classes and subsequently taking the duties of chairing the department at the university. The immediacy of these personal and work realities shaped my ability to conduct research and write at the time in more direct or immediate ways than the colonial conditions I lived and worked in. In my attempt to acknowledge the immediacies of my context, I did not do the same for my own situatedness as a working mother. The "immediate, local, and particular place in which we are in the body" (Smith 1990, 17) specifically in terms of motherhood, I had concealed in order to forefront the politics of settler-colonialism.

Yet these factors were also constituted through one another or, to use the words of Donna Haraway, "where the tones of extreme localization, of the intimately personal and individualized body, vibrate in the same field with global high tension emissions" (Haraway 1991, 195). My teaching and family commitments I located in defiance of settler-colonial workings to eliminate Palestinian society, and the self-reflection on my writing was informed by feminist questions of process and accountability that were integral to my teaching, parenting, and relationships with others. As I embarked upon my next research project on theater-based productions of gendered violence in Palestine, the awareness of how I had separated out these realities from my process of knowledge production became central to my research and writing practice.

Limits of Representation and Process

The focus of my research was a mode of art-making that I called issue-based, because a major trend among theaters in the West Bank within the last ten years was the production of plays that targeted a specific issue in society by bringing it to public attention through art. Theater practitioners conducted research on the proposed issue by studying reports, statistics, relevant laws and regulations, and at times conducting personal interviews. The plays were supported and often initiated by international and foreign governmental, cultural, or development agencies that promoted a normative, global rights-based, and development discourse. The increased dependency on international funding, in addition to the institutional dynamics of theaters as registered nongovernmental organizations, shaped the ways theaters work to produce and perform these plays, as well as how the work is evaluated and documented.

I understood the production of issue-based plays within a longer trajectory of institutionalization in the Palestinian cultural sphere and dependency on international resources. I thought of the relationship between theater artists and funding agencies as one of "mutual instrumentalization," however uneven in practice (Rui 2016). I borrow this term from Taniele Rui who discusses the way the international agency that funded her ethnographic research in São Paulo, Brazil, made use of her work to promote its political agenda on a global scale of policy. She, in turn, used the influence of the funding agency to be able to gain access to official data and government actors for her research. In my research, I saw how international funders positioned theater practitioners to be local researchers of an issue under study and how the theater play they produced served to promote funding policies and ideological perspectives on globalized issues. On the other hand, such funding enabled the work of these theaters to continue as it also encouraged theater artists to explore new ways of producing theater that was community-based.

As gender violence and inequalities in Palestinian society received noticeably high attention from development and humanitarian organizations, political figures, and researchers, "gender-based violence" became constructed as a major issue in local Palestinian society (Hammami 2019). I chose as my focus one theater project that was commissioned by the UNESCO office in Ramallah as part of their investment in the cultural sphere as a resource (Yúdice 2003) for advocating for gender equality and specifically for addressing violence against women in Palestinian communities. The project involved a series of interactive workshops a group of theater artists conducted with communities of women across the West Bank in 2014. The artists drew on and transformed these women's narratives into a public cultural performance for targeted audiences and for the general public. I was conscious of my research on issue-based theater projects that take gender as a main issue being implicated in a wider network of policy-oriented and normative and rights-based discourses, specifically of gender and gender-based violence, in addition to culturalized analyses of Palestinian women (Abu-Lughod 2011; Johnson 2008; Shalhoub-Kevorkian 2009). As one of the theater artists in the project noted about the way the project was structured, "to work with women is already a project that enters into a social system," and specifically one circumscribed by particular assumptions about violence and Palestinian society.

I had attended a number of plays that addressed violence against women in such areas as inheritance rights, the question of infertility, and murder by family members. I was critical not of the content or aesthetic realization of these issues but of structurally how these plays were meant to fulfill their declared aim of intervening in societal perceptions. Considering that a social issue is not a fact but is produced, I was interested in how these theater productions came to be. Where did the issue-based theater production come from? What were the theaters' ways of evaluating if the plays achieved the goals for why they were produced? Was the declared goal of shaping societal perceptions the only criteria from which to evaluate the plays? How did the theaters that define society, societal perceptions, change? What were the limits of my understanding to categorize this art production as issue-based? What discursive networks may my writing about violence against women partake or challenge?

My initial research on the project was based on a reading of textual and multimedia documents that the hosting Theater, the sponsoring agency, and media coverage produced, leading up to the art product. This was the most accessible and only way I could imagine beginning my research as I had limited mobility because I was teaching five days a week and my time otherwise was with my young children. I was on deadline to present the preliminary research at an academic conference and in between teaching and family commitments, I was additionally able to conduct five lengthy phone interviews with select theater artists and administrators and the main representative from the project's funding agency. My preliminary reading that was based on this data gathering examined how conditions of funding embedded in the project served a performative function, generating more gender-based theater projects. I showed how the condition of producing specific forms of documentation of all stages of the production process served to represent the project in a narrative of success and accomplishment, thus becoming a main mechanism for institutionally evaluating the work of the project. I argued that processes of documenting the work came to stand in for the work, in effect replacing the liveness that not only constitutes theater practice but forms the foundation for the declared aim of the project to intervene in societal perceptions.

I presented versions of this preliminary research in two different academic forums where representatives from two funding organizations were present, albeit not the one that sponsored the theater project I was discussing. The representatives were present because one had sponsored my research project and the other the conference panel that I was participating in. One representative, who was the program officer of the regional office for one of the largest funding foundations for civil society initiatives, research, and media work globally, gave me her card following my presentation and told me she was interested in the dynamics I was laying out regarding funders and artists and wanted to follow my research as it developed. The other representative, the executive director of a much smaller organization that gave small grants to support academic research on a particular region, wrote me a long email detailing the dynamics of navigating larger funding agencies' conditions and requirements for obtaining the funds for the grants. Both made it clear that they were interested in my research because it detailed power dynamics and hierarchies of their work (although in different ways and to different degrees) that they wanted to alleviate. These two representatives, both women who had various affinities to the Arab World and Palestine in particular, actively responded to my analysis. I respected their responses, unexpected as they were, for I had not imagined representatives of funding organizations comprising my audience. However, as I perceived how my research may be instrumental to such representatives, I wanted to understand the dynamics, communities, and experiences that the project of producing such a play created for those involved, particularly the artists.

I wanted to understand the nuanced ethical and political positionings of those involved within the larger infrastructure of investments in the cultural sphere that also embodied North–South global relations and was mediated by the settler-colonial conditions in Palestine. I wanted to know more about the women who participated in the theater workshops from which the play's content was drawn. A set of logistical questions emerged for the research: What if I could not access the women whose stories comprised the content for the play? Even if I did locate some of the women, would they remember participating in a three-hour theater workshop two years prior? Under what conditions would I engage the women to discuss their experiences? How do I attend a relevant three-day conference held by the Theater I was researching that was scheduled midweek, while still nursing my young baby and teaching full-time at a university a two-hour trip from the Theater? How can I be accountable to those I was writing about while also being critical of the dynamics implicated in their work? How can my scholarship be useful to those I was writing about?

While I wanted to also engage with the women whose stories the artists used to produce the theater play, I knew it was difficult to carry out that research predominantly because the women resided in a number of different localities far from my own. Because of my family and work commitments, I would not be able to travel across the West Bank and spend appropriate amounts of time with the women. As a result, I came to more clearly define my research subjects as the theater artists, moreover because I saw resonance in the artists' work with my own. Questions of research ethics, and specifically feminist methods regarding process and representation that were at the forefront of my thinking at the time, became the focus in my research. Not without its own problematic concerns, I saw the theater artists I was studying as conducting gender research, as they engaged with communities of women to draw the narratives of the play they would later perform. The artists created a platform for the participating women to share their personal stories and then conducted select interviews to listen and record the testimonies. The facilitated interaction between the artists and women, and the artists' acts of representation and narrative production I linked to accountability and ethical responsibility of researcher to researched subject. What ethical-political questions did they face? Who did they feel accountable to? Where did they see value in the project? In effect, these sets of questions mirrored my own reflection on the scholarly work I was doing.

Privileging Reflections

As I positioned the artists I was studying as researchers of women's experiences of violence, I focused my analysis on their understanding of the work they were doing. In part, this focus also emerged from my attraction to certain artists I was interviewing because of their articulations of the work they do. I kept returning to these same artists for follow-up interviews and communication as their concerns about their artistic work in some ways paralleled my own about my scholarly work. These concerns were largely about accountability to those we work with and represent, considering the value in our work within the wider politics of colonial violence, and being conscious of our modes of self-evaluation.

In an interview I conducted with one of the theater artists involved in the gender-based theater project, she explained how: "With the recorder in front of you, they see you as someone who can help them, not as a theater-maker." She was referring to the interviews she and the other female theater artist of the group conducted with women participants as part of the interactive workshops that served as the main basis for producing the script of the play. Near the end of each three- to five-hour theater workshop, the group of theater artists identified one or two women to record an interview with, whose personal story could serve as source material for the play with the women's consent. The artist I was interviewing described the multiple roles she played in the theater project: her self-defining role as a theater artist, her role as recorder and witness to the women's personal testimonies, her role in the project as a female Palestinian artist from 1948 (which she highlighted to me in our interview), and her role as someone commissioned to complete certain tasks. She reflected on these various roles and the tensions they raised.

My own recorder sat between us during our interview. I did not believe that she had expectations from my interview with her in the way that she related to me that she felt the women had during her interviews with them. The questions that I asked coupled with the time that had passed since the project (as it was now approximately two years later) brought out a series of self-reflective comments from her. The concerns that she raised became central to my understanding of this particular project and also to the genre of issue-based theater projects in general. A paraphrase of some of her main concerns: Why was she, an actress from 1948 Palestine, cast in the project and not an actress from the community in which the Theater was based? Why was the play not performed in the communities in which the workshops were conducted? What was the goal of having only one workshop in each community and only one play? Why did the project need to be built from "real stories"?

Her pointed questions spoke to the colonial geography in place, structural concerns of the project, and the "two-edged sword" of personal testimony (Roof 2012, 532). The politics of casting in this case, while based in the settler-colonial division of Palestinian society, foregrounded the nuanced and overlapping layers of insiders/outsiders found in the Palestinian context. The structural dynamics of the project built on the artists working in marginalized communities not their own and for short durations of time spoke to the "terms of engagement" of the project instituted by the sponsoring agency (Wood 2001). The value attributed to real stories raised ethical questions regarding the use of someone else's personal experience, particularly as a mode of representational authority. Moreover, as the artist stated, the project as conceived—a UN-commissioned project to work with women to publicize in an aesthetic forum the multiple forms of violence they live—was already implicated in questions put forth by feminist researchers regarding hierarchy, exploitation, authoring, and authority.

I came to realize that as I positioned the artists as gender researchers (parallel to my own positioning researching the gender-issue theater project), I privileged certain kinds of reflections, such as this one. I conducted follow-up interviews with these artists and theater administrators and built my analysis around their understandings and articulations over other interviewees. My research was thus not about how theater artists perceived their art as an agent of gender and social engagement but rather how certain individuals in the cultural sphere critically understood their positioning and their work on gendered violence in a settler-colonial context. I was attracted to these individuals because I felt that their critical-ethical reflections, not their positioning or work, resonated with my own.

My interview with this theater artist, for example, came on the heels of five interviews I had already conducted. Each of those interviewees was articulate in their responses to my questions and communicated a clarity in their thoughts. In other words, they felt convincing. And yet my reading of the project felt different from what was communicated through those interviews. It was only when I interviewed this particular theater artist did she put into words my sense of the project. She spoke openly in a self-critical manner, explaining that what she was saying now she had not realized then. I felt that she, in part, did the work for me in her analysis of the project. I was conscious that my privileging of certain interviewees produced a particular reading of the project that otherwise may have been represented differently. Yet I also understood that how I perceived the artists' work was not equal to their own perceptions nor was it parallel to my own work. What I and the theater artists were doing was measured according to different standards and did not carry the same forms of accountability or expectations.

The relationship between the theater artists and myself can also be characterized as one of mutual instrumentalization that varied from interviewee to interviewee. I had been asked by different theater artists over the years to help document particular moments of theater history, to assist in writing funding proposals and make international links with artists and institutions, to serve as a dramaturg or teach in local theater training institutes, and to share scholarship on Palestinian theater work via books and pdfs of articles and book chapters that have been written in English and Arabic. As I have developed relationships with certain artists over the years, the kinds of reflections that I privileged have been based on an affinity with my own drive to bring the dynamics of process into focus rather than an analysis of the final product as such. In contrast to the interviews conducted for this particular theater project that demonstrated certainty and clarity of the work to produce the final project, the questions on process brought out uncertainties and discomfort. My investment was in the unfinished, incomplete understanding of process and its legacy on future work.

Getting "Lost"

In 2016, as part of my fieldwork for this research project, I attended a conference hosted by the Theater that initiated the gender-based play. The conference extended over a few days, and the trip took approximately two hours from where I live. At the time I was nursing my son of four-and-a-half months and teaching full-time at the university (as maternity leave was a maximum of three months). I organized makeup sessions for my missed classes, chose to take my son with me for the two days I would attend the conference, and inquired with two colleagues if they would like to accompany me on the trip to the conference. The desire for company was predominantly to help care for my son while I was participating in the conference, but just as significant was their very presence during the two-hour drive.

Getting lost was not a mere detour or loss of time and gas only. In any two-hour drive within the West Bank, one passes by a number of Israeli colonial settlements and military checkpoints or bases with armed soldiers. Some months before I had lost my way back home to Ramallah from another research site and landed alone in an Israeli colonial settlement. I was unexpectedly confronted by the above-ground light rail system that divided the road, which is part of Israel's colonial infrastructure in its West Bank settlements that are not found in the rest of the West Bank where Palestinians reside. I stopped my car to call a friend for directions. I felt marked as a Palestinian, an unwelcome or perceived threatening presence in a settlement for Jews only, and I did not feel comfortable stopping to ask for directions in Arabic or English. I did not want to be in a position of vulnerability and weakness. I was also conscious of numerous cases of violence based on a colonizer's perception of being under threat because of the colonized being "out of place," "lost," or "hesitant."

Because of this earlier driving experience, I preferred not to be alone for my travel to the theater conference. I also preferred to go by car rather than public transportation because I had my young child with me. As we embarked, I was armed with some handwritten notes based on a friend's explanation for directions as I had not made the drive before. At that time, Israel had placed a ban on 3G services for Palestinian mobile telecommunications in the West Bank, and I did not have a smartphone in any case. However, one of my colleagues on the trip who grew up in Jerusalem had an iPhone with an Israeli telecommunication number. She was, therefore, able to make use of Israel's 3G services to its settlers in the West Bank. Waze, a GPS navigation application developed by an Israeli company, was installed in her phone and guided our way north alongside Palestinian villages and Israeli colonial settlements.

My other colleague who joined us was considered to be illegally residing in Palestine by the Israelis who control the population registry of all residents in the occupied territory of the West Bank, Jerusalem, Gaza strip, and the Golan Heights, in addition to the colonial state. Born in the United States to Palestinian residents of the West Bank, her parents moved the family back to Palestine when she was 17 years old, one year past the age limit where Palestinian children must be registered by the Israelis to obtain a local Palestinian ID. She was only given a three-month tourist visa, and till this day years later her application for family reunification is pending with the Israelis. My status at the time, as registered by the Israelis, was an extended six-month tourist visa, obtained via an application submitted to the Israeli regime on the basis of my being married to a Palestinian resident carrying a local ID number in the West Bank. As was the standard, my visa was restricted to the West Bank only.

While my immediate concern for company was to help care for my young child once I was at the conference, having two colleagues with me on the way to the conference reduced a layer of anxiety about getting lost yet also added other layers of risks. The labor involved to plan for a two-day trip to a Theater two hours away, to conduct fieldwork for two days, included also imagining the potential consequences for myself and my colleagues. The factors embedded in the labor of movement were not just multiple but also extended beyond myself to a collective of people around me. The field site, as is my positioning, is a construction that is also in flux. On the one hand, Israel has since lifted its ban on 3G services for Palestinian mobile service, and one can navigate across the West Bank using navigation mapping applications. On the other hand, I can no longer make the drive to this Theater in my car because of Israeli restrictions placed on my visa.

The way that I relate to and attempt to define the context of my field research is not fixed as the context itself also undergoes changes. As my research developed, so did the research site, and both were constructed by daily, interpersonal interactions and dynamics. What I initially located as a tangible, geopolitical, and sensory space of settler-colonial violence that circumscribed my knowledge production, I realized did not alone define my context. I understood the context of my knowledge production as more inclusive and relational comprising arenas where I also teach, raise a family, interact with my colleagues and research subjects, and fight against a colonial regime of control to maintain my very residency and presence in the field.

Notes

1 Local Palestinian ID cards are issued by the Palestinian Authority as a bureaucratic procedure only after Israeli state approval. The Israeli state controls the Palestinian population residency, regulating who can be considered "legally" a resident of the occupied Palestinian territory (oPt). Israel continues to refuse putting in place official procedures for individuals without local residency who, like myself, are married to Palestinian residents and/or are employed by Palestinian institutions to obtain long-term residency permits.
2 The subtitle is a variation of Caroline B. Brettell's edited volume *When They Read What We Write: The Politics of Ethnography*. Westport, CT: Bergin and Garvey, 1993.

Bibliography

Abu-Lughod, Lila. 2011. "Seductions of the 'Honor Crime.'" *differences: A Journal of Feminist Cultural Studies* 22 (1): 17–63.

al-Haq. 2019. "Engineering Community: Family Reunification, Entry Restrictions and Other Israeli Policies of Fragmenting Palestinians." Last accessed 7 April 2019. http://www.alhaq.org/cached_uploads/download/alhaq_files/images/stories/PDF/Family_Unification_14%20February%20(1).pdf, accessed 16 December 2021.

D'Amico-Samuels, Deborah. 1991. "Undoing Fieldwork: Personal, Political, Theoretical and Methodological Implications." In *Decolonizing Anthropology: Moving Further toward an Anthropology for Liberation*, edited by Faye V. Harrison, 68–85. Washington, DC: Association of Black Anthropologists, American Anthropological Association.

Hammami, Rema. 2019. "Follow the Numbers: Global Governmentality and the Violence against Women Agenda in Occupied Palestine." In *Governance Feminism: Notes from the Field*, edited by Janet Halley, Prabha Kotiswaran, Rachel Rebouché, and Hila Shamir. Minneapolis: University of Minnesota Press.

Haraway, Donna J. 1991. *Simians, Cyborgs, and Women: The Reinvention of Nature*. New York: Routledge.

Johnson, Penny. 2008. "'Violence All Around Us': Dilemmas of Global and Local Agendas Addressing Violence against Palestinian Women, an Initial Intervention." *Cultural Dynamics* 20 (2): 119–32.

Joseph, Suad. 1988. "Feminization, Familism, Self, and Politics." In *Arab Women in the Field: Studying Your Own Society*, edited by Soraya Altorki and Camillia Fawzi El-Solh, 25–47. Syracuse, NY: Syracuse University Press.

Moghnieh, Lamia. 2017. "'The Violence We Live In': Reading and Experiencing Violence in the Field." *Contemporary Levant* 2 (1): 24–36.

Nast, Heidi J. 1994. "Women in the Field: Critical Feminist Methodologies and Theoretical Perspectives." *Professional Geographer* 46: 54–66.

Roof, Judith. 2012. "Authority and Representation in Feminist Research." In *Handbook of Feminist Research: Theory and Praxis*, edited by Sharlene Nagy Hesse-Biber, 520–43. Los Angeles, CA: Sage.

Rui, Taniele. 2016. "On the Mutual Instrumentalization of Funders and Researchers." Paper presented at the *Institute for Advanced Study's Summer Program in Social Sciences*, Paris, June 2016.

Shalhoub-Kevorkian, Nadera. 2009. *Militarization and Violence against Women in Conflict Zones in the Middle East: A Palestinian Case-Study*. Cambridge, UK: Cambridge University Press.

Smith, Dorothy E. 1990. *The Conceptual Practices of Power: A Feminist Sociology of Knowledge*. Toronto: University of Toronto Press.

Wood, Cynthia A. 2001. "Authorizing Gender and Development: 'Third World Women,' Native Informants, and Speaking Nearby." *Nepantla: Views from South* 2 (3): 429–47.

Yúdice, George. 2003. *The Expediency of Culture: Uses of Culture in the Global Era*. Durham, NC: Duke University Press.

6 FIELDWORK IN THE PALESTINIAN COLONIAL CONTEXT: SEARCHING FOR THE VOICES OF PALESTINIAN WOMEN

Samar Kassis

Introduction

For anthropologists, fieldwork is the foundation of knowledge and the fundamental activity of anthropologists themselves (Moser 2007, 243). The field is a physical and epistemological space for knowledge production that reflects the life experiences of men and women, and the power relations that exist in specific historical environments. It also reflects the values, beliefs, hopes, fears, and prejudices of individuals and groups in concrete social settings (Pole and Hillyard 2016, 80).

In the Occupied Palestinian Territories (OPTs), fieldwork as a generator of knowledge production takes on a very different role and assumes a very different set of meanings for Palestinian researchers and their research subjects. The realities of living under the harsh conditions of a colonial occupation shape the context for both the researcher and the human subjects of research. What emerges in this kind of environment is what some scholars refer to as "engaged research" whereby both the researcher and the interview subjects share common experiences from bonds of empathy. The result is that the research generated from fieldwork in this kind of environment has a purpose well beyond the written word and is instead a more highly charged reflection of lived experience.

This chapter is based upon my personal experiences as a Palestinian woman researcher conducting anthropological research with Palestinian women ex-political prisoners in the West Bank in the OPT. My aim is to highlight important incidences in my fieldwork and to consider crucial questions that include: What does it mean for a Palestinian woman to do research on resistance activities conducted by Palestinian women ex-political prisoners who spent long sentences in Israeli colonial prisons? What form of relationship is formed between the researcher and the Palestinian women ex-political prisoners? How does this relationship affect the knowledge produced about the women's narratives? What are the ethical responsibilities toward the narratives of these women and their experiences in this form of research? Lastly, how do ethical challenges tend to raise difficult choices for me as an indigenous researcher?

In addressing these questions, I consider some aspects of my research with Palestinian women ex-political prisoners who were detained during the 1970s and 1980s and released in 1997 following the Oslo Accords. The narratives of these women embody the paradox of being detained for resisting acts and being released by a peace agreement that forced them to sign a document rejecting their own acts. For them, the Oslo agreement was a form of submission, as Edward Said described it, "an instrument of Palestinian surrender" (Said 1993). The women ex-political prisoners had sacrificed the most precious for them, their freedom, their lives, and their family members for liberating their land. The Oslo agreement was not perceived by them as a peace agreement but an expansion of the Zionist settler-colonial project of occupation in peaceful circumstances (interviewee 2016). Following the Oslo agreements, Palestinians continued to suffer multiple forms of colonial practices including mass imprisonment. As of 14 July 2021, the number of Palestinian political prisoners and detainees is estimated at 4850. Out of the total number 41 are female and 225 are children under 18 years old (Addameer 2021).

Based on my experiences living under settler-colonial occupation and conducting research with women ex-political prisoners, I argue that the female indigenous anthropologist studying her own society can provide a deep analysis on the role of women in politics and resistance due to the perspective of being an insider and having an intimate knowledge of the material realities and the intercommunal discourse about resistance. Indigenous status, though, entails various challenges as will be clear in this chapter.

Since anthropological fieldwork had been historically linked to colonialism, I sought a new way of defining "indigenous" in the context of Palestine. Prior to the Israeli occupation, Palestinians had no need to define themselves as native or indigenous and therefore I had to seek a different research paradigm for understanding this different environment. I did this by looking at how academics within indigenous studies use these terms not to label themselves within the colonial definition of the indigenous status but to bring the understanding back to a land-based ideology that shows that we historically come from and exist upon the land versus the constructs of a Western nation-state ideology that fixates the indigenous/native person within the pejorative confines of settler-colonialism. This left me looking for scholarship and techniques that helped me put into practice a methodology that would allow me to employ and use this discipline in a critical manner to reflect on the narratives of Palestinian women ex-political prisoners.

In addition to conceptual challenges, there are numerous real-life restrictions on indigenous Palestinian anthropologists such as myself trying to conduct fieldwork under conditions of Israeli occupation. Most obvious of them is the restriction on free movement. Throughout my research I could not get a permit to pass Israeli checkpoints as I was rejected for security reasons. This had limited my ability to reach interviewees.

The brutality of life under Israeli occupation affects all Palestinians and ultimately shapes the research field in profound ways. As any Palestinian woman living in the OPTs, I experience the colonial practices on a daily basis: the violent murders of Palestinians by Israeli soldiers at checkpoints, the constant arrests of Palestinians at roadblocks and from their homes, the demolition of Palestinian houses, the oppression that occurs in Israeli prison and interrogation centers, as well as all the types of extensive forms of humiliation and acts of injustice perpetrated against the indigenous Palestinian communities. Besides all this, I have two brothers who were arrested, tortured, and imprisoned during the second intifada. From this unique position of being an insider, I have the ability to reflect on the role of Palestinian women in politics, society, and resistance. Nevertheless, with the advantage of being an insider there are numerous challenges. There was no way for me to detach myself from the women and their stories. Their words became a part of my own personal narrative, the narrative that my family and I lived through the two intifadas. The deep intimacy with their cause and their sacrifice was not something I could leave in the space of the fieldwork. Emotional attachments and the range of emotions experienced were all integral to this research and were very much part of my methodology.

Exploring Painful Experiences

Women who participate in research are actually doing research in their daily lives, as they construct the meanings of the experiences that later become the data that researchers interpret (Olesen 1994). It is challenging to write about someone's life, especially if that person is a woman from Occupied Palestine who spent long periods captive in Israeli prisons. There are a series of cultural and personal barriers that even an indigenous researcher must cross before they can conduct their fieldwork. As a feminist indigenous researcher who was born under and has lived through the Israeli Occupation, my key point is to produce knowledge about

Palestinian women ex-political prisoners based on how they understood and interpreted their experiences, besides how they demonstrated themselves during the interview with the insight of an insider's lens. It is during these encounters that I found the formal traditional approach for conducting these interviews, with its disregard for the colonial context of Palestine, to be insufficient for this case study.

Yes, the participants traditionally are the ones who cooperate with the researcher in reflecting their stories and experiences. However, an important variable that influences the interpretation and analysis of data is the ability for me as the researcher to be able to connect and understand the multilayered consequences of their sacrifice and how their gender both complicates and conceals their efforts and revolutionary acts within a patriarchal society. Through my life experiences, my status as a Palestinian woman and an educated feminist researcher in Palestine affected my methodology, as well as the criteria used in the interpretation and analysis of the narratives of Palestinian women ex-political prisoners and how their sacrifices and their experiences are placed among the collective political and historical narrative of Palestine.

For conducting my research, I found that the traditional methodology for creating my research community was not going to be sufficient and instead looked to a more organic method in order to gain access to these women and their narratives. Due to political, cultural, institutional, and geographic restrictions, I had to rely on a more personal form of recommendation and introduction to this highly protective community. From the first woman ex-political prisoner I was introduced to, and from thereon, each interviewee became the subsequent link to the next woman I would eventually interview in the process known as "snowball sampling." I delve into how a Palestinian woman researcher must play the role of the intermediary, she can engage the gaze of her interlocutors through these profound stories and experiences while being cognizant of the delicate and careful process of community building in order to bring their voices into the academic arena. I reflect on how ethical dilemmas constructed difficult choices for me, first as a researcher and secondly as a woman studying other women in her own society.

In approaching the research, I utilized a range of methods including focus group discussions, in-depth semistructured interviews, and field observations. In order to be able to begin finding a research community I relied on the communal and cultural connection to try and identify and find the contact information of these women in order to create and establish my research community. These connections were also cultivated through my activism and the sit-ins that I attended. First, I chose to conduct a focus group discussion with some of the target group, in order to generate data which could facilitate my interviews. I then made sure to give the interviewees the opportunity to talk about their experiences collectively; this portion of the discussion guided me in order to build the structure of the individual interviews with the Palestinian women ex-political prisoners. The research community was drawn from different political organizations, socioeconomic backgrounds, and various governorates from the West Bank and East Jerusalem.

I want to emphasize that this research went beyond the words and analysis written on the pages of my study, and it created a community between myself, the women ex-political prisoners, and my students. These women became an integral part of my teaching. They came and spoke directly to my students sharing their stories, building from their individual narratives a collective oral tradition that imprints upon the youth this important history and the role of the women in their communities within the resistance. I and my students had the ability to understand and feel how the experience of imprisonment and the changes of Palestinian lives after the Oslo agreement had affected these women because these events had a direct impact upon my life, while bringing to life the events that define the world my students now live in. These women who are members of our families and communities are the part of the Palestinian movement that has been left out of our history books. Yet, it is their sacrifices, actions, and ideologies that have been and currently are a part of our feminist revolutionary history and important for the building of the feminist and political movement of the future.

I was overwhelmed with many feelings that oscillated between sadness, anger, embarrassment, and exasperation. The pain and the difficulties experienced from active resistance was not restricted or dominated by men; women ex-political prisoners had proven that Palestinian women are capable partners in the struggle and resistance against the Israeli settler-colonialism. It struck me how aware they were that their acts of resistance were significant beyond the goal of resisting the Israeli settler-colonial occupation, but that they were also fighting a double form of patriarchy. Their difficult and painful experiences were not some distant and unintelligible story that existed outside of me; though I set out a particular method and criteria for the interview process the narratives of these women viscerally and emotionally had and still have an effect upon me. They taught me a deeper level of persistence, determination, and the importance of pursuing a life of resistance at all costs. It is their deeds, words, and experiences that will intergenerationally transfer to future young girls and women, reviving concepts and values of silent sacrifice and struggle. The important lesson learned from painful narratives and experiences not only is relevant for the academic research I conducted but has also become a part of the lived experience I personally carry and hold.

Lack of Data

I faced many challenges in finding interviewees due to lack of data or information recorded by the Ministry of Detainees and Ex-detainees[1] about Palestinian women ex-political prisoners who were released in 1997, as part of the Oslo agreement after signing the Hebron protocol[2] on 18 January 1997 between the Palestinians and Israelis (Ferwana 2010, 31). The head of information and data for the ministry admitted that before (he meant before 1997) the Palestinian Authority (PA) was in the stage of building institutions and the organizations, computers were found but not as highly used as today, so there was not any kind of documentation or following up to all ex-political prisoners. He also mentioned: "Today our documentation system is developed and became more operative and well effective." The Ministry of Detainees and Ex-detainee was established in 1998; this was one year after the women were released and subsequently were not included in the database.

At this realization, I was confronted with the contradiction that we, the indigenous Palestinian society, have become so dependent on empirical methods of creating knowledge and validating facts through documents that these women and their role within the resistance was nowhere to be found in our collective memory. Sadly, they were silenced and forgotten both from our oral tradition of remembrance and from the now-official records being institutionalized within the new Palestinian government. The Israeli Occupational military and penal institutions have ample documentation on Palestinian political detainees. However, today the security sectors for the PA share all the information with the Israeli colonizer through the computerized system that is used to record all information related to all Palestinian political prisoners. This is actually what the Oslo agreements generated security coordination between the Palestinians and the Israelis' settler-colonial security and military forces.

This exchange of information regarding acts of resistance serves only to further the occupation and not to aid in Palestinian sovereignty. I was promised to have a list with names, phone numbers, marital status, and places, in order to contact my research group. Unfortunately, apart from a phone call with two or three names, nothing happened. I also visited Addameer[3] and the Palestinian Prisoners Club[4] in Ramallah. Addameer did not have any statistics or names for all the Palestinian women who were released in 1997. But they published a report in 2010 about Palestinian women political prisoners; it mentioned that 21 women political prisoners were freed in February 1997 (Addameer 2010). However, the team provided me with a list that included 58 names and demographic information about Palestinian political and ex-political prisons with phone numbers. The list was based on the date of what at the time was the arrests for the last five years and did not include the women ex-political prisoners from 1997. Another report for Abdul-Nasser Ferwana[5] published in 2010 mentioned that 31 Palestinian women were released at that time (Ferwana 2010, 30). The Prisoners Club shared the same problem with the other organizations. No documented list was available, so I had to depend on the members who participated in the focus group. It was apparent to me that the discrepancies between these two institutions and their documentation of Palestinian political prisoners at this time were something that I would find commonplace. There are many reasons for these discrepancies, part of it due to the fault of the PA, and the other due to the Israeli practice of kidnapping and arresting people without formally documenting them within the database. The interconnected database and the complicity of the PA with the illegal practices of Israel greatly contributed to the disappearing of the political prisoners from the PA's records, as well as the failure for us to have any truthful and transparent documentation of the people that have been held captive inside Israeli military and penal institutions. Through the appearance of transparency there is still a disappearance of Palestinian political prisoners, and the women who were released in 1997 had seemed to be not only lost to the database that would only start a year later but also wiped from the memory of the Palestinian struggle.

Their sacrifices have been eliminated and neglected as part of the design of the Israeli colonial project. A critical part of Israeli colonialism is to erase the Palestinian collective memory and impose a kind of social amnesia on Palestinian society in order to inhibit Palestinians from knowing how to resist in the future. Sadly, this truncated social memory has made it difficult for Palestinians in the present to learn from those who struggled in the revolutionary movements before them. This is especially true for Palestinian women ex-political prisoners whom the Israeli occupiers want to silence. As a researcher, my aim is to let the voices of these women speak in order to elevate their stories of resistance to the level of national collective memory.

Here I recall one of the interviews I conducted with a Palestinian woman ex-political prisoner in 2016. She mentioned that Palestinian women ex-political prisoners established a "league of women who were detained for freedom." She said that the fundamental aim of establishing the league in 2003 is to form an independent entity regardless of political affiliations, in order to document the individual and collective narratives of the Palestinian women ex-political prisoners. In addition to creating an archive that includes all their experiences and stories that one day will be recorded and documented as a part of the Palestinian national history, it also enriches the Palestinian women movement's history.

One of the most ironic aspects of these women prisoners is that many were released during what was supposed to be a watershed moment in the Palestinian struggle, the Oslo Accord. Sadly, in the aftermath of the so-called peace agreement, the struggles and sacrifices of this group were almost completely neglected and forgotten. These women, who from their prison cells were unbreakable and the true meaning of a revolutionary Palestinian community, stopped at nothing to make sure that every last woman who was being held captive inside an Israeli prison and detention center was released during the Oslo prisoner exchange, and yet not a word of their struggle and contribution to the movement was documented anywhere. Again, it is worth noting that not even one piece of paper exists in which their names are documented and remembered or their whereabouts known. I, as a Palestinian woman, was flooded by a torrent of emotions ranging from anger, embarrassment, sadness, and indignation. How is it that a group of women who were so integral to the movement after Oslo, like so many prisoners at that time, were to be swept away from the official national narrative and, worse, the collective memory of their communities for which they gave the ultimate sacrifice? As an indigenous academic, it was something that I could not reconcile and it made me realize how this study was that much more pertinent not just for the academic community but for me to make sure to bring these women and their voices and stories to the students I teach; to help reconstruct a community destroyed by the false promise of Oslo and the PA.

Interviewer–Interviewee Relationships

Some anthropologists have claimed that this relationship is so unique that there are no conventional words available for the relationship between the fieldworker and his or her "key informant." (Driessen 1998, 44)[6]

If the researcher forms a close relationship with the interviewees, this allows for a higher likelihood that they would reveal their personal feelings and thoughts (Kirsch 2005, 2164). I found that during my fieldwork throughout the several research projects that I worked on, friendships and significant relationships had been built with the participants who became part of my research communities at the time. I met many women ex-political prisoners in various occasions and activities, demonstrations, protests, strikes, and sit-ins in the middle of Ramallah. The sit-in engaged me more with women ex-political prisoners and their families on a personal level. Sitting under the tents where the protests were taking place situated me within an environment where my relationships with these women were built on a mutually felt solidarity and trust. While talking with these women and listening to their stories and demands during the protests, a bond was built that far exceeded what I, as a researcher, could have created with these women. I became personally invested and attached to this community of women and to the Palestinian struggle as viewed from their position. My research made me committed to all aspects of the Palestinian prisoners' issues and causes, as well as with the women and their families personally.

The interviewees appreciate interest, attention, sincerity, and warmth shown by the interviewer (Kirsch 2005, 2164). I believe that "The more comfortable participants are, the more likely they are to disclose information and reveal the nature of their lived experiences" (Streubert, and Carpenter 2011, 14). During previous research in which I engaged with women ex-political prisoners, I recall in one of the interviews that took place in Betunia—a town near Ramallah—with two teenagers (a boy and a girl) that their mother was an ex-political prisoner. The mother insisted on sharing her story and experiences with me before I met her children. I welcomed and respected her desire and listened attentively to her story. My positionality as a Palestinian woman from the West Bank working with a team of researchers from Birzeit University—a university that is known by the ex-political prisoner community to always stand in solidarity with the prisoner's movement—made her feel comfortable and safe enough to share her story with me. She described her experiences inside the walls of Israeli prisons, the challenges she faced after she was released, and how the PA governmental organizations dealt with her and with other women ex-political prisoners. The words of the woman I interviewed continued to echo inside me and provoked important concerns. I became keen to dig more and find answers to all the questions that this interview struck in my mind.

However, there are scholars who prefer to maintain distance with interviewees in order to be objective. Many of these researchers utilize the approach of positivism, where the role of the researcher is restricted to data collection and interpretation in an objective method. In my research, I found that friendship and community-based relationships are fundamental to the method I was creating. The traditional and neutral approach that positivism calls for was not one that the women I had come to know would have responded to. It was imperative that they felt trust, and this could only be cultivated when I engaged with the participants in the research on a personal and communal level. These personal alliances not only created important connections that allowed the participants to provide my research with invaluable knowledge and experiences that impressed themselves not only upon my research but led me to create a new method of teaching through community building by bringing these women to my classroom to connect and share with my students not just through academic writing about the women. This intergenerational connection and transmission of these women's history, sacrifice, and lives in their own words to the young students is essential to realizing how indebted we are to them. This ethnographic form of education that is based on direct relation-building not only facilitates a space for knowledge and memory but also leads to healing for the women and the community.

The idea that a researcher can be purely objective and that subjectivity will lead to biased findings is, itself, a subjective judgment. While I was conducting the interviews, some of the interviewees complained against the researchers, journalists, and activists who remembered to write about their stories and experiences only during national occasions such as Prisoner's Day or hunger strikes (interviewee 2015). My responsibility as a researcher is to not exploit the researched community for my personal benefits. I felt it was my responsibility to document their experiences and help create a counternarrative to show the other side of the story outside the male-dominated discourse on resistance. Palestinian women ex-political prisoners are not passive victims; they continue struggling and resisting in their daily lives, and as a researcher, it is my duty to document their experiences as a part of the narrative of the Palestinian resistance.

My role as an indigenous researcher allowed me to delve deeper within these women's lives and their communities than I would have been able to if I were not taken in by them. I found that it does not take away from the researchers the ability to be fair and measured in their research. It allowed me to be a more effective and dynamic researcher, and enabled our team to open an academic space for these women to emerge from the invisibility imposed on them following their release in 1997. Most importantly, it enabled these women to become agents in telling their own stories of struggle and resilience to students, scholars, and the broader society.

The interviewees were aware of the importance of their stories during the interviews. When they mentioned their children and the life they lived while held captive inside Israeli prisons, the interviewees talked about specific events such as the chats they had when their children when they visited them in prison, life with their children after they got released, and very little about how their children were affected by their long absence. After two or three visits, the interviewees became more open, and talked in detail about their daily life, their concerns and constant fears of being rearrested after their release from Israeli settler-colonial prisons, their children, and political beliefs. So, the more successful I was at forming close relationships with the interviewees, the more they would reveal their personal feelings and thoughts and the more valuable and informative their stories became (Kirsch 2005, 2164).

Feeling ethically responsible toward the interviewees and their narratives, according to Tillmann-Healy, when you become a friend with the participants it means you should be available to listen and to participate in their activities as well (Tillmann-Healy 2003). From time to time I received invitations from the Palestinian women ex-political prisoners to attend their activities especially through social media. When I engaged with the participants' struggles, their stories, humanity, and harsh experiences, I found that I cannot leave the field by turning off the recorder, turning my back, and exiting as soon as the research has been completed. Because, in truth, their stories and lives are not stagnant and the important work in which many still participate to this day should be brought to light, this in essence makes this research one that must constantly grow and evolve, and I find that I too must constantly engage and be a part of these women's lives in order to push forward their right to be represented and defended in our collective story (Personal Narratives Group 1989).

Small Talk

When I started to visit the field in 2005, my colleague—the coordinator of the project—whispered in my ear, "Be attentive to the informal 'small talk' during or at the end of the interview, because often the most important data is generated from that talk." Not only does such informal conversation enhance good relationships with interviewees, but it also provides access to information from interviewees otherwise difficult to obtain (Driessen and Jansen 2013, 250). In one of the interviews, when I and the participant finished our conversation and were on the way out, we had an intimate conversation. At that moment the participant shared a significant incident about her personal life with me. The information that she shared was very valuable and reflected her own story and experience deeply. The "formal research" stays formal, therefore with turning off the recorder, other more intimate and crucial levels of the relationship appear.

Small talk is also fundamental in facilitating access to a wider network of interviewees for research (Driessen and Jansen 2013, 252). In my research, one of the most daunting challenges I faced was locating Palestinian women ex-political prisoners released in 1997. In all of my interviews, I shared this obstacle with interviewees sometimes at the beginning or at the end of the interview. So, when we go back together to that date the participants started to remember the women political prisoners who were with them in the same room or who shared memories with them or strikes that they went through together. From such small talk, I gained the information needed about others I could interview. At the same time as I was relying on these women for this important information, I realized that this process was allowing the women to get back in touch with each other. One of the interviewees fetched her old diary during the interview and opened it, then she read a note written by her roommate in prison, and all of a sudden she decided to call her and inform her about my visit. Some, due to getting married and trying to move forward with their lives, had not been able to stay in contact with their fellow women resistors who were held captive by the Israelis, and one by one they not only led me to the next woman but also to each other.

Outsider and Insider

The "relationship between researcher and participant cannot be determined a priori such that a researcher can be categorically designed either an insider or an outsider" (Ergun and Erdemir 2010, 17). Through the first interview I had the feeling that I am both simultaneously an insider and outsider. Despite the differences, I had lines of commonalities with the research participants such as our nationality, gender, language, cultural identity, and political and social situation. This assisted me to access the interviewees without any obstacles. As an indigenous fieldworker, I am an insider who has conscious and unconscious knowledge of the studied community. The indigenous fieldworker may be quicker in understanding the indicators of the social situation of the researched community—regardless of the effects that gender may have—and the common language, the historical and political experience, and the integration within the society all are very important factors for the indigenous researcher and fieldworker (Altorki and El-Solh 1988, 16). During the first interview, which was held in a nongovernmental institution that supports the Palestinian political prisoners, *Nadie al-Aseer* the Prisoner's Club, I sat with an ex-political prisoner who worked at the Prisoner's Club. She was responsible for following up on the legal issues related to prisoners and to contact their families. As we sat down and became acquainted with each other, she recounted specific incidents that happened to her, and as she received calls from prisoners and their families, she would describe their stories and how she supports them through the club. Here I felt deeply that I am an insider; she felt comfortable answering her phone and talking in front of me. As the interview proceeded, it became apparent to me that the formalities with which she began the interview started to melt away and she became more candid about not only her experiences but also of all the prisoners that the club deals with. She spoke to me about all of the protests and strikes that are held by the families and the public in support of the political prisoners not as a person explaining these events to an outsider but to someone who is very much knowledgeable and a part of these events. She recognized me as a fellow activist who is not only intrinsically knowing of the political realities of the political prisoners but very much active and coming from the inside of this community.

Another example of the importance of the communal and political connections that exist between an indigenous scholar and the research community occurred during an interview I conducted in Deir Balout, a village in the Salfit Governorate in the North of the West Bank. I recall the warm welcome I received, which is typical for Palestinian hospitality; as in other interviews, they all asked about any difficulties I faced on my way to the village, if there were Israeli checkpoints, and if they stopped me at the main checkpoint. They asked me if I would drink coffee with them before the interview. What ensued from this kind of intimacy was an informative story about the importance of cultural and social moments of connection and of building trust, and is one that I intrinsically understood.

As a researcher, I found myself writing both "We" and "They" during data analysis. It is not that I sometimes saw myself as an outsider instead of an insider. It was instead a question of how to deal with such a familiar community in the space of my academic work. I constantly had to figure out how to negotiate my language and situate myself and my perspective of this research in a manner that privileges the voices of the women who had become part of my research community, and yet not erase myself completely. When I used "we" I was dealing with an issue related to Palestinian women living in the OPT, while when I used "they" I was referring to them as Palestinian women who experienced imprisonment and painful episodes during their lives. I did not personally share the experience of being a political prisoner or ex-political prisoner. I did not live this experience personally, though my two brothers were both tortured and imprisoned by the Israelis during the second intifada, and so I still have a connection to the reality of political imprisonment and what it does to the families of the political prisoners. From this angle, though I felt deeply connected to the interviewees due to the shared struggle and political reality that causes all Palestinians to be affected by this tactic of war used by the Israeli settler-colonial occupation, I still considered myself as an outsider. And to some degree, as much as the women I spoke to took me into their confidence and into their communities and homes, they still felt a degree of separation due to the fact that "You did not live our experience. You cannot feel exactly what I mean. Here is prison too" (interviewee 2015).

Not only within the prison did these women feel separated from the rest of the community that they fought so selflessly for, but when they were released from prison, there was a further degree of separation due to the fact that the state and the people did not remember them, incorporate their sacrifices into our communal history and struggle, and did not help them to deal with the scars of being an ex-political prisoner. On top of the intercommunal failure to be there for these women and uplift them, they were under the constant fear of Israel harassing and rearresting them and their children. I figured out that in this part of the conversation I am an outsider, so I considered myself a learner through active listening. Showing the understanding and reflecting the importance of "her-story" (7) are essential elements through the interview. The interviewee added, "Being with men and women who were detained and experienced Israeli detention, and lived the same circumstances, made me feel comfortable. They could understand me, they have the same way in dealing with most of the issues, they did not see me as a stranger or unlike them" (interviewee 2015).

In order to get closer to understanding the experiences of this community, I turned to the academic writings of other indigenous academics such as my colleague and ex-political prisoner, Rula Abu Duhou. In her master's thesis "Palestinian Prisoners' Movement, 1967–1992: Struggle for the National Identity," Rula explained the term "community and prison community" in Israeli detentions. This community is the main component for the preservation of the national, political, and human subject. It is also a way to build the national, political, and communal personality. This group and community are a protective shield for strengthening and building individuals to face constraints and challenges (Abu Duhou 2014, 52–53).

Fieldwork is an area of learning. I read about Palestinian women and their experiences in Israeli prisons from the women themselves, but when I was in the field with the participants, hearing their stories with their own voices, watching their anger and happiness, their excitement and disappointment, hearing their voice tonality and seeing their tears, realizing that they spoke to me despite the liability upon their lives and their families brought out a whole new dimension to something that, though I am intrinsically connected to, the written word and the common knowledge of political captivity does not bring to light. To tell the whole story of their imprisonment and freedom impacted me greatly as both a researcher and as a fellow Palestinian woman. From my personal history of living among the systematic imprisonment of Palestinians and witnessing these women's narratives, I felt that I am now closer to being part of their world and my research had a deeper meaning and purpose. From the first interview, the women pulled me in and engaged me more with their stories. They showed me the need to find the best way I could to share and connect the lived experiences of these revolutionary women inside the Israeli prisons with the younger generations. This, coupled with the tremendous disappointment they both felt and lived from the betrayal of the agreements made under the Oslo Peace Accords, and the way the PA and the other cultural institutions of the society that they fought so hard for disappeared and erased them from the collective revolutionary history of Palestine, caused me to feel a deeper need to help document the experiences and deeds of these women for future generations to learn from.

Conclusion

The key imperative of feminist research is to produce knowledge that enhances understanding of (women's) experience while providing critical insights about the research process. I found that the personal process and development of my understanding of the act of conducting a field-based ethnographic research within my own community at times shifted and greatly augmented my perception of what the purpose of this research is in the larger context of Palestinian society, as well as for me personally as a feminist indigenous researcher. The ethnographic fieldwork that I conducted in Occupied Palestine endeavored to understand the experiences of Palestinian women ex-political prisoners who experienced two important historical eras in Palestine. It became a personal and academic commitment to shine a light on the stories of this particular group of women who were effectively silenced and erased from the national historical narrative since the signing of Oslo.

Being part of the process, through the medium of academia, to help these women bring their stories to the classroom and to document their words and sacrifices permanently sought to rekindle the communal connections the younger generations should have with these strong, dynamic, and selfless women. It also allowed me to reposition the elite and at times colonial role of academic research to be a tool not just of higher learning but also make it a working document by placing it within the context of the community and within the hands of the women on whose lives it is based. As highlighted throughout this reflection, there are enabling factors to being an insider, an indigenous researcher, and a Palestinian feminist that can provide smooth access to research communities, the field, and facilitate space for people of different backgrounds to come together. At the same time, many political and social boundaries and constraints existed that affected and informed how I conducted my fieldwork.

Writing about my own experience in the field and my reflections on the process was challenging. It took me a while to reorganize my thoughts and to focus on what I was going to present in this short chapter. Like other researchers and field workers, many challenges appeared such as ethics, emotions, reflexivity, positionality, collaboration, identification, intersubjectivity, and authority as interpreters (Bloom 1998, 2). I found that this was a vital journey and one worth going through in order to demonstrate the experiences and narratives of Palestinian women ex-political prisoners who were released after the signing of the Oslo peace agreement, to be a part of securing and attaining their right to their historical place within the collective memory of the Palestinian resistance movement, and to give them their due recognition in the consciousness and minds of the future generations—for it is their sacrifices that are and will always be indebted to.

Notes

1 The Ministry of Detainees and Ex-detainees' affairs was established in 1998, but it was transferred to a commission in 2014 upon a presidential decree on 29 May 2014 by Mahmood Abbas, the president of the state of Palestine. The commission is the official, legal, social, and political reference for Palestinian and Arab detainees in the Israeli occupation prisons to defend their humanitarian and legal rights in accordance with the international law, international resolutions and charters, and human rights organizations. The commission seeks to release all detainees and provide legal protection for them without any political, social, or ethnic discrimination. The commission looks forward to obtaining human justice and to consolidate freedom, democracy, culture, and values of human rights. In addition, it seeks to support the right of Palestinian people to freedom, independence, a decent life, and dignity. http://cda.gov.ps/index.php/en/.
2 The text of this document is available in Arabic language in a report written by Abdul-Nasser Fewana (head of the Palestinian Detainees Committee) in 2010 on page 29. www.palestinebehindbars.org/asra.pdf.
3 *Addameer* (Arabic for "conscience") Prisoner Support and Human Rights Association is a Palestinian nongovernmental civil institution that works to support Palestinian political prisoners held in Israeli and Palestinian prisons. Established in 1992 by a group of activists interested in human rights, the center offers free legal aid to political prisoners, advocates their rights at the national and international level, and works to end torture and other violations of prisoners' rights through monitoring, legal procedures, and solidarity campaigns. https://www.addameer.org.
4 The Palestinian Prisoners Club is a nongovernmental organization that was established in 1993 to support political prisoners in Israeli occupation jails. https://www.facebook.com/ppc1993/.

5   Abdul-Nasser Ferwana is head of the Palestinian Detainees Committee and a member of its follow-up committee in the Gaza Strip.
6   Henk Driessen cited the quote from: Prell, Riv-Ellen. 1989. "The Double Frame of Life History in the Work of Barbara Myerhoff." *Interpreting Women's Lives: Feminist Theory and Personal Narratives*, edited by The Personal Narratives Group. Bloomington: Indiana University Press.

Bibliography

Addameer Prisoner Support and Human Rights Association. 2010. "Palestinian Women Political Prisoners Systematic Forms of Political and Gender-Based State Violence." Last accessed 23 January 2019. http://www.addameer.org/sites/default/files/publicati ons/palestinian-women-political-prisoners-december-2010.pdf.

Addameer Prisoner Support and Human Rights Association. 2014. "General Briefing: Palestinian Political Prisoners in Israeli Prisons." Last accessed 1 August 2021. https://www.addameer.org/advocacy/briefings_papers/general-briefing-palestinian-political-prisoners-israeli-prisons-0.

Addameer Prisoner Support and Human Rights Association. 2021. "Statistics." Last accessed 1 August 2021. https://www.addameer.org/statistics.

Altorki, Soraya, and Camillia Fawzi El-Solh. 1988. "Introduction." *Arab Women in the Field Studying Your Own Society*, edited by Soraya Altorki and Camillia Fawzi El-Solh. Syracuse, NY: Syracuse University Press.

Bloom, Leslie. 1998. *Under the Sign of Hope: Feminist Methodology and Narrative Interpretation*. Albany: State University of New York Press.

Driessen, Henk. 1998. "The Notion of Friendship in Ethnographic Fieldwork." *Anthropological Journal on European Cultures* 1: 43–62.

Driessen, Henk, and Jansen Willy. 2013. "The Hard Work of Small Talk in Ethnographic Fieldwork." *Journal of Anthropological Research* 2: 249–63.

Emerson, Robert M. 1981. "Observational Field Work." *Annual Review of Sociology* 7: 351–78.

Ergun, Ayca, and Erdemir Aykan. 2010. "Negotiating Insider and Outsider Identities in the Field: 'Insider' in a Foreign Land; 'Outsider' in One's Own Land." *Field Methods* 1: 16–38.

Kirsch, Gesa E. 2005. "Friendship, Friendliness, and Feminist Fieldwork." *Signs* 30 (4): 2163–72. https://www.jstor.org/stable/10.1086/428415.

Moser, Stephanie. 2007. "On Disciplinary Culture: Archaeology as Fieldwork and Its Gendered Associations." *Journal of Archaeological Method and Theory* 14: 235–63. https://doi.org/10.1007/s10816-007-9033-5.

Olesen, Virginia. 1994. "Feminisms and Models of Qualitative Research." In *Handbook of Qualitative Research*, edited by Norman K. Denzin and Yvonna S. Lincoln, 158–74. Thousand Oaks, CA: Sage.

The Personal Narratives Group. 1989. *Interpreting Women's Lives*: Feminist Theory and Personal Narratives. Indiana University Press.

Pole, Christopher J., and Sam Hillyard. 2016. *Doing Fieldwork*. Los Angeles, CA: Sage.

Said, Edward. 1993. "The Morning After." *London Review of Books* 15 (20): 3–5. https://www.lrb.co.uk/the-paper/v15/n20/edward-said/the-morning-after.

Stephenson, John B., and L. Sue Greer. 1981. "Ethnographers in Their Own Cultures: Two Appalachian Cases." *Human Organization* 40 (2): 123–30.

Streubert, Helen J., and Dona R. Carpenter. 2011. *Qualitative Research in Nursing*. Philadelphia, PA: Lippincott Williams & Wilkins. https://oysconmelibrary01.files.wordpress.com/2016/09/qualitative-research-in-nursing-advancing-the-humanistic-imp.pdf.

Tillmann-Healy, Lisa M. 2003. "Friendship as Method." *Qualitative Inquiry* 5: 729–49.

Arabic Bibliography

أبو دحو، رلى. 2014. "الحركة الفلسطينية الاسيرة 1967-1992: النضال من اجل الهوية الفلسطينية." لبنان: منظمة التحرير الفلسطينية.

(Abu Duhou, Rula. 2014. "*Al-Harakah Al-Falistinyyah Al-Asera 1967-1992: al-Nidal min Ajel al-Hawiyah al-Wataniyah.*" *Risalet Magester. Birzeit: Jamiat Birzeit.*) (Abu Duhou, Rula. 2014. "Palestinian Prisoners' Movement, 1967–1992: Struggle for the National Identity." *Master's Thesis*, Birzeit University, Birzeit, Palestine.)

فروانة، عبد الناصر. 2010. حرية الأسرى: ما بين صفقات التبادل والعملية السلمية. مؤسسة أسري خلف القضبان.

(Ferwana, Abed al-Naser. "*Hurriyat alasra: ma bayna safaqat al-tabadul wa al-amaliyah al-silmiyah.*" *Mu'assasat asra khalf al-quḍbān.* http://www.palestinebehindbars.org/asra.pdf.) (Ferwana, Abed al-Naser. 2010. "The Freedom of Prisoners: Between Exchange Deals and the Peace Process." *My Family Behind Bars.* http://www.palestinebehindbars.org/asra.pdf.)

7 THE FEAR FACTOR: FIELDWORK AWAY FROM THE SAFETY BLANKET OF DEPOLITICIZED NOTION OF GENDER AND WOMEN'S ISSUES

Sara Ababneh

Introduction

In this chapter I trace the role fear played in my fieldwork of the Jordanian popular movement (*al-Hirak al-Sha'bi al-Urduni, Hirak* in short). I examine the fear of going to protests with the presence of thugs and riot police, which was heightened by my pregnancy and the fear I had for my unborn child. I also scrutinize my fear of "red lines," fear that study participants seemed to have overcome and often argued with me about. Finally, I study the fear of the secret service and the role that played in my fieldwork. The fear I felt was a direct result of my decision to move away from the safety blanket that doing research about women and gender had provided me with until then. Having long been critical of what Islah Jad (2004a) called the NGO-ization of most Arab women's movements, I saw many ways in which gendered research in Jordan was complicit in depoliticizing the struggle for women's rights. In the context of the Arab Uprisings and popular movements it became increasingly rare to see any women's rights activists on the streets of Jordan, or to hear of any explicitly "gendered" demands. I realized that doing research about the *Hirak* required me to separate myself from the "invisible list" of gendered issues in order to study the radical nature of the movement (Ababneh 2020). Doing so, I also let go of the protection that the depoliticization of doing research on women and gender had given me until then. This chapter is about the struggles of doing research while attempting to say no to depoliticized gender and the search for what a more radical form of gender studies, which takes seriously intersectionality and communal struggles against structural oppression (Abu Lughod 2002; Crenshaw 1991; Halley 2006; hooks 1981), might look like.

The Security of Doing Gendered Research

My initial research interest was in the diverse means of women's empowerment. While writing my PhD thesis at a British university, my audience was liberal Arab and Western feminists who did not see Islamism as potentially empowering to women. I was interested in how women active in Islamist organizations in Jordan and occupied Palestine were able to use Islamic teachings to empower themselves and women around them.

With the occupying Israeli authority too, studying gender made me less of a threat. When I tried to enter Palestine, the Israeli officer investigating me was put at ease that I was "only studying women." This was firstly due to the Orientalist—if not outright racist—attitude of the officer, which I did not seek to counter in this case as long as it enabled me to enter Palestine, that looking at women in Palestine would expose the patriarchal sexist practices of Palestinians (Hammami 2016; Shalhoub-Kevorkian 2008). For him, Palestinians were the culprits and the politics of occupation and apartheid would be left untouched. The second reason gender has become analogous to being apolitical is also because of the change in work of local women's rights NGOs, in what Islah Jad (2004a, 2004b) calls the NGO-ization of women's movements. Working through an NGO framework, most women's rights issues are often seen as projects, isolated from wider social and political structures. This enables women's rights NGOs and researchers to study gender relations in severe cases like occupation or in nondemocratic societies, without ever having to confront these structures of authoritarianism or occupation. Indeed, their "project"-centered work can actually serve to entrench and consolidate those oppressive structures. Furthermore, most NGO-ized modes of work assume a development mentality, in which the main source of women's oppression is the communities in which these women live. To go back to the example of occupied Palestine, it is Palestinian men who are seen as the reason why Palestinian women do not leave the house, and not Israeli settler-colonialism. The Israeli Officer seemed to have internalized the assumptions surrounding the oppression of Arab women and asked me how my Jordanian father allowed me to travel alone.

In Jordan, while I was researching the Jordanian Muslim Brotherhood (MB) and its women, I was never approached by anyone, or offered the dreaded invitation to have coffee at the *Dai'ra* (the Jordanian General Directorate of Intelligence (GID)). This all changed when I became increasingly interested in more traditionally political topics: that is, protests. By the time I had started my second research project, which was studying the Jordanian popular protest movement (the *Hirak*), I had become increasingly interested in class as a source of marginalization. Due to the depoliticized nature of gender and of women's rights NGOs in Jordan, I moved away from focusing on women alone and started studying marginalized communities as a whole and the politics of marginalization. This shift deprived me of my main security blanket: the ability to appear harmless because I was "only" studying women and gender. With my interest in protest groups beyond their gendered demands, my research could now be seen as being more dangerous and potentially more political, leading me in fact to eventually receiving the dreaded phone call from the GID.

Mind over Body

I had just moved back to Jordan when the Arab Uprisings started in late 2010. Around the time of the first protests in Tunisia, Jordan, and Egypt, I was pregnant (in my first trimester), feeling physically nauseous yet politically inspired and elevated. My body and hormonal state taught me valuable lessons about how much I was really in charge of myself and made me question the notion of individualism on a whole new level. Whereas before I had seemingly endless amounts of energy, now I only wanted to sleep. Before pregnancy I had seen myself as a strong woman who would let nothing and no one stop her. Now my body made me question how much my mind was actually in charge. Things improved during my second trimester: I felt in charge of my body once again and was able to join the protests, first in front of the Egyptian and Libyan embassies and later the weekly Friday protests in front of the Husseini mosque in downtown Amman and the 24th of March protest at the Ministry of Interior. However, my quest to conquer my body with the force of my mind was short lived. Overall, I had to content myself with participating from afar: through watching the protests on television, following social media, and by organizing discussion groups and workshops on the Arab Uprisings at the University of Jordan, my place of work.

In addition to bodily impediments, pregnancy also brought fear with it. I found that I was far less willing to take risks than I would have liked to take. At any sign of potential violence, I left the scene quickly. I was constantly checking where thugs were and whether their stones would reach me. During the 24th of March 2011 protests I stayed at the margins, making sure that I could run away if things became violent.[1]

Leila was born in July 2011, at the same time as the Jordanian popular movement moved out of Amman toward the governorates. I was unable to join fellow Ammani activists who traveled to governorates to protest alongside governorate activists there. While I had been still somewhat able to follow what was happening while I was pregnant, after giving birth I found myself completely preoccupied with our miraculous new family member. I had to wait almost four years, long after the *Hirak* had ceased to exist, until I could go back to participating in the Jordanian popular movement, this time by writing about it.

Moving toward Real Politics

As Soheir Morsy wrote in 1988 for many indigenous researchers the goal of research is to study "our people ... for our benefit" (Morsy 1988, 72). Mine was not a project of exploring otherness but rather a personal quest (Gupta and Ferguson 1977, 17). With the start of the Arab Spring protests all over the region, I too was interested in whether gendered demands would be included in popular demands and would be part of the demands of the nation. I started researching women in the day-wage labor movement (DWLM) and later the Jordanian popular protest movement in search of "women's demands."

At first, I wanted to learn more about the DWLM, a movement that had started in May 2006 to fight for the right of all workers to be hired permanently in accordance with Jordanian labor law. What was so striking about this movement was the high number of women in both its leadership and rank-and-file. More surprising was the fact that this group staged an overnight sleep in protest in which the male and female workers stayed in front of the royal court (Ababneh 2016). I was interested to see how this group was able to engage in such culturally radical acts and how it was able to create such a gender egalitarian structure that really suited women's needs. After finishing this project, I became increasingly interested in the Arab Spring (2011–12) as it played out in Jordan. Initially I wanted to study how gendered demands were made. I wanted to understand how national demands could be gendered to include women's problems. I wanted my research to recognize that national struggles are for all people, that is, women as well as men.

Throughout my fieldwork, however, I could not find what I was looking for. I asked protestors if they had demanded that Jordanian women have the right to give their children Jordanian citizenship. I asked whether there had been women protesting. I asked whether any demands were made for women specifically. The answers were mostly negative. The men, and women, whom I asked insisted that the biggest issues that faced Jordan was poverty and policies of economic marginalization and impoverishment. As hard as I searched, I could not really find any "gendered" or women-specific demands being made. In certain groups, in particular nonlabor groups, it was even hard to find women.

It was after a year or two into the research that I began to realize that the way the literature and I myself had been conceptualizing gender had fallen prey to the depoliticization that results from NGO-ization. In other words, the *Hirak* activists were not demanding the gendered demands that I was searching for because these gendered demands were part of the status quo they were fighting. I could not "see" gender, because an invisible list had already been formed in my mind that restricted what fighting for women's rights and gender justice meant. This list had been formed through the work of women's rights activists, NGOs, donor initiatives, and academics writing about these initiatives.

Jordan's so-called civil society has developed an invisible list of problems facing women. These problems have been considered "women's issues." The main issues on the list are gender-based violence, legal restrictions facing women, women's political marginalization, and economic disempowerment (in the narrow sense of the word, which does not include structural economic marginalization) (Ababneh 2020). Since the women in the DWLM and later *Hirak* activists did not directly face and resist any of these issues, I (and women's rights organizations and the media at large) did not recognize their struggle as a woman's struggle. None of the Jordanian women's rights NGOs or civil society actors stood by the women of the DWLM or *Hirak* activists. Studying the DWLM and the *Hirak* made me question the work of women's rights organizations in Jordan, many of whom are incapable of standing in solidarity with these—predominantly women's—movements.

More importantly, my research made me question this invisible list. While the problems on the "women's issue list" are certainly important, for the majority of Jordanian women they are not the most pressing problems. The problems most women face every day are poverty and unemployment. I was still interested in seeing how poverty and economic marginalization affected women specifically. I also wanted to study the activism that sought to fight them. I saw that women shared these problems with the men in their communities. While the impact of poverty and unemployment is gendered for sure, I did not want my focus on gender to blind me to the other injustices being committed (Halley 2006).

Protestors conceptualized poverty differently from organizations that give microfinance loans to women and speak about women's economic empowerment. These projects assume that women somehow face poverty on their own as individuals or that these women are poor because of their communities. Due to the NGO-ized nature of their work that disregards "structures," there is no acknowledgment that the communities in which these women live have been impoverished by neoliberal economic policies. For many NGOs and women's rights organizations, poverty becomes an individual problem that women face because they are women. While poverty is gendered, it is not true that most women are poor just because they are women. They are poor because their "communities" have been impoverished. When a community is impoverished, so are its women and children.

Most women's rights NGOs do not engage in critical analysis of the structural problems that have impoverished entire communities and, by extension, the women in them. The problem with the women's list is that it is a list of problems that women do not share with their communities. The problems women share with their communities are missing from the list. Yet, they are the most pressing problems women face.

I realized that I too was looking for "gender and women's" issues, using that old invisible list. I needed to put gender (at least in the old/established sense of the term) aside for a while to truly be able to hear and grasp the messages that were coming my way from my participants. I therefore stopped looking for women-only groups or groups that addressed "women's issues." Rather I started studying *Hirak* groups focusing centrally on economic marginalization. Doing so, I never stopped looking for gender, of course. First, I looked for female activists, as I wanted to see how they conceptualized their struggle and whether they understood their activism differently than their male counterparts. I was interested in gathering life histories of these activists, be they women or men. I also wanted to see how male activists described their experiences in terms of gender. I wanted to see why certain issues were seen as important "national" priorities and others not. While I still had gender on my radar, the way I looked for it changed. I no longer went to the predefined "women's spaces" and struggles. I expanded my research to encompass the national (incorrectly also perceived as a male-only space). I wanted to understand how women experience these communal and national problems differently, whether there were different problems according to one's gendered subject position inside certain marginalized communities. I was also interested in finding solutions that would address the needs of all who made up these communities. Most importantly, I wanted my research to shed light on these communal problems as women's problems. I felt strongly that women's rights initiatives should join the labor and governorate activists. I hoped that my research could show how these communal struggles were gendered and how women's rights groups could join these movements.

In order to study the *Hirak* I needed to repoliticize gender, and the first step to doing so was to move away from studying women and women's issues in the traditional sense as issues separated from wider communal issues. Once I did this, I soon realized that with the move to repoliticize gender I had also lost the security blanket that studying gender had provided me with until then. I had been protected and cushioned during my previous research projects because I was only looking at gender in isolation to class, religion, and race and women's struggles in isolation from wider communal struggles against structural marginalization. Now, in my quest to find a more radical definition of gendered demands, and thus refusing that blanket I was exposed as researching "real" politics, I started appearing on the radar of the secret service.

Confidentiality

The encounter with the GID made me reconsider whether I should indeed use participants' real names or whether pseudonyms were a safer option. I kept going back and forth. I called a participant from each group to inform them about my visit to the GID and ask them if they would like me to use pseudonyms. All refused.[2] I was still not convinced. What if a statement on paper would lead to convicting a participant? The political climate was very different in 2015/16 to how it was in 2011/12. Certainly in 2011—and even in 2012—when participants had publicly crossed some red lines, the euphoria of the Arab Uprisings was still high. Things had not "gone wrong" yet in Syria. The regime did not know the outcome of the protests and was treading a careful line. But by 2015 there was no *Hirak* anymore that could protect activists. Activists were still being tried for treason away from public support and the media. I finally reached a conclusion while speaking to Mahdi al-Saafeen, one of the youth activists I interviewed extensively. Al-Saafeen argued that I needed to respect the agency of my participants. He continued that they were adults who knew the risks they were taking. I needed to respect their decision and not assume that I was more aware of their interest than they were themselves.

I have also been disturbed by literature on Jordan in which—mostly Western—authors provide information and analysis that is clearly not their own without making any references to the locals who are the sources of this information. In order to avoid appropriating the ideas of others as my own, I have kept the real names of participants when it comes to their involvement in the *Hirak* and their ideas. I have, however, changed the names in this chapter when I have discussed personal stories of participants. When I have changed the name I only put a first name. When I mention a participant by first and last name this is an indication that I have used the real name of that person.

Logistics

Since I did not participate in most events of the Jordanian *Hirak*, I needed to build new connections and be introduced to activists. My way in was through Amman-based friends who had been *Hirak* activists themselves. Their vouching for me gained me entry into different *Hirak* circles, from workers' groups to governorate activists and youth groups that formed in Amman.

Two people in particular enabled me to gain access and the trust of activists by vouching for me: Abu Kalthoum and Nadim.[3] Both Abu Kalthoum and Nadim had been very active in Palestine-related activism in Amman prior to 2011, which is how I met them. They grew up with the liberation of Palestine as their primary target. When protests erupted in early 2011, they too joined protestors. Initially, they were close to friends their own age who were active in Leftist political parties based in Amman. When these parties were hesitant to join the *Hirak* in the governorates and to fight for issues of social justice, however, Nadim and Abu Kalthoum, both of whose families were displaced from Palestine in 1948, moved toward making new networks and working with East Bank Jordanian governorate activists directly. A whole new way of doing activism emerged in the *Hirak*. Abu Kalthoum would come over to my house and we could discuss how much his image of Jordan and East Bank Jordanians had changed. He became very critical of the chauvinism that many oppositional political parties reproduced by portraying East Bank Jordanians as an extension of the regime and the monarchy. Abu Kalthoum would tell me about the activities that the protestors were planning to contest the old form of identity politics, to move beyond the division of Jordanian-Jordanians versus Palestinian-Jordanians to an understanding of solidarity based on class.

We both thought that it was extremely important to write about this process, in addition to focusing on the economic demands of protestors that the liberal press continuously silenced. We started conducting interviews in early 2013. However, Abu Kalthoum got married shortly afterward and moved to the United States with his wife, leaving me to undertake the reminder of my research and writing on my own.

Main Participants

Abu Kalthoum had left me with a long list of activists with whom he had worked closely. In addition, Nadim was kind enough to help me set up a lot of the meetings and eventually go with me on many of my fieldwork trips. He organized and accompanied me to my fieldtrip to the South where I met activists from Karak, Tafileh, and Aqaba. Nadim also planned and accompanied me to my interviews to Huwwara in the North, near Irbid, and to Hay al Tafileh in Amman. These were all activists with whom Nadim had closely worked during the *Hirak*. He had organized activities with them, often staying overnight, since their work extended well into the night. By not only introducing me to them but also accompanying me to the interviews, Nadim gave me access not just to the trust of many participants but also to interviews that I could not have conducted on my own. He often jumped in asking questions, remembering certain instances, and asking about certain events (many of which I had no prior knowledge about).

Doing so, Nadim became intimately familiar with my research. During the hours we spent in the car together we mostly discussed the interviews, analyzed what participants had said and thought about identity, economics, and gender.

Nadim was also one of the main activists I interviewed. I interviewed him seven times, adding up to over 15 hours of recordings. Nadim played a key role in enabling my research, introducing me to activists, and allowing me to gain their trust. He was also key in my thinking and analysis process. Interviews with him functioned not only as a valuable source of information—no other participant has spent this much time trying to recapture all events for me—but also as a main source of analysis. The interviews were a conversation in which Nadim challenged, built on, or refuted some of the many topics we had discussed. In that, Nadim was the truest "participant" of my study. He was far more than an interviewee: without his help my research would have been completely different.

Being Someone Else's Daughter and Wife

Most of the study's participants were men. While some groups, like the DWLM, were overwhelmingly composed of women, other groups, like the Hay al Tafaileh group, barely had any women in its midst. Even though I tried to search for women in most places and ask about women, many of the groups were either exclusively male or had very few female activists. The men I interviewed had no issue being interviewed by women, neither did my gender prevent me from doing interviews with the men. As I will explain shortly, this was mostly because the men in my family (my husband and father) did not place any restrictions on me as a woman to do so.

Nadim accompanied me on most of my fieldwork trips. Throughout the years many of my interns at the University of Jordan's Center for Strategic Studies (CSS) also came to interviews, took fieldwork notes, and transcribed the interviews. Doing so, they too became intimately familiar with the material. After a day trip to Mleih, a town to the south of the city of Madaba, to interview Mohammad Sneid, for the fourth time, Tasneem, an intern who accompanied me on multiple visits, commented how strange she found it that we ate together with Sneid and his colleague while Sneid's wife had prepared the food but did not join us.[4] Tasneem observed that there seemed to be a different set of rules for the wives and female members of participants and us, as women. Tasneem was surprised at the different way Sneid and his colleague interacted with us as women and their own family members. Tanseem wondered why Sneid's wife did not eat with us, while Sneid and his colleague did not seem to find it problematic to mix with us.

Tasneem's observation connects to the discussion of the role of family in many communities in the Arab world. Many feminists have identified the family as one of the main sites to (re)produce or challenge the subordinate position of women in Arab society. Suad Joseph (1994, 2018), for example, writes that a kin group organizes the social, economic, and political life of its members more than any other social structure, including the state (55). Wilhelmina Jansen points out that women's identity is even more dependent than men's identity in the family in Jordan (Jansen 1998, 81).

It can be argued that the family determines the choices many Arab women have (Joseph 1994, 62; Rubenberg 2001, 35). In other words, people's application of taboos and restrictions mostly applies to women of their own family. Most people do not see it as their role or duty to enforce any moral conduct (even if they adhere to it in their own family and in relation to females in their families) to women outside their family. The study participants assumed that my and Tasneem's family (i.e., male members of the family) seemed to have approved of our interaction. Or the participants simply did not think it their role to question the conduct of women who are not their immediate family members.

For Sneid and his wife a different set of rules applied to Tasneem and me. That set of rules concerned the social and not the workspace. Through my research on the DWLM I had learned that women and men did indeed mix together in work-related protests. More than this, they even staged a sleep-in. However, the lunch to which Sneid invited us was a social activity in which social practices were once again observed. Tasneem and I, however, were not seen as part of this social milieu in which men and women do not mix, which for myself, at least, was true.

In Tafileh, a city in the south of Jordan, I had a very different experience. While most of the people I interviewed in Tafileh were men, I also met with Um Nibras. Um Nibras was one of the main female activists in the Tafileh movement. Her husband Abu Nibras and herself had both been communists and had been active in the events of 2011/12. I interviewed Um Nibras individually—she also joined Nadim and myself when we invited all the activists we met on our first day in Tafileh to the lobby of the eco-lounge in which we were staying. There she contributed loudly, smoked, and did not seem to mind mixing with fellow activists and Nadim and me. These two contrasting examples show that it is problematic to generalize about gendered social practices based on my fieldwork experience.

Surveillance and Censorship

The question of who was imposing self-surveillance and censorship—my participants or I—became one of the main questions I asked myself. Matters came to a test after my field trip South first to Karak, then to Tafileh, and finally to Aqaba. On the second day of my Tafileh trip, I conducted a focus group at night. I had interviewed activists all day and a group of the core organizers had agreed to come to my hotel. I was staying at the Dana travel lounge that is run by the Royal Conservatory of Nature (RCN) in Dana village. I started doing individual interviews with activists, but after three hours the interviews turned into a focus group discussion. Earlier on when I asked about pseudonyms, Um Nibras had said to me: "We are happy for you to use everything we say. The question is whether you will be able to really write about everything that we tell you. We are not adhering to any red lines (*khutut h'amra'*), will you adhere to any?" Her question was in relation to the critique many had made of the royal family. I told her that she was right to ask me, because I would indeed not be able to write about these things. I knew that I had to adhere to certain red lines.

Nadim and I were the only guests at the RCN's lounge in Dana that evening. We did the interview in the lobby/communal space near the breakfast area. The guards and the receptionist were sitting close by. It was February and cold outside. One of the guards had started a fire in the fireplace. We had bought cookies and ordered tea. I was quite aware of the presence of the eco-lounge's staff. I was worried about the type of discussions we were having. My participants were not only loud, they also did not shy away from crossing any of the common "red lines." I was scared that any one of the staff could write a report about us. The participant was right: I was actually more afraid than my interviewees. They had already put themselves on the line, openly critiquing the regime and the monarch. And I was not willing to go as far as they had gone.

After the interviews in Karak and Tafileh I went on to Aqaba to interview worker activists there. Upon my return to Amman, the director of the CSS where I work called me to his office. He told me that he had received a phone call from the GID (the secret service, that is, the *Mukhabarat*). The officer who had called him had asked him if he knew where I had been this week. The director told him that he knew that I was doing fieldwork in the South. The officer asked him to arrange a meeting with me and the *Dai'ra* (GID). I was quite shocked to hear this. While I had always joked that at some point I would have to have the proverbial coffee with the GID, when the call came, it created within me a deep fear that I had not expected, translating into three months of sleep disturbances and insomnia.

This meeting also made me wonder who had told the GID. Was it a random person on the street? One of my colleagues at work? One of my interns? Maybe even one of the participants? Growing up I have been taught to be particularly weary of those who challenge the system, since they might be undercover informants waiting to lead others to make similar reckless demands. I became increasingly entangled in suspicion, doubt, and fear.

Prior to my field trip to the South my father had started getting increasingly more worried about my research. His deepest fear was how this would affect my foreign husband and non-Jordanian children (Ali had joined our family by then).[5] His fear was not unfounded. A close friend of mine and oppositional activist who is also married to a foreign husband and whose children are—like my own children—also not Jordanians received numerous phone calls from the GID. During the last phone call the caller said: "You don't seem to be worried for yourself, but you should at least think about your foreign children." My friend took this to be a clear threat to her children's ability to stay in Jordan and has since emigrated.

My father was adamantly opposed to me going to the South. He was also uncomfortable with the fact that I was going with Nadim. When I told him about the meeting with the GID, he insisted that he attend any meeting between me and the GID. He called his friend to arrange the meeting himself, instead of going through the director of the CSS. He also called a relative of ours who works in the GID to ask him about the procedure. Arranging my visit himself, my father was hoping that he could protect me and my "foreign" family.

After weeks of back and forth, the date was finally set and we were invited to the GID building itself. The outcome of the negotiations between my father, the vice president of the university, the director of my center, and the GID was affected by the discovery of a "terrorist cell" near Irbid. The GID had been very busy with this event and we did not feel that given the severity of the situation in Irbid we could negotiate any further.[6]

We called the GID and were told to park in the parking lot of a big supermarket adjacent to the new GID building. We were told that this is where "visitors" usually parked. We had arranged the visit with the university professor coordinator in the GID. He sent us a car that took us from the supermarket parking lot to the main building of the GID. Later on, my father remarked they could have made us walk, which would have been a real *bahdaleh* (humiliation). We were taken into the university professor's coordinator's office, which was nicely furnished with leather sofas and wooden paneled walls. The coordinator and my father chatted for about 20 minutes. I hardly said a word. My father talked about his work and his patients and doctor's service to this country, especially those working in the public sector for as long as he had worked there. The coordinator assured us that we should not be worried at all, that the GID really liked knowing the work of professors and that it was a great opportunity for all of us to meet one another.

Lila Abu Lughod describes how hesitant she had been when her father insisted on accompanying her to the Awlad Ali Bedouins in Egypt when she first started her doctoral research. She writes that while her father did most of the talking, she was silent, "feeling distinctly unlike an anthropologist" (Abu Lughod 1986, 12). Similar to Abu Lughod's father, my father was keen to do whatever he could to protect me by showing that I was not an isolated, and thus vulnerable, individual but belonged to a family and more importantly was an extension of my father himself. It was this relational capacity that my father sought to underline, and that I did not try to dispute, understanding that being seen as an "individual" was far less advantageous for my case. However, despite lip service to respecting these familial ties, the GID was far from letting the visit pass in this fashion.

After about 20 minutes the coordinator said that, if we did not mind, I should meet his colleague while he continued chatting to my father. My father's attempts to keep things social, by having me seen as an extension of him, not as an individual researcher but as the daughter of a known surgeon who had spent over 30 years in the public sector, were only the introduction to our visit. Despite preforming the social rites and maintaining niceties, I was eventually separated from my father to be interrogated on my own.

I was taken to a much less grandiose office. Unlike the coordinator, the man in the room did not address me using my doctor title, a gesture that I interpreted as an intentional show of strength and disrespect. He said, "Are you Sara Ababneh? Give me your ID." I said I was and that I had not caught his name. He told me his name was Abu So and So. Later I was told that in interrogations officers never gave their real names and went with a *kunieh* (Abu or Um so and so, in Jordan many people are addressed as the father or the mother of their eldest son (or daughter if the person does not have any sons)) instead. While the meeting with the coordinator had been very respectful and amiable, Abu So and So's tone made it clear that this was an interrogation.

He started off asking me about whether I had ever traveled. I said yes. He asked me where to. He asked me if anyone during my travels had asked me to write this chapter. I said, unfortunately, not many people were interested in the Jordanian popular movement. He then asked me about my paper. When I started speaking about the main focus of my paper—mainly the struggle against economic marginalization—Abu So and So became friendlier. He clearly related to the demand and did not seem to classify it as a security threat. We talked for about an hour and a half.

Even though the meeting ended well, and I have not heard back from the GID since, I was nonetheless shaken by the visit. I found myself far more hesitant while conducting interviews in the coming weeks. While acting as a participant observer at a workers' protest against Royal Jordanian Airlines employment policies, I found myself more scared than I had ever been participating in a protest. I also experienced, as noted earlier, insomnia for the first time in my life. I started suspecting that my phone was being surveilled, noticing that the battery was depleting faster than normal, which might have been normal Apple marketing tactic, of course, but in my mind everything was suspicious these days. In sum, I became suspicious of everyone. I do not know how the GID found out about my trip to the South. In my mind anyone could have told them. The trip showed me that the same state that had tortured some of my study's participants could potentially move against me too.

My fear was heightened by the stories that my study's participants told me about the real violence they had encountered. Latifa, a female activist of *al-Hirak al-Shababi* Amman, told me that many of the women she worked with stopped attending demonstrations after their brothers and fathers started receiving fabricated videos and images of their daughters. These images intended to smear the reputation of these female activists. Latifa herself was also exposed to a smear campaign. Her father—a religious preacher—received messages telling him that his daughter had a boyfriend. Simultaneously, images of Latifa and—her later husband—Karim were circulated on various social media outlets claiming that the couple were expecting a baby. This was before the two were engaged.

My experiences with the GID, coupled with what happened to my friend whose children the GID had threatened, also made me realize that I was more vulnerable as a woman doing this type of research, not only in my individual capacity as a woman but precisely in my social capacity as a mother and wife. This social vulnerability was a by-product and intersected with the legal discrimination against women, in my particular case my inability to transfer my Jordanian citizenship to my children and husband. As an individual the impact on me and a male researcher might be similar, we could both be jailed, maybe even experience violence. But a male researcher would not have risked having his family expelled from Jordan. A Jordanian man has the right to give his citizenship to his wife and children. Doing critical research would not threaten the legal status of a Jordanian male researcher's family, the way it could potentially threaten my family life. My father's efforts to have his patriarchal right to have his family reside in Jordan extend to his non-Jordanian grandchildren have provided us with much security over the past years. Socially, despite not being Jordanians my children feel at home in Jordan. However, the encounter with the GID showed me that my family's precarious legal condition could be easily used against me. My own "relational" vulnerability showed me how little an individual lens is able to expose about underlying structural and legal threats and risks researchers face.

An Insider to Trust?

Did being Jordanian make my participants trust me more? Maybe in some ways, but not necessarily in others. From consulting UN organizations in fact-finding missions I have often observed how open Jordanians are with (Western) foreigners. When teaching foreign study abroad students I have to always remind my students that they are not to quote any of their local professors or people they had conversations with. I think that the main reason for this openness is that while any Jordanian could potentially be an undercover GID agent—a testament to the success of the GID in planting fear and mistrust between Jordanians—foreigners are perceived as not being close to the status quo. People therefore tend to not self-censor themselves as much with foreign researchers or students. This trust is often misplaced as many foreigners do not appreciate the real dangers reckless words can cause their Jordanian interlocuters, nor are they of course more trustworthy.

Inside a state in which the security apparatus still often functions as a form of public surveillance people's distrust of each other often is the strongest deterrent of critical words or action. The activists I interviewed sought to disrupt the culture and system that rules the lives of many Jordanians. In their activism they used their bodies and words to challenge red lines and create a new patriotic discourse. Doing so, they sought to protect themselves and their work from the accusation of treason and/or being hostile to the national interest of Jordan. The biggest factor enabling my research was thus the participants' belief in their mission and their struggle to make their voices heard. Most had overcome their fear and gave me frank and honest answers.

I experienced very little suspicion in the field. This was mostly because I was introduced directly by Abu Kalthoum and Nadim, and accompanied by Nadim. Mostly, participants appreciated my interest in the topic. Doing the fieldwork four to six years after the events proved difficult in terms of participants' memories of certain events, the politics of the present, and accuracy of the details. Quite a few contacted me after the interview telling me how speaking to me had reminded them of how important their work had been. Others felt that it was crucial to document the *Hirak* and were happy that I was doing this. Many saw my work as an extension of their own: namely to contribute to a new reform discourse, and even as an extension of patriotic work.

Tribalism and Identity Politics

The only time someone refused to be interviewed by me was when I tried interviewing a distant relative of mine who had been part of a group to which Nadim did not have direct relations. I had never met this other Ababneh before but thought that being related to him would be enough of an introduction and that I needed no other form of introduction. I was wrong. This was the only participant I approached who refused to be interviewed. When I finally did interview him, it was only because he accompanied a friend of his whom I was interviewing.

This story problematized my own assumed access to most "East Bank" activists just because I am of East Bank descent myself. To this day I am unaware of why he distrusted me; it might have been my urban accent or the fact that I live in Amman and not in Bishra and Sal (the rural villages in which most Ababnehs live). It might have simply been a matter of reaching this participant through the wrong network. It later transpired that this Ababneh and the person who had given me the Ababneh's contact information had had a disagreement. It might have also been the difference in class background. This encounter challenges the assumption about Jordan that family affiliation or place of origin is the main source of identification and trust. The common wisdom about Jordan is that most Jordanians identify as either Jordanian-Jordanian or Palestinian-Jordanian, and that this form of identification supersedes all other forms of loyalty. *Hirak* activists sought to challenge this common wisdom, by forming class-based alliances.

While much of what they told me concerned this topic of identity, this fieldwork encounter with a family member who should, by family ties alone, have been my greatest ally and participant provided me with a personal example of how false these assumptions can be on the ground.

Another element of this common wisdom is that Jordanian-Jordanians are first-class citizens (as opposed to Palestinian-Jordanians) who the state will not dare touch. Many colleagues would joke that I could write what I wanted since I was Jordanian-Jordanian. Much of my research experience directly contradicted this belief. Most of my research participants were East Bankers (Jordanian-Jordanians) who had paid a high price for their activism, and whose "East Bank" status had done little to protect them. In fact, in many ways it worked against them, in particular when they were active in groups that were not based in the governorates from which these participants came. The most extreme example of how dangerous it was to be an East Bank activist away from your city of origin was what happened to Karim. While Karim's family originally comes from the Southern city of Karak, Karim grew up in Amman. He joined an Amman-based youth group during the events of 2011/12. Like many of his peers he was eventually arrested. While most activists told me that the police did not physically harm them in any way, Karim was severely beaten and tortured while in custody. He told me that those who beat him kept alluding to the fact that he was Jordanian. Karim and all those who worked with him testified that he was tortured the most precisely because he was Jordanian-Jordanian. Other Jordanian-Jordanians who were in mixed groups experienced similar treatment. I was told of one Jordanian-Jordanian whose first cousin was brought in to torture him. Many of my study participants concluded that Jordanian-Jordanians were disproportionately targeted by the security apparatus and beaten more than West Bankers, precisely because these East Bankers were seen as being traitors to their East Bank origins. Hearing these stories heightened my own sense of insecurity. While I had never seen myself as untouchable or above the law, seeing the physical scars on Karim's body served as a clear reminder of the huge gap between discourse and reality.

The Boldest of Them All

Research and literature that is critical of the regime in Jordan is almost nonexistent. Inside Jordan, the politics of GID surveillance and more importantly self-censorship play a big role in maintaining this situation. However, even foreign researchers rarely forward any bold critiques. In my work, too, I applied self-censorship. I decided early on that I would not include any material that was critical of the monarchy. Instead I focused on demands and wider structural critique that focuses on the economic structures.

Yet, despite my self-censorship, I hoped that my work would bring forward voices that are not heard in most international academic work on Jordan either: a public common sense that is highly critical of neoliberal economic policies, fights for social justice and economic sovereignty, and that believes in the Palestinian cause. It is not just that the English literature on Jordan is hesitant to critique the regime and monarchy, it is also that most of the literature seems unable to hear this common sense. It is not just foreign researchers, however, who do not acknowledge this public common sense but also local elites. Together these researchers assemble a picture that not only does support the regime's neoliberal economic reform agenda but also celebrates it.

It is here that being a native researcher helped me the most. I was also someone who despite living in Amman, and living an upper-middle-class life, had family who lived in a village. I grew up seeing my uncles struggle to make it. I watched as my extremely intelligent cousins graduate from universities and yet be unable to find employment year after year despite their high grades. Whenever we were in Sal, a village near Irbid in the North of Jordan in which my father was born, the critique of a state policy was, day in and day out, the main topic of conversation.

My research really became participatory in my attempt to recapture the common sense of the *Hirak*. I used the interviews for many reasons: to find out what a certain group had done; to recapture events; to trace networks; to understand demands; to discuss challenges; and to learn more about participants' life stories. After conducting the initial interviews, I would go back and think about what discourse different groups were advancing. After analyzing interviews, I often met with participants again and asked them what they thought about my analysis. These meetings were less interviews and more conversations about wider discourses of economic reform and identity. Some participants had written about their work, but most had lived the *Hirak* and did not have much time to reflect. The second, third, fourth, or fifth interviews (follow-up discussion) functioned as a way to think through the common sense of the *Hirak* (or a particular subgroup). It was this process that turned the research into more of a participatory project.

Doing Research in Our Own States

In the groundbreaking book *Arab Women in the Field: Studying Your Own Society*, Altorki and El-Solh (1988) discuss the importance of doing research in one's own society. The different contributors speak about the challenges, limitations, and opportunities such research provides. In anthropology this volume and other articles started a debate about the importance of doing research in one's own community and enabled generations of future researchers to embark on important research.

Yet, most of the writers of the volume, while having ethnic and familial links to the communities which they researched, had come back to do the research, their families having immigrated to the global North. Thus, while these researchers certainly researched their own societies, they did not research these societies while they lived there permanently.

From the perspective of fear, a new challenge emerges when one conducts research in one's own society, or should I say state, and which is also one's permanent abode: that if the state registers critical (and therefore potentially subversive) research, the researcher will have to live with these consequences. The researcher cannot simply take refuge in another state/return to another state. While I hold another passport that would allow me to move to another country in case I had to, this scenario is not one that I seek to live. Jordan is my home. I plan to stay here. One security blanket is writing in English for an English-speaking audience. This enables many researchers living in Jordan and other Arab countries to write about topics they might not be able to get away with if they wrote them in Arabic. In my research I impose self-censorship and refrain from challenging any of the official red lines. But I still attempt to critique and shake the economic power structures that marginalize so many.

Conclusion

In this chapter I examined the role fear played in my fieldwork studying the *Hirak*. As with many Arab feminist academics, I too sought to align my research with my activism. Having been critical of what Islah Jad (2004a) calls the NGO-ized nature of women's rights projects and research on gender that comes out of "civil society" institutions, I sought to move away from studying the struggle for gender justice apart from wider struggles for communal justice. In researching the Jordanian popular movement, instead of focusing on gender exclusively I tried to repoliticize gender by connecting it to wider struggles. Doing so, however, I also let go of the protection that depoliticization of doing research on women and gender had given me until then. This chapter explored some of the ways this fear manifested itself in the research process.

Notes

1   An anonymous Facebook post called for a protest on 24 March 2011 on the Circle of the Ministry of Interior. This was an effort to find a symbolic space for protests in Jordan replicating Egypt's protests in al Tahrir square.
2   One participant asked to be interviewed under a pseudonym from the beginning.

3   Abu Kalthoum and Nadim are both pseudonyms that we agreed on in late 2021 when participants' circumstances changed.
4   Mohammad Sneid was the leader of the Day Wage Labor movement(2006–14). He was also one of the key activists during the *Hirak* and a leader of the Dhiban youth movement.
5   Being married to a non-Jordanian, unlike Jordanian men, I am unable to transfer my Jordanian citizenship to my children. My husband and children have to renew their residency permits each year. In the future, my children will not be able to work in many sectors and will not have the unconditional right to live in Jordan.
6   Many accuse the government of disregarding human rights conventions as part of their antiterrorist campaign.

Bibliography

Ababneh, Sara. 2016. "Troubling the Political, Women in the Jordanian Day-Wage Labor Movement." *International Journal of Middle East Studies* 48 (1): 87–112.

Ababneh, Sara. 2020. "The Time to Question, Rethink and Popularize the Notion of 'Women's Issues': Lessons from Jordan's Popular and Labor Movements from 2006 to Now." *Journal of International Women's Studies* 271–88.

Abu Lughod, Lila. 1986. *Veiled Sentiments, Honor and Poetry in a Bedouin Society.* Berkeley: University of California Press.

Abu Lughod, Lila. 2002. "Do Muslim Women Really Need Saving? Anthropological Reflections on Cultural Relativism and its Others." *American Anthropologist* 104 (3): 783–90.

Altorki, Soraya, and Camilla F. El-Solh. 1988. *Arab Women in the Field: Studying Your Own Society.* Syracuse, NY: Syracuse University Press.

Crenshaw, Kimberlé. 1991. "Mapping the Margins: Intersectionality, Identity Politics and Violence against Women of Color." *Stanford Law Review* 43 (6): 1241–99.

Gupta, Akhil, and James Ferguson. 1977. "Discipline and Practice: 'The Field' as Site, Method, and Location in Anthropology." In *Anthropological Locations: Boundaries and Grounds of a Field Science*, edited by Akhil Gupta and James Ferguson, 1–46. Berkeley: University of California Press. https://www.degruyter.com/document/doi/10.1525/9780520342392-002/html.

Halley, Janet. 2006. *Split Decisions How and Why to Take a Break from Feminism.* Princeton, NJ: Princeton University Press.

Hammami, Reema. 2016. *Follow the Numbers: Global Governance and the Agenda-Setting "Violence against Women" in Occupied Palestine.* Birzeit: Birzeit University.

hooks, bell. 1981. *Ain't I a Woman: Black Women and Feminism.* Boston, MA: South End Press.

Jad, Islah. 2004a. "The NGO-isation of Arab Women's Movements." *Institute of Development Studies* 35 (4): 34–42.

Jad, Islah. 2004b. "Women at the Cross-roads: The Palestinian Women's Movement between Nationalism, Secularism and Islamism." Ph.D. Dissertation, University of London, London, England. Retrieved from http://ethos.bl.uk/OrderDetails.do?uin=uk.bl.ethos.413154.

Jansen, Wilhelmina. 1998. "Contested Identities: Women and Religion in Algeria and Jordan." In *Women and Islamization: Contemporary Dimensions of Discourse on Gender Relations*, edited by Karin Ask and Marit Tjomsland, 73–102. Oxford: Berg.

Joseph, Suad. 1994. *Gender & Family in the Arab World*. Washington, DC: Middle East Research & Information Project.

Joseph, Suad, ed. 2018. *Arab Family Studies: Critical Reviews*. Syracuse, NY: Syracuse University Press.

Morsy, Soheir. 1988. "Fieldwork in My Egyptian Homeland." In *Arab Women in the Field: Studying Your Own Society*, edited by Soraya Altorki and Camillia Fawzi El-Solh, 69–90. Syracuse, NY: Syracuse University Press.

Rubenberg, Cheryl A. 2001. *Palestinian Women: Patriarchy and Resistance in the West Bank*, 35. Boulder, CO: Lynne Rienner.

Shalhoub-Kevorkian, Nadira. 2008. "Gendered Nature of Education under Siege a Palestinian Feminist Perspective." *International Journal of Lifelong Education* 27 (2): 179–200.

8 RESEARCH IN THE JORDANIAN CHILD WELFARE SYSTEM: NAVIGATING TABOO SUBJECTS

Rawan W. Ibrahim

Introduction

This analysis draws on my experience studying the Jordanian child welfare system. I conducted six research projects between 2010 and 2018, three of which were independent. Three were carried out with partners, including partners from the Global North. Reflecting on these fieldwork projects, I have found that my experience as a Western-educated binational female researcher has been shaped by a complex web of interrelated contextual layers. These involve the cultural context, the political and practice dynamics of work, and research in the child welfare system. The web of layers intersected with personal and professional factors: (1) my social status; (2) the topic of research; (3) my professional record; and (4) my relationship to those in power. The intersections between this web of layers and the personal and professional factors significantly influenced my access to participant interviews and data collection, as well as shaped the contours of ethical dilemmas. Some of these variables facilitated my research and some hindered it. I had to be constantly cognizant of these variables. The question of what the "field" of field work is is profoundly shaped by time, site, location, as well as the personal (Gupta and Ferguson 1977).

At times, I took for granted that these factors are part of what is required to carry out research. Their profound impact on one particular study, on the transitional experiences of unmarried pregnant teenagers who had been taken into residential care to protect them from so-called "honor" crimes, forced me to consider them more seriously. My reflections, in this chapter, largely focus on experiences from that research project. Below, I introduce the personal and professional factors as they unfolded in my research experience.

Contextual Layers: The Cultural Context and the Research Field

The cultural context and political and practice dynamics within the child welfare system wove into each other to impact the fieldwork experience. The predominant elements of the broader cultural context that I identified as affecting my experience are patriarchy and tribalism. Prioritization of the rights and dominance of males and hierarchical and authoritarian gender roles are pervasive in the field of child welfare in Jordan. Decision-making is dominated by men, who are largely culturally conservative.[1] Despite the appearance of a less segregated workplace where women and men work alongside each other, there are expectations (by both genders) of how women should dress and behave, especially around men. To be worthy of respect, women are expected to be conventional and pious. They are not to challenge men, especially men in higher positions.

Patriarchy, in Arab society in general and in Jordanian society in particular, is interlinked with tribalism. The inherent value of individuals lies in their membership in a kin group—their tribe. The size, success, and affluence of an individual's tribe significantly impact the perceptions of their professional, political, and social standing. This can provide many opportunities for individuals who are part of dominant tribes, impacting their status in the social hierarchy and their affiliation to power and privilege. The most politically powerful tribes in Jordan are the East Bank Jordanians, as opposed to those of Palestinian origin and "West Bankers." While I myself am privileged in many ways, I am of Palestinian origin. In my field, I often have had to rely on personal and professional attributes beyond those conferred by my family, such as my qualifications and professional track record, and to earn the trust of those in power.

My research experience in the child welfare system has been influenced also by the fact that it is a top-down system. The child welfare system in Jordan lacks specialization. Professionalization of social work remains nascent. It is strongly influenced by cultural and religious issues, is not evidence-based, and is cautious about allowing research access. The media continually subjects the child welfare system to scrutiny, often overlooking its positive contributions. As a result of these dynamics, I faced lack of trust about how the data I collected would be utilized. A number of decision-makers, gatekeepers, and child welfare staff feared exposure. How these elements unfolded and intersected with my own personal and professional attributes to impact my research is the story of this chapter.

My Background and Social Status

By Jordanian standards, I am an unconventional single woman, with a Christian Palestinian background. I was born and raised in Jordan in a liberal household, although it was not without its patriarchal elements. Both my parents encouraged me to become a self-reliant, educated, professional woman. As a teenager I migrated to the United States, completed high school and college, and became a naturalized American citizen. Later, I completed my postgraduate studies in the UK. Between studying for my degrees, I returned to Jordan and worked in the social work field, gradually advancing my postgraduate qualifications and my career.

Palestinian Jordanians who question or critique the status quo may be regarded as disloyal. Their involvement in political domains has historically been restricted.[2] The Christian community is respected by many Jordanians for its contribution to the broader economy. It includes many who are highly educated, competent, and with a good work ethic. In comparison to their actual size as a community, Christian Palestinian Jordanians are overrepresented in a number of critical domains. Nevertheless, Christians, and especially Christian women, can indeed be stigmatized by the more conservative Muslim community. Many in the more conservative Jordanian Muslim community believe that the Christian community's more liberal lifestyle and Christian women's greater freedom of movement is unacceptable, if not blasphemous and decadent. Professional Christian women often must exert much more effort to earn acceptance and equal respect. They need to be aware of their attire, behavior, and adherence to gender norms. Christian women affiliated to East Bank tribes tend to be in a stronger social and political position than their peers originating from the West Bank and Palestine.

The milieu in which I was socialized throughout my childhood and adulthood in Jordan, the United States, and the UK was liberal, valuing individual character. I was brought up to discuss and state my opinions respectfully. The notion of being subordinate, because I am female, was alien to me. I was naïve in this regard. I had to learn anew, as a professional and scholar, how to interact professionally with my conservative male counterparts in the Jordanian child welfare system.

Coupled with this is my physical appearance. My attire is professional but tends to be considered too simple. My hair is naturally curly, larger than average, and often unruly. To secure the respect I need to obtain access to research materials, I had to somehow remake myself. To be taken seriously, I needed to dress the part that reflected my credentials, gave me gravitas, and countered my other attributes. Despite "remaking" myself, my outspokenness has been at times labeled as "privileged," "Westernized," "arrogant," and "out of touch" with local decorum. Labels, such as these, are, at times, used as excuses when a woman presumes she is equal and challenges conservative colleagues.

My background, social status, and related issues have been important factors in all of my research projects, and particularly in obtaining access to participants. My professional record, institutional support or affiliation, and research topic also influenced my access to participants, as many field researchers have observed (Altorki and El-Solh 1988).

Choice and Background of Topic

My postgraduate qualifications and work experience have always centered on child protection, the continuum of alternative care settings for children and youth, and young people's transition from residential care to adulthood in Jordan. These experiences deepened my insight into the alternative care system, including the power dynamics within the hierarchical structure, cultural and religious influences, and how notions of honor in the system can profoundly affect decisions made on behalf of children. This is particularly the case for unmarried birth mothers, who are at risk of so-called "honor" crimes. My research topic focused on understanding how young women taken into the care system because they are unmarried and pregnant transition and reintegrate into the community.

Subjects relating to honor are a taboo area and a source of political dilemma. Conservative members of the Jordanian government and society see women's group activism, related to issues of honor, as threatening the social order. They take criticism of crimes of honor in the Western media as unwelcome interference from "the decadent West" and a continuation of the hegemony of Western culture. Local female activists who engage in initiatives to combat discriminatory social and legal practices are often accused of conspiring with the West for their own personal glory. My research falls within these taboo areas, both socially and politically. My embarking on my research topic, as a liberal and unconventional woman, made several of the officials, who served as gatekeepers of the areas to which I needed access, uncomfortable.

My Indigenous Insider–Outsider Status

Prior to submitting my formal request to the government for permission to access this population of young women, their families, and the professionals who worked with them, I knew that embarking on this sensitive project would require some groundwork. Given that several government officials found the topic unsettling,

I needed to ensure that the most important stakeholders had clear and precise information about the aims of my research and understood that the process would be inclusive. I had to persuade them that my intended outcomes were aligned with their own priorities and concerns for the young women. The results of the study would have a genuine impact on the lives of the young women. Because of that, I needed government approval.

I met with the officials of key institutions to whom I explained the purpose of the study and that the process would be inclusive. I clarified that I understood the sensitivity, and particularly the political sensitivity, of the area I sought to study. I explained that I was intending to meet with those officials several times throughout the research process to share my preliminary findings, seek guidance, and listen to any concerns that they might have. I requested permission to include the names of their institutions and to indicate their interest and support in my request for government approval. The majority of these stakeholders agreed to collaborate with me on the project because they knew me as a practitioner, through my work in the field over the years. They respected my contribution to the field. I had worked directly with a number of them. They saw me as a serious professional. I was an insider, in that I am part of both Jordanian society and the field in which I sought to carry out my research. I was not employed by any of the organizations that I approached. Both the stakeholders and the government officials knew that I was well aware of both the challenges and the contributions of Jordan's child welfare system.

I established contact with some nongovernmental organizations (NGOs) that provide psychosocial and legal services for the young women I proposed to study and their families. Although both stakeholders and NGOs were interested in the study, the NGOs would not allow me to access the young women in their care without written government approval. This was despite the fact that I could ethically obtain access to willing families. This was understandable: if they were to continue serving and supporting the young women once they left the facility, they could not jeopardize their relationship with the government or any of the major stakeholders. Fortunately, some stakeholders and NGOs offered to support my access to the young women, albeit on the condition of government approval.

My Professional Record

I was living and working in two very different worlds: a liberal social and familial world, and a largely conservative working world. My continued work in the same field has allowed me to build long-term professional relationships. Those with whom I have developed strong relationships appreciate my commitment to the field. Over time, they no longer find my liberal and unconventional views threatening. I often justify the reasoning behind my decisions to them by using language and terminology that aligns with their religious and conventional views.[3] We enjoy open, respectful discussions. Over the years that I have worked in the child protection field, colleagues and government officials with whom I have worked understand that, despite my awareness of significant challenges in the system, I have a history of addressing and resolving these matters confidentially.

Nevertheless, my outspokenness and the fact that I carry myself as an equal to colleagues has often been held against me. Female colleagues often have told me that the problem is that I consider myself equal to male managers. My more conservative male colleagues, and even some female ones, saw me as an unacceptably bold woman who, despite evidence of my achievements and ethical practice, threatened the status quo. The realization of the implications of my background, my social status, and my individual personality has been disheartening. To survive and navigate the system, I continuously tried to find a balance between remaining authentic and faithful to my principles and learning how to carry myself differently.

Attempts to Achieve Access

Given that the child welfare system is at risk of scrutiny, officials and practitioners can be guarded about sharing information. Gaining access through institutions to potential participants with their genuine consent requires jumping through a number of hoops. The young women and their families in the unmarried pregnant teenager study are an exceptionally difficult population to identify, due to the stigma and risks attached to their experience. The two main access points are the government and NGOs. Access through NGOs is possible and ethical. However, NGOs require government approval and need to protect their relationship with the government. Although obtaining approval from the highest level was essential, fieldwork entailed covert pressure on middle management and practitioners to participate and facilitate the research by granting me access to the young women.

Obtaining ministerial approval was the safest approach. Yet, I did not want middle management to feel pressured. I thought that a bottom-up approach would help to resolve this issue. I conducted a series of meetings with middle managers. The meetings were cordial. Nevertheless, my research was rejected at first. I could not bypass middle management. This meant that I would have to wait for a change in leadership and try again. A ministerial change did occur, accompanied by a change among the middle managers. On my second attempt to obtain permissions, I was told that they would cooperate provided I had ministerial approval. They imposed conditions: I would not publish or present my results on any platform without prior approval. I agreed and submitted all the necessary documents.

I was verbally informed that I had received the minister's approval but that I must wait to receive this in writing. Then, a third, sudden, ministerial change occurred. The following day I inquired about the written approval and was informed that it had been revoked by the minister herself, before leaving her post. It was obvious that the middle managers were not on board. They had required me to obtain ministerial approval to buy them time to resist the research. To their surprise, however, the minister had approved it. When I requested a formal rejection letter to prove that the minister had indeed revoked her approval, I was informed that "that's not how things work."

I still did not want to bypass middle management because they tend to remain in posts longer than ministers. I would have to deal with them whomever was in the ministerial post. I nonetheless decided to request an appointment with the new minister. Fortunately, he was aware of my work and track record. We had met previously and he and I worked in the same field. During our appointment, I explained the whole process. He called in staff and requested the paperwork that I had submitted. I was surprised to see that my application had become a sizeable file. I sat quietly as he carefully examined the file, going through every page, using his pen to follow the lines. He tapped on one page and informed me that I had indeed received approval from his predecessor. It was clear to him that middle management was "afraid."

To my surprise, and dismay, he called the middle managers and reprimanded them for not following through with ministerial decisions, even after a minister had left. Although I appreciated his support, I was concerned about the ramifications of his tone and reproach of them. Ministers often change, while middle management are merely shuffled around. He informed me that he wanted this research to take place under the conditions to which I had previously agreed. He added another condition: if I learned of any misconduct during my research, I was to contact him, and only him, directly. Of course, I agreed.

A fourth ministerial change took place. Again, I had to wait to hear the status of my request. However, now I was aware that middle management had been insulted. There was no way I would get their approval. After the latest minister had settled into her position, I informed middle management that I was requesting an appointment with her. At the appointment, she called them in and asked them what the issue was. They were reluctant to disclose anything beyond stating that this topic was "not a priority." It was a diplomatic way of stating their disapproval without giving a reason for it in my presence. She attempted to solicit their consent by trying to convince them that this research would support their position by helping to prove the necessity of Article 308 of Jordan's Penal Code, which was being challenged. The Article allowed rapists to avoid a jail term by marrying their victim. The young women in question are minors and often victims of statutory rape. I was not willing to negotiate access in a manner that would serve a political agenda, and certainly not one that serves rapists in the name of honor.

At that point I decided to bypass governmental approval, at least for the time being, hoping for another ministerial change. One NGO, that was especially interested in the research, agreed to provide access on the condition that their participation was confidential. I was able to interview a handful of participants: three practitioners and the father of a teenage rape victim who had become pregnant and had been taken into care. Two of the three practitioners were extremely cautious. The third, whom I had known for several years, was comfortable in the interview. She facilitated access to the girl's father, who trusted her. Although he was outspoken and discussed the torment in detail, the interview was very difficult.

Personal and Professional Attributes in Data Collection

In all the projects that I have worked on, the area of my research has involved difficulties and struggles that people, mostly young people, have had to endure. The literature on interviewing has been an important element of my preparation. However, the experience of conducting interviews, especially with young people with difficult life journeys, has taught me far more than the literature. When reflecting on my experience of conducting research, I have found that conducting interviews has been the most humbling experience. I am always amazed at the participants' courage and willingness to share their difficult and deeply personal stories with a total stranger, and by their immense generosity in imparting their wealth of knowledge. Listening, conversing, and reflecting on each life story is enriching. It is from the participants, and especially the young people, that I have learned that a successful interview rests first and foremost on the quality of the connection and "their" experience of the interview process.

Conducting interviews in the field of child welfare has also taught me that while the personal and professional attributes discussed above are important, they can take on different meanings for participants and for decision-makers. My doctorate, the fact that I am in my mid-forties, and my professional record in the field gave me credibility when conducting interviews with both young people and practitioners. For practitioners, however, these attributes and my choice of topic were at times intimidating unless they understood that; having been a practitioner myself, I understood the difficulties inherent in a hierarchical system that is publicly scrutinized.

With the young people, I am acutely mindful of how my background and social status may negatively affect the power dynamics in an interview. I remain professional and adhere to cultural requirements such as gender distancing. I have found that my unconventional demeanor puts them at ease. Many have expressed that they expected our first meeting to be more formal, if not tense. Moreover, unlike officials and often practitioners, who may be concerned about my choice of topic, young people are intrigued by my interest in their experiences, and especially by my desire to learn from them. Many of the young adults with whom I conducted interviews and who continued to participate in my long-term longitudinal research regarded my ongoing long-term involvement in the field as a form of continued solidarity with them.

Despite this experience, embarking on data collection, regarding the unmarried pregnant teenagers, was challenging. This was partly because, although I did not have governmental approval, the manner in which I had obtained access to the participants was in line with ethical standards: they were consenting adults. Another challenge was the difficult experience of the only parent that I was able to gain access to: the father of a teenage girl who had been sexually assaulted by a man twice her age and impregnated. The third challenge was that, during that interview, I realized that I knew the child who had resulted from the rape.

The father came to meet with me in the office where I was conducting my interviews, accompanied by the practitioner whom I had interviewed earlier. I was surprised that he was willing to talk to me. The practitioner who introduced him had done me a great service by easing his concerns. She informed me that she had reassured him that she and I have known each other for some time, and that I have been in the field for several years and can be trusted. He clearly had confidence in her judgment. My background and social status were not as relevant in this interview as my professional record and my relationship with this colleague, which probably made all the difference. Without the latter's reassurance, I doubt I would have had access to the father.

This was the first interview I had ever conducted where I truly did not know where to start. How and what does one ask a father whose daughter has been sexually assaulted and impregnated? Emotionally I was walking on eggshells, but I was careful to conceal how I felt. Any discomfort on my part would be clear to him and might very well make him feel uncomfortable too. I was grateful that he was willing to share his story. After going through the consent process, I asked him where he would like to start. I wanted him to be in control and to share what he wanted to share and what he thought was important for me to know. In a frustrated tone of voice, he said, "We were treated like criminals. My daughter was the victim and we were treated like criminals." A few minutes into the interview he was in tears. The pain was so fresh and raw for him that I felt pangs in my stomach. I questioned the appropriateness of what I was doing and asked him if he wanted to stop. He wanted to continue.

The father recounted how his daughter had been mistreated by the authorities, until she got to the care home. He was angry that she had been insulted by a policewoman and placed with adult criminal women. Not only did they take her from him, as the authorities were afraid he would take her life to redeem the family's honor, she was also transported to court together with the rapist. To make matters worse, some relatives and officials suggested that he should consider Article 308. Giving his daughter in marriage to the criminal who had assaulted her was inconceivable to him. He wanted the rapist punished.

He recounted the measures he had had to take to be reunited with his daughter and the torment of his child having to go through the pregnancy and deliver the baby. He was angry that some practitioners had tried to foist the baby onto them when his daughter had clearly stated that she did not want to hold or even see her. While the baby was also a victim of this ordeal, to her young birth mother and her grandfather she was the embodiment of terrible abuse. He was grateful that a few practitioners and officials had stood by him throughout the whole process. His focus now was on a good education for his daughter. He was worried about her future. He doubted that she would find a husband. I was impressed at how dedicated he was to protecting her and how he was planning for her future. I remember realizing that I had assumed that most fathers would resort to marrying off such a daughter to protect the honor of the family, if not wishing her dead.

Coming Full Circle

Because I was the director of the project that established foster care in Jordan, what was also very difficult about this interview for me personally was that I knew the child that had resulted from the rape. As soon as the father started describing the details of his and his daughter's experience, I remembered the child. During the interview I thought she looked a lot like him. In my practice experience, the individual story of each child is always important. However, some children's stories or characters stand out more than those of others, and this was one of them. Although she was only a toddler when I met her, she was very quiet, kept to herself, and avoided most people whether she was familiar with them or not. Her eyes were strikingly beautiful, with dark thick eyelashes that enhanced their almond shape. I had to arrange the necessary steps needed to formally inform her birth father, who was in prison, that his daughter was being enrolled in the foster care program to give her a chance to live with a family rather than be raised in the institution. I was also one of the people who interviewed the foster father who was interested in fostering her.

Children can be taken into care following abandonment or removal by the state for being born under taboo circumstances such as unmarried pregnancy or rape. Irrespective of the quality of their individual journey through the care system and beyond, abandonment or rejection by the birth parents inflicts a most painful wound. Many of the young people whom I have interviewed over the years describe it as a wound from which one "never quite heals." It felt surreal to be interviewing the child's grandfather. I understood how many mothers who become pregnant as a result of sexual assault reject their infants. Knowing how their children experience this rejection is also painful. When the biological grandfather told me that he wanted nothing to do with the child, I hoped that the decision we made on her behalf with the family who fostered her was a sound one for her. I also realized that if I was to gain access to further such families and young mothers, I would need to be emotionally prepared. I needed to be prepared to hear and absorb their predicaments and to come full circle, since I know a number of young people with a care history and many of the practitioners who work with them.

Conclusion

I have reflected on my experience as a binational, Western-educated female studying the Jordanian child welfare system. My experience has been influenced by two sets of factors: (1) contextual circumstances including the cultural context and the practice dynamics in the child welfare system, and (2) my personal and professional attributes. I had taken these factors for granted until I realized their profound impact on one particular study of the transitional experiences of unmarried pregnant teenagers who have been taken into residential care to protect them from so-called "honor" crimes. This chapter has explored how the intersection between these contextual layers and my personal and professional attributes significantly influenced my ability to gain access to the sample I sought to interview, my interviews with the participants, and my collection of data, and created ethical dilemmas.

Notes

1   It is noteworthy that there has been an increase in the number of women appointed as ministers. However, there is a high turnover of government officials, even at the ministerial level.
2   For example, a Jordanian prime minister of Palestinian and Christian background is unlikely in the near future. Allowing those of Palestinian origin to hold what may be considered politically sensitive positions, such as in the Jordanian Intelligence (Mukhabarat), the Army or the Ministry of Interior Affairs, is also unlikely. However, people with Palestinian and/or Christian backgrounds do of course serve across the whole range of the public and private sectors and are very active in the economic sphere.
3   One such example is the request to officials to allow the fostering of children by single women, as opposed to only couples. When examining the types of foster care backgrounds needed to increase family-based care for institutionalized children, I made this recommendation to colleagues whom I had not known for long. The

initial response was anger at the idea of condoning the forbidden state of single motherhood, potentially implying that having children out of wedlock is acceptable. I put the issue aside for some time while those particular colleagues and I became better acquainted. I raised it again, having ensured that other respected Muslim colleagues were in agreement and willing to express their support for my suggestion. Eventually it was included in the criteria for fostering, and a number of single women came forward and were approved as foster-carers.

Bibliography

Altorki, Soraya, and Camilla F. El-Solh. 1988. *Arab Women in the Field: Studying Your Own Society*. Syracuse, NY: Syracuse University Press.

Gupta, Akhil, and Ferguson, James. 1977. "Discipline and Practice: 'The Field' as Site, Method, and Location in Anthropology." *Anthropological Locations: Boundaries and Grounds of a Field Science*, edited by Akhil Gupta and James Ferguson, 1–46. Berkeley: University of California Press. https://doi.org/10.1525/9780520342392-002.

9 CONDUCTING RESEARCH WHILE DEATH SURROUNDS YOU: THE RESEARCHER, GENDER, AND WAR IN SYRIA

Saja Al Zoubi

Introduction

Being a female Syrian researcher conducting fieldwork particularly in rural areas presents for interesting and thought-provoking challenges and experiences. I will highlight the challenges and constraints that female researchers face and how these became more complicated during the war. This discussion is based on my own experiences over several years of conducting on-the-ground fieldwork in rural areas in Syria before and during the war, and in neighboring Lebanon with Syrian refugees. My fieldwork often consisted of face-to-face interviews using structured and semistructured questionnaires as well as focus group discussions (FGDs). Interviews and FGD were lengthy and would take anywhere between 30 minutes to more than two hours, which often provided for a rich source of qualitative and quantitative data.

These experiences bring to the fore feminism and gender roles, fieldwork constraints and precautionary processes, the general research challenges, and the price of being a female scientist in one's home country and later in exile. In this chapter, I take a closer look at the scientific environment and the knowledge production of Syrian female researchers.

Because of my own movement, the geographic scope of this chapter includes Syria, Lebanon, and the UK and covers the period from roughly 2005—when I became an agricultural engineer in a governmental scientific agricultural research center—until 2019. This time frame covers two periods: before 2011, when the war broke out, and wartime.

Syrian War Scene

The day of 15 March 2011 was a turning point for Syrians. On this day everything changed, and many people had no idea of what was going to happen or where they would end up—myself included. The war began as a conflict between Syrians themselves, but it soon became an international conflict as we witnessed soldiers from different countries arriving to fight for different purposes. By 2019, the war had entered its eighth year and there is still no accurate information or statistics about the full extent of the damage caused. It is nonetheless heartbreaking to see the tremendous loss and damage to the lives and livelihoods of the Syrian people. Before 2011, the population of Syria was estimated to be 20.5 million, but since the outbreak of this war, more than 13 million Syrians have fled their homes, over 6 million are internally displaced, and there are roughly 13.5 million people known to be in need of humanitarian assistance within Syria's borders. Around 5.2 million people have become refugees in neighboring countries and around 1 million in Europe (Al Zoubi et al. 2019; Connor and Krogstad 2016; Connor 2018; UNHCR 2017; World Bank 2017). United Nations agencies estimated that 540,000 people were still living in besieged areas in 2017, with more than 470,000 having died since 2011 (World Bank 2017).

Women and Gender Norms

"Do not waste your time and get married," my professor advised me when I was preparing my master's proposal in 2006 in Syria. It is challenging to be a female academic in a highly patriarchal society, especially for someone who also explores gender and feminist issues in their research.

There is a stricter adherence to and policing of gender norms and patriarchal values among rural communities in Syria, although, at the same time, women's contribution to their families, societies, and rural development is also valued. Studies show that rural women are the fundamental pillars of agricultural labor in their villages (Al Zoubi 2010), yet their work is not considered as economic work. Women are more involved in the domestic work. In some areas where women are allowed to work outside of the home, the payments go to the men. The lack of capacities due to the traditions and gender norms forces rural women to limit themselves solely to farm work and homemade processes (dairy, food, handcrafts). They rely on men to market their products because traditionally, markets are exclusive to men in these areas (Al Zoubi 2010). This is the main reason that prevents these women from having their own income or alleviating their benefit margin (Galia 2013).

In these rural communities, many women suffer from losing their right, according to family tradition, to inherit property. The tradition in these rural areas is to force women to give up their share in the property to their brothers or the father divides his property between his sons only before his death, to avoid any problems with daughters or sons-in-law. During one interview with a woman in the southern region of Syria, I learned that her husband was angry because she was refused her portion of the family property. During the interview, her daughter told me: "They are going to do the same with us, the daughters." My informant's husband concurred, saying: "Yes, our son might financially support us, but our daughter will go to her husband's home and will not support us!" Unsurprisingly, I met one woman who refused to give up her share and was able to regain her property through the courts. Unfortunately, she had to pay the price of family connection as her brothers did not want to be in contact with her anymore. Moreover, some of these women lacked the autonomy to make fundamental decisions in their families (Al Zoubi 2010). Traditions and habits in some areas make even speaking about women's role in society seem pointless because nothing will change. These practices enhance male dominance and female dependence. Some of these women surrender to this dependence syndrome and do not appreciate their contribution to their families and communities. Thus, gender norms and consequences of male dominance increased women's challenges when they became the breadwinners of their families since the war broke out. These women with dead, disappeared, or jailed husbands feel the war's tragedies and violence most acutely.

While I was conducting oral interviews in rural communities, I saw how such opinions about the difference between men and women's role in society were strong and that perceptions of women and men are strictly divided. Amal (a pseudonym), for example, is a displaced woman working as a house cleaner. She explained to me that her husband prefers playing football to working. Although Amal is the breadwinner of her family, her husband insults her and abuses her physically. She said, while avoiding making eye contact with me, that "He is the man and he can do what he wants. Hitting me is his right and my life now is better than getting divorced." Amal was conforming to ideas and practices she learned from her family and community. Nonetheless, many women managed to adapt to the loss of their families' livelihoods in the displacement context.

Scientific Environment and Feminism

The scientific community at some point was an extension of the patriarchal society that housed it. While there is a language of equality under the regime, the reality is very different as some managers and supervisors in charge of scientific centers don't believe in women as scientists and do not believe that researching issues that may be important to women's lives are valid topics of research. I faced some who detracted female participation in the sciences. Hence, women do not get enough support as researchers. The same manager who calls for gender equity was also the one who put obstacles in front of female researchers. When I asked him to print the references I traveled and collected from different countries to keep them in the work library, he replied: "Women always can't separate their work at home from their work here!" He said that because the books were about home economics science. I tried to explain the notion of home economics science and the need of these references since there were no other references available in Syria about this topic. Finally, he approved printing 25 pages only, while he had approved providing a printer for male researchers in the same center so they can print at their whim. Later, he asked my boss to stop my work in this domain and find "more useful work in another domain" although the department I worked in was focused on socioeconomic research that was related to home economics science.

Professors were opposed to my master's research in this domain because it was new and there were no related scientific references in Syria. Their rationale was that this research requires great effort that cannot be done by a female researcher. Because I believed it was important to produce knowledge on these issues, I moved to another university in Aleppo province, 361 kilometers away from my home in Damascus, to pursue my studies. Two years later, I graduated with honors and my research was converted to a book, *The Role of Women in Home Economics*, which was selected by the Arab Women Organization (an affiliate of the Arab League of Nations) as the best Arabic book about women in 2010. This book was the first scientific reference on home economics in Syria. Nonetheless, while one of the professors who teaches home economics courses at Damascus University started using the book as a reference, he refused to coteach the course with me, literally saying: "There is no place for this young girl here."

I was involved in a project with Action Against Hunger (ACF) and Arab Centre for the Studies of Arid Zones and Dry Lands (ACSAD) during the war that was based in the northeastern part of Syria. The situation was dangerous there, yet I felt it was important to try and do the fieldwork to ensure that people could find alternative sources of funding. The national team was supervised by two male professors, both of whom made snide, insulting comments insinuating they were not happy nor felt confident that I could do the work as I am still "a young girl." Even though I did the majority of the work including designing the questionnaire, conducting individual and focus group meeting in these dangerous areas, training the rest of the team to conduct fieldwork, and reporting the results and potential interventions, my name was not on the report because I had to quit just before it was finalized.

Additionally, some people believe that working in the field of gender studies is a breach of Arab family principles and indicative of a desire to adopt Western values. One of my previous supervisors even considered working with international organizations in this field of study as being fraught with hidden agendas.

The governmental agricultural research center I used to work in had more than 800 employees, where all the high positions were often held by men, with one female exception who was the relative of the minister. Even as a deputy of the general manager, her position was subject to patriarchy and was subsequently eliminated as soon as her relative was no longer in office. There were few female researchers working as leaders for smaller departments or research projects and they faced continuous challenges and had to overcome numerous obstacles to stay in these positions of leadership. The leader of my research group was replaced by a younger man with less experience without any explanation as to the reasons or rationale for the decision.

As the research center relied on fieldwork research, some female researchers avoided traveling alone with drivers or male colleagues, just to be safe from criticism and gossip, even though that meant they could not do their jobs to the best of their abilities. This is the extent to which policing and monitoring of women and women's behaviors can intrude on their ability to do their work.

Syrian Scientists: Inclusion and Exclusion

Routine procedures were not conducive to scientific researchers, in particular researchers who are employed by governmental institutions. In 2010, my direct manager decided to report me to the minister of agriculture by claiming that I was contacting a foreign organization without permission in order to receive my book award. Fortunately, the minister considered my award an honor for my institution and for Syria's agricultural sector. However, a few days later, a new decision was taken, which outlined that any connections with foreign institutions should be through the ministry. Otherwise, hard sanctions will be issued. This felt like a blow to our ability to connect with the scientific community around the world and to be able to further advance our research agendas. I felt particularly targeted when my male supervisor decided to shame me by asking me whether I had seen the minister's statement in front of the entire office staff.

Governmental employees were not allowed to cooperate or work with foreign organizations outside of Syria without permission. Most researchers work in governmental agencies as has been the norm in Syria. Getting permission was almost an impossible process, which takes a long time and has no guarantee of approval. Similarly, attending external seminars, workshops, and conferences without permission was very risky. These processes have resulted in keeping scientists away, especially after bans and sanctions against Syrians were imposed. International projects were closed, research funds stopped, and exchanges came to a halt.

While fear during the war period did limit work productivity, there were other factors that also impacted the ability to conduct research. The war led to the destruction and/or stagnation of many research centers and universities; buildings were destroyed, items and equipment were stolen, and researchers were scattered and displaced. The agricultural research center I worked at was located in Duma, in Eastern Ghouta in the rural part of Damascus until the middle of 2012. Since Duma was an active conflict area, many employees suffered numerous tragedies. The Center moved its office to the city and by the time I left this work in early 2016, the socioeconomic team's workplace consisted of a small room, with two desks, one computer, and 14 researchers. The work environment became even more chaotic and confusing. It became even more important to secure data and ensure no one has access to your sources or data.

Many male scientists and researchers fled leaving the research centers largely dominated by female researchers. They nonetheless were not supported financially and logistically. In addition, security and safety conditions limited the research areas and the researchers' movements. This combination decreased the quantity and the quality of the research and knowledge production. The bright side of the male immigration was the designation of women scientists in high-profile positions. This period is critical, and the knowledge that is produced might play a main role in the current situation and later. It has made it also possible to talk about things that were previously not accepted. I once spoke about food insecurity on a television program, stating that the study I conducted showed that more than 81 percent of Syrians live below the poverty line. I was later reprimanded by my supervisor who insisted that I should not have mentioned this data. Recently, there seems to be more space to publish such statistics and describe the miserable situation under which Syrians live.

Nevertheless, this kind of intimidation has not stopped me from cooperating with international scientific institutions since my priority is to keep up with developments in socioeconomic studies. Blocks to international connections for Syrian researchers have become commonplace since 2011. Unfortunately, I have faced obstacles in applying to or procuring awards and fellowships due to my Syrian nationality, limitations on travel, and sanctions. In 2016, I was awarded the Civil Society Scholar Award by the Open Society Foundation, United States. However, it was cancelled after six months due to the ban against Syrian nationals by the United States. These restrictions can cause a lot of trauma, and mental and physical exhaustion as researchers feel their opportunities for scientific development and professional growth constantly dwindling. Some of these limitations are more severe when it comes to female researchers. When I succeeded in connecting with a Japanese institution, which had announced an award competition, to include

Syrian research centers, my institution was not receptive to my application but encouraged the other three that were led by men. The head of the committee making decisions did not believe in female researchers or feminist issues and used his position to limit the importance of the socioeconomic department's work in this area of research. At an annual meeting of the different departments, he stated: "What is the benefit of these studies, they are a waste of time, effort, and money, the ideal place for woman is the home." Surprisingly, the decision was supported by my direct male supervisor.

To ensure that I was still able to conduct my work, I had to come up with a strategy that involved me having two sets of resumes: one for use within my governmental work circle, which excluded any mention of my international awards or cooperation, and one for everything else that included this information. Yet, these precautionary processes were not enough especially in a world dominated by social media. On one occasion, a photo of me at an ethics of science workshop in Egypt was posted on a Facebook page, which immediately generated questions about how I had been able to attend this workshop without formal permission. I received a reprimand letter from my manager and was warned not to do it again. He told me: "This time it is a verbal warning" after I explained the trouble I went through to get permission from the previous manager who thought my attendance there was a waste of time. I recognized later that a female colleague stole the photo from my unsecured laptop and published it. These kinds of restrictions were among the reasons I chose to leave my governmental job. My story is not unique, I am but one of many researchers unable to benefit from the scientific opportunities available because so much of what we do is decided at the whims of managers who are invested in power structures—bureaucratic and patriarchal—that slow down research.

Fieldwork in War Zones: Challenges and Obstacles

Fieldwork is the skeleton of my research. Building up this skeleton is challenging work, but it has become more complicated since 2011 because it became more difficult to find communities in place. Displacement, migration, death, and disappearance have affected the ability to develop research samples or at times find just a few people to interview. On one occasion, I was searching for one of my informants in a town in Sweida, which is a province in the southern part of Syria. When I went to her town, I was told that she had gotten divorced and had gone to live in her family's town. I went to her family's town but discovered that her family had fled Syria and that she had been remarried to another man, but no one knew where his town was. Situations like this were becoming more common. There was also the fact that many people refused to meet with me. Um Amer burst into tears as she said to me: "Death is everywhere in Syria and you want me to answer your research questions." All Syrians have been affected in a way or another. Once, when I arrived at the home of an informant after a long trip, I was told that her brother had been killed two days before my meeting with her and that she obviously could not talk to me at that time.

Finding proper places to hold focus group discussions, meetings, and interviews was a complicated measure, but it became more complicated during the war with the lack of safety in damaged villages and the need of security clearance in others. Before the war, it was easier to use a private house or a room in other places such as a government building, religious place of worship, or a private rented space in a town. This dilemma forced me sometimes to make changes in my targeted area's list. This was the case in a refugee camp in Kafar Zapad in Lebanon. Although I did in-person interviews with Syrian refugees there, the information was not enough since I could not hold an FGD. The solution was to look for another camp in the same village, which meant more time, effort, and cost. On the other hand, when I could not meet a farmer's group for safety and security issues in Darya, which was an active conflict area in rural Damascus, the key informant helped me to gather them and meet outside of Darya.

Similarly, finding accommodations for myself was another significant challenge. The governmental center where I used to work had branches in all provinces. Mostly, these branches had guesthouses providing accommodation for the researchers during their work visit. Unfortunately, the war destroyed many of these guesthouses and others became unsafe. I wanted to use one guesthouse during my fieldwork in Salamiyah in the central area of Syria; however, it was surrounded on the western and the eastern sides by al-Qaeda and ISIS. In spite of this, it was a relatively safe area and included various sects, so I was planning to stay there. Yet when I arrived at the guesthouse, I was informed that al-Qaeda was just one kilometer away and that it was not advisable to use light at night especially during armed clashes! I had not been told about this when I called to ask about the accommodation. The boss of the center explained, "Al-Qaeda may hear our telecommunications, so we didn't want to mention that. However, your colleagues used to stay here, nothing happened." This missing information would have been detrimental to my ability to conduct research had it not been for the fact that I had friends who lived in the area. So, I put my luggage in the guesthouse but slept at my friend's house. Every day after conducting the survey, I went to the guesthouse to take a shower and to change my clothes quickly so I could leave it before nightfall. It was hard to use these facilities in my friend's house. Five months later, this guesthouse was attacked by armed groups. The guards were killed, several persons were abducted, and the property was looted. Some researchers were threatened, and their money, mobiles, and identity papers were stolen—fortunately, all survived.

In some areas in Syria such as Sweida, Aleppo, al-Hasakah, and Qamishli, I used to stay at hotels for safety and security reasons, but in areas close to Damascus such as Daraa and rural Damascus, I went back and forth every day. In the context of the war, the notion of safety and security changed. In al-Mofakker al-Sharqi, a town in Salamiyah, which I assumed was considered safe, one of the women in the FGD told me: "Look at the wall behind you, there was a hole caused by a mortar attack last week, but we repaired it." I realized that all persons in the home were under the fire of ISIS, which had attacked the town several times but had failed to capture it despite causing major damage and fatalities.

Having good knowledge of the targeted area before going there is a way to stay as safe as possible. Knowing the traditions, the religious and political positions, checking the safety levels of villages and towns, communicating closely with key informants (local leaders, relative institutions), and knowing something about the life history of the targeted community helped to facilitate my fieldwork under such challenging circumstances. Collecting this information early on, relying on different informative sources rather than just one, and keeping this information updated were strategies I used to avoid unpleasant surprises. As a researcher working to support those impacted by this war and women in particular, I had to work in unsafe areas. Wherever I worked, I had to have a good idea about each area and its residents before visiting it to collect data. Some of the risks included: abduction, murder, injury, and robbery. I tried to avoid active conflict areas, but there was unrest in most of the Syrian rural areas and things were shifting constantly. Once while working as a member of a humanitarian organization in one of the besieged areas in rural Damascus that was controlled by the Tahrir al-Sham and al-Nusra, I helped my female colleague to put on headscarves and conservative clothes. While we were leaving the checkpoint, one of the armed men criticized my colleagues' clothes saying, "Next time wear a longer T-shirt, this is unacceptable." I will never forget how frightened my colleague was and that she could only whisper: "Thank God that I had put the scarf on."

Given the difficult security situation and my understanding of rural traditions around women's behavior and how they do not accept women traveling alone without their kin even if it is a necessary component of their work, I was keen to be accompanied by male facilitators during the field surveys. The facilitators guided me through the safe roads to use and facilitated my communications especially with men in some rural towns. This strategy removed some obstacles that could have stood in the way, but not all obstacles. Tragically, my colleague and facilitator in al-Hasakah, which is located in the northeastern part of Syria, was killed by ISIS in his town because he was a government employee. In Salamiyah, while we (driver and teamwork) were moving from one town to another, my colleague from Salamiyah was driving his car ahead of us in order to protect and guide us. This was necessary so as not to mistakenly take a wrong turn on the road and end up in ISIS or al-Qaeda territory and be most likely captured and held.

The war in Syria imposed its scenarios. Sectarianism and identity became the fundamental concern of all fighting parties. I faced some of these problems. Surprisingly, I was told in different areas that I was not supposed to survive, just because some of the interviewees noticed that my surname is matched with that of a high-profile person in the Syrian government. Hence, the strategy of being "neutral," diplomatic, and avoiding any political opinion or debate was key to my survival. These arguments happened in a besieged area in rural Damascus and in some camps in Lebanon. Although I was calm, I was scared enough to finish the interview quickly and leave the camp without any hope of return. I learned to avoid telling people my surname in some communities since it was better to introduce myself as a researcher explaining the aim of the organization I am involved with and the aim of my research. I would also tell the interviewees from the beginning that there is no need to know their names since that would help me to protect my own identity.

I come from a town in Daraa province. Daraa had been implicated in the war as an area of clashes located near al-Sweida in the south of Syria. In Sweida, it was better for me to be accompanied by persons from the same province because some residents in al-Sweida province were harmed by armed groups in Daraa province, generating obvious animosity to people from Daraa. However, I was prevented from entering some villages located nearby Daraa province despite the fact that I was accompanied by a person from there and I was moving from one area to another by his car. One time, the government checkpoint guards did not let me through as they were afraid of the residents' reactions because some persons in this area were abducted by armed groups in Daraa and there were some cases of revenge being taken on behalf of Sweida residents from people who fled Daraa. Nonetheless, the residents were very kind and welcoming. Some employees in the relative centers in Sweida offered to help by linking me with my targeted community, but they apologized later to avoid problems and criticism they might face from their residents when they recognized my identity. Among this chaos, I had to continuously calculate when I could use my governmental ID, as I did in al-Hasakah at government checkpoints, and when to use my humanitarian organization's ID at other checkpoints.

One of the consequences of war is inflation and the drop in the value of the Syrian pound. Since 2011, the cost of living had increased by more than tenfold. The hike in prices affected daily life tremendously in addition to the shortage of petrol and energy sources. The lack of services was common all over Syria. Transportation became harder and more costly, especially in rural areas, and sometimes, when I needed work, transportation was not available. I often had to decide whether to use private cars or governmental cars as the latter are marked; this required a specific budget allocation and modification. Internet connections were limited in rural areas, while telecommunication was a little bit better. In some areas, such as al-Hasakah, where there were no connections, I used to walk long distances in the city center to find a place that provided satellite communications but with a very high cost. One day, I was very happy to finally find a print shop in al-Hasakah city after more than one hour of searching. I needed to update the questionnaire and print it to be able to continue with the field. However, the electricity was not good enough to print. It took several days to get the updated questionnaires printed by a colleague from the main office of the organization I worked for in another province (four hours away). In some rural areas, there were no opportunities to get these services at all and conditions were harsher during the winter season.

Discussion and Interview Management

It was not easy to gain the confidence of local dignitaries in some of the rural communities as they often were elderly men or state employees who did not like to work with a young woman. I look years younger than I am and this was an obstacle during my meeting with the dignitaries (head of Municipality, head of Extension Unit, elderly persons in the town, etc.), who tried to direct the discussions and tell me what I could and could not do in the town. They insisted on attending the focus group discussions with the targeted people, which was problematic because few wanted to speak about their problems in front of local dignitaries. My strategy was to get the facilitators to stay with the dignitaries somewhere else to get more information about the situation of the town, while I conducted the focus group meeting. I used various communication skills to manage the discussions without upsetting anyone. It was necessary to be strict sometimes and friendly at other times to control the discussion. Moreover, it was necessary to explain the research and its goals in detail.

Fieldwork requires a lot of negotiation and understanding. This includes ignoring comments that can be deeply offensive or problematic to ensure access and the ability to gather data. I often observed what I felt were patriarchal tensions during the fieldwork. This was particularly so when I held discussions with some wives in the presence of their husbands. In the microfinance research I conducted, I found that some women had received loans from programs specifically offered to women. However, it was the husbands who controlled the loans. The husbands were trying to give answers in my discussions with their wives, so I resorted to fabricating excuses to stop the discussion in order to return when the husbands were not at home. I was also surprised that it was not only men who underestimated a female researcher's work but also a lot of the women. Once, when I asked a woman if she would let me interview her, she replied with a tough tone: "Why, you are a woman, tell me what can you do? Do you want to cook with me? (laugh). I prefer to prepare food for my husband than making this interview with you." I used the same logic of tradition to convince her to talk to me, where I explained that I had expected her to invite me for lunch, saying: "Generosity and kindness are the habit of people in this town, isn't?" After a conversation lasting about 50 minutes, I learned that she was displaced with no official documents or assets and that her husband is a casual worker, who can only find work occasionally. Unsurprisingly, when I connected her with a humanitarian agency, which helps displaced families to renew their documents and enhance their living, she apologized. The interview with this woman provided me with a lot of useful information for my research.

Maneuvering around cultural norms was also tricky and at times costly to the research. I was interviewing a woman in my province of origin, Daraa, accompanied by my female colleague. While I was registering some notes, she provided us with coffee and slowly passed a small piece of paper in front of me. The note said: "Could I get your number; my brother is a handsome engineer, and he is looking for a good wife." I admit I was caught by surprise and did not know how to respond. Finally, I said that I do not accept offers like this. This was not a good answer despite my very polite demeanor. The result was that she got upset and I could not complete the interview successfully.

Being a Scientist and a Mother in Exile

Toward the end of 2016, I received a job offer to work for an international organization in Lebanon. I resigned from my humanitarian work in Syria and extended the unpaid leave from the governmental work I supposedly still had as they had refused to accept my resignation and moved to Lebanon with my husband. I was happy to be close to Syria to be able to visit. Soon after I started my work with Syrian refugees, I became aware of the hostility that many Lebanese felt toward Syrians. This hostility is the reflection of the political tension between the Syrian government and some Lebanese parties that has lasted for years since the Syrian army was in Lebanon for almost 30 years (1976–2005). The peak of this tension was in 2005 after the Lebanese prime minister, Rafiq Hariri, was assassinated. Thus, the Syrian influx was not welcomed in Lebanon since the Syrian war broke out. The Foreign Ministry rejected the organization's request to obtain a work residency visa for me. So, I could only enter Lebanon via my engineering syndicate card, which allowed me to get a residency visa for one month. This meant I had to leave and come back every month. I avoided using my Syrian car during my fieldwork and made sure to be accompanied by a Lebanese driver who had a good reputation in the organization I worked for. My fieldwork timetable thus became contingent on his availability. Using a Lebanese car with a Lebanese driver minimized the questions we faced at the checkpoints and gave me more space for free mobility.

In late 2017, I faced those hostilities first-hand on the borders. After a short visit in Syria to renew my visa, I was coming back to Lebanon to cross first the

Syrian border and then the Lebanese. A Syrian border officer did not allow me to leave Syria despite me having had governmental permission in the past. It took around 45 minutes to convince him to let me leave. The negotiation drained me emotionally and I burst into tears as I left his office worrying it may be the last time they let me cross. An hour later I was in the long queue in front of the Lebanese border officer who also challenged me aggressively saying: "Why are you working here, go and work in Syria." I left the customs and immigration office after a long discussion, which included me having to call my work to help me get permission to enter Lebanon. Finally, after all that they issued me a temporary residency visa for one week. Although my work succeeded in renewing my visa for one month, I did not feel safe or secure in Lebanon anymore, and later understood the feeling that Syrian refugees in Lebanon had identified during the field survey when they told me that "in Lebanon, we live in constant fear." Finally, in January 2018, I got a position at the University of Oxford in the UK. In addition to my happiness that I have become affiliated with the university that I was dreaming of for around 20 years since my father had first told me about it, I was happy that I was going to be able to continue with my research but also sad that my husband and I were going to be so far from Syria. On the flight to London my husband asked me if I thought we would be able to go back to Syria one day, but I could not answer.

Being forced to leave your country distorts all the happiness and accomplishment one has, especially if one was pregnant for the first time and suffers all the side effects of pregnancy. Our decision to avoid seeking asylum under any conditions meant that our stability in the UK is limited to the work residency visa availability. This adds more pressure. Adjusting to life in a new place was hard and it carried with it the complications of being a foreigner and having to adjust to new customs and language, including new ways of working. It is also complicated by being helpless about what is happening in Syria and constant worrying about family, obsessively checking the news. Being away from family and loved ones was even harder when I had my first born, Victor, and faced various difficulties with the birth and adjusting after, as an employed woman with a very short maternity leave. Visa conditions have required that I go back to work with long hours and keep watching my tiny Victor through mobile screen and expressing milk in my office.

Securing a safe place doesn't mean the cheerful end for individuals whose home, people, memories are still under fire. I still remember that day when we had received the pictures of my husbands' destroyed home in the south of Damascus. The house was occupied by different armed parties. They had stolen every piece of furniture, even the electricity plugs, the bookcases but not books. The picture of my husband's scattered books on the ground was even more of a shock than the destroyed home. Honestly, these challenges and sorrows have consumed us, making research and scientific inquiry even more challenging.

However, the key to succeed in exile is being open to being surrounded by warm new connections, such as friends, colleagues, neighbors, and work connections.

Figure 9.1 Photo of my husband's books on the floor.

This might eliminate the exile obstacles and open new opportunities for the future. At the same time, the pressures of managing work, while not a luxury, is often a prerequisite to save your mental health and head to success.

Yet, exile always imposes its conditions that forced me to shift my research interest. Being in exile constrains my work on women's empowerment, rural development, and affected households in Syria. Instead, my focus shifted to researching ways to enhance refugee households, policies, and politics that reshape their livelihoods, and forced migration and migrants' laws and conventions. In 2017 I contributed to *Science in Exile* (https://twas.org/ScienceInExile), a documentary exploring the story of four researchers who were forced to suspend their work and flee the conflict in Syria, Yemen, and Iraq. The film has won global recognition, screening more than 50 times in two dozen countries, at film festivals, major science centers, international conferences, and universities. In early 2021, I became a member of the steering committee of *Science in Exile* initiative (https://twas.org/about-science-exile-initiative) which aims to create a network of like-minded organizations

Figure 9.2 Photo of my husband's family home destroyed.

that will work together to develop a platform and roll out a coordinated advocacy campaign, so as to foster a cohesive response for the support and integration of at-risk, displaced, and refugee scientists.

Discussion and Conclusion

In this chapter, I illustrated the challenges that female researchers in general and feminists in particular face in the fieldwork and scientific environment in line with other feminists' perspectives that go through these challenges in Arab countries where social and gender norms are not always conducive to women and women issues. In some ways, my experience in 2011 is similar to that of Suad Joseph when she experienced "the comforts of the certainty" that her familiar family gave her during the fieldwork in Lebanon before the civil war (Altorki and El-Solh 1988). I do follow methodologies that enable me to merge with the informants (Keller 1983). Although I am an economist, I have been trained to be an anthropologist as well during the fieldwork. I really focus on the transparent observation; I follow Gupta and Ferguson's (1977) advocacy to consider the field as one element of my methodologies to reach the "situated knowledge." Indeed, these tips help me always reach my targeted community, live with them sometimes, and gain such rich information to serve my research and policy makers.

Yet, during the war, these methods were not enough to conduct research and fieldwork successfully, where the whole environment is dominated by sadness, depression, chaos, confusion, lack of trust, safety, and security. Wartime imposes new tactics; researchers should protect themselves first and then conduct research. Among the chaos they live, researchers not only seek safety from the armed parties but also have to find safety within. Feelings of isolation are very common among scientists and researchers during the war. This is increased by the effects of international sanction that do not respect science and scientists.

Unfortunately, there is a lack of literature that tackles fieldwork and knowledge production during the war from a gender lens. Meanwhile, few studies speak about the challenge of conducting scientific inquiry science while scientists are in exile, which is why I wanted to bring forth this important global case using a gender lens. Although they face severe challenges to create and add value to their home and new home, female scientists' life in exile is dominated by fluid conditions that might not be in their favor personally or professionally. Questions persist as to what happens after scientists migrate. What is the future of knowledge production in the home country? What are the chances to rebuild the home country? Where are female scientists in all of this?

Answers to these questions can summarize the future of scientific work, science, and knowledge in destroyed countries that were/are controlled by patriarchal and extremist parties. Yet, supporting and incubating these scholars by the community and authority to adapt to their new host countries is the way to enhance their contribution to the science and knowledge production. This creates a twofold benefit to the host country and their home countries in one way or another.

Bibliography

Altorki, Soraya, and Camilla F. El-Solh. 1988. *Arab Women in the Field: Studying Your Own Society*. Syracuse, NY: Syracuse University Press.

Al Zoubi, Saja, Aden Aw-Hassan, and Boubaker Dehebi. 2019. "Enhancing the Livelihood and Food Security of Syrian Refugees in Lebanon." Beirut, Lebanon: International Center for Agricultural Research in the Dry Areas (Issue January). https://repo.mel.cgiar.org/handle/20.500.11766/10065.

Connor, Phillip, and Jens Manuel Krogstad. 2016. "About Six-in-Ten Syrians Are Now Displaced from Their Homes." *Pew Research Centre*. http://www.pewresearch.org/fact-tank/2016/06/13/about-six-in-ten-syrians-are-now-displaced-from-their-homes/.

Connor, Phillip. 2018. "Most Displaced Syrians Are in the Middle East, and about a Million Are in Europe." *Pew Research Centre*. https://www.pewresearch.org/fact-tank/2018/01/29/where-displaced-syrians-have-resettled/.

Galia, Alessandre. 2013. "Identity as Farmers: A Case Study from Ten Households in Syria." *NJAS Wageningen Journal of Life Sciences* 64–65: 25–33. https://doi.org/10.1016/j.njas.2012.10.001.

Gupta, Akhil, and Ferguson, James. 1977. "Discipline and Practice: 'The Field' as Site, Method, and Location in Anthropology:" *Anthropological Locations: Boundaries and Grounds of a Field Science*, edited by Akhil Gupta and James Ferguson, 1–46. Berkeley: University of California Press. https://doi.org/10.1525/9780520342392-002.

Keller, Evlen Fox. 1983. "Feminism as a Tool for the Study of Science." *American Association of University Professors* 69 (5): 15–21.

UNHCR. 2017. "Syria Emergency." https://www.unhcr.org/en-us/syria-emergency.html.

World Bank. 2017. *The Toll of War: The Economic and Social Consequences of the Conflict in Syria*. Washington, DC: World Bank. http://documents.worldbank.org/curated/en/811541499699386849/pdf/117331-WP-v2-PUBLIC-The-Toll-of-War.pdf.

Arabic Bibliography

الزعبي، سجا. 2010. دور المرأة في الإقتصاد المنزلي. دمشق، سوريا: دار نينوى للنشر.
(Al Zoubi, Saja. 2010. *Dawr Al-mar'a fi al-'iqtisad al-manziliy*. Dimashq, Suriya: dar ninwa lil-nashir.) (Al Zoubi, Saja. 2010. *The Role of Women in Home Economics*. Damascus, Syria: Ninwa Publishing House.)

10 FEMINIST RESEARCHER IN A CONSERVATIVE ISLAMIC SOCIETY, IRAQ

Ilham Makki Hammadi

Introduction

I did not expect that the experience of my doctoral field study would carry so many difficulties, obstacles, and challenges. My study focused on Islamic women from the Shi'a community studying *Mantiq* (Logic), *Usul al-Fiqh* (Principles of Jurisprudence), *Fiqh* (Jurisprudence), and *Tafsir al-Qur'an* (Qur'an Exegesis) in the most important Shi'a religious seminaries called "Hawza" in the cities of Baghdad and Najaf between 2014 and 2016. I use the term "Islamic women" to refer to women who adopt Islam as an identity and a way of life, interspersed with the finer details of daily practices and behaviors. The women in my research are distinguished from other women by their commitment to perform religious/cultural rituals that have become a distinct cultural pattern, different from any practiced by other Muslim women. The religious ritual practiced by these women includes a communicative action that revives the Shi'a belief system/structure as a group.

I was in a real confrontation with my religious identity, and my role and status as a feminist secular researcher trying to study a group of Shi'a women, which put me in a situation of vulnerability and weakness. My experience studying female students in Hawza seminaries, considered one of the most important components of the Shi'a religious institution, made clear that the religious/political context restricted people to invisible borders, societies semi-closed to all except those who share the same political affiliation. Despite being an indigenous researcher, sharing the same culture, religion, and social class, speaking the same local language,

I looked like an outsider when I conducted my field study, trying to intrude and infiltrate; my reasons and justifications for being among these Shi'a women were deemed suspicious.

This chapter examines the difficulties, complexities, and challenges I encountered during my doctoral field study. I reflect on the issues that surrounded my religious identity as a researcher conducting research utilizing feminist frameworks. I illustrate the moments of confusion, vulnerability, and psychological pressure that I experienced during my field study as I moved from one Hawza to another. I discuss how I addressed the issues of representation and my positioning with the women interviewees, I reflect on the power dynamics present in the research process, and I illustrate how the political context impacted the research results.

Context: Iraq after 2003

Identifying oneself as Sunni, Shi'a, Kurd, or Arab became a very important aspect of relationships among Iraqis after the fall of the political regime in 2003 and the occupation of Iraq by the US-led coalition forces. Adhering to the traditional identity, be it religious or ethnic, and seeking the protection of the clan were the people's way of protecting themselves following the collapse of the state's official security apparatus, especially the army and the police. The day of 9 April 2003 was a historic day in Iraq; the fall of the authoritarian Ba'th regime was announced. Amidst international and regional bewilderment and surprise, the Iraqi army did not put up much resistance to the American military campaign. The Bush administration's decision to change the political system in Iraq was not coupled with a clear vision or a precise plan for the post-Saddam era. The United States made multiple "strategic mistakes" where it only planned the war it wanted to fight against the debilitated Iraqi army, not against a prolonged insurgency.

The US-led coalition forces faced resistance from some armed factions and groups; chaos and insecurity followed in most provinces. The invasion resulted in the demise of the infrastructure and widespread killings, kidnappings, and car bombings in residential neighborhoods. The breakdown of security reached its peak following the explosion of Askariya Shrine in 2006, a holy shrine for Shi'as. The incident led to a civil war between Sunni and Shi'a armed groups. US policies co-opted and reinforced sectarian divisions and the institutionalization of ethnic/sectarian politics in the ruling bodies. Sects have indeed always existed in Iraq throughout its history. However, violent sectarianism did not, certainly not in the way it came to be in 2003.

The new Iraqi constitution of 2005 did not establish sectarian divisions, but we can see the divisiveness of sectarianism in Article 41, which stipulated: "Iraqis, are free in their commitment to their personal status according to their religions, sects, beliefs, or choices, and this shall be regulated by law." Indirectly it stipulated the annulment of the progressive personal status law of 1959 with all its advanced amendments for women. Sectarian division became a political custom in the three governmental key positions. The president of the republic is Kurdish, the prime minister is Shi'a, and the parliament speaker is Sunni. These sectarian divisions of power spread to all levels of the state and expanded to the daily life practices of people.

Research and books prohibited under Ba'th rule spread like never before, and every single group, persecuted and marginalized under the Ba'th one-party system, recreated its own new narrative based on its perspective, and no one had the right to object or criticize. One of the most noticeable characteristics of the new political system is the rise of Islamic movements, especially Shi'a, controlling and monopolizing power. Never before in Iraq's history have the Shi'a participated in politics and monopolized power as became the case after 2003 (Alnafisi 2011; Khursani 1999; Niqash 1996).

All of the moments of confusion, vulnerability, and psychological pressure during my field research are forever engraved in me as I moved from one Hawza to another. Before my field study, I was not aware of the depth of repugnance against Saddam and the Ba'th among the Shi'a, as a consequence of the persecution and marginalization practiced against Shi'a during the Ba'th rule. After 2003, the country turned very sectarian and those in power threatened those of different sects. In 2006 due to the civil war, my family and I were compelled to leave our house of 30 years for a safer neighborhood. However, since then we have never felt completely safe or protected. During field research, there were many instances where I did not feel very reassured, in large part because of the reality of my family's religious identity being Sunni while I was studying and interviewing Shi'a women.

Women's Positioning after 2003

My choice to study women's experiences in Hawza seminaries, as part of the requirements to obtain my PhD, was inspired by my MA field research in 2009–10 on the nature of the political culture of Iraqi women in the parliamentary period of 2005–10. Women made up 25 percent of parliamentarians (MPs) in large part as a result of a quota system. It was clear that the number of Shi'a women was larger than Sunni women, and greater than secular women, as a result of the sweeping win of Shi'a political parties and blocs.

The fall of the Ba'th regime was an important turning point for women, especially Shi'a women. The political discourse of the Islamic/Shi'a blocs and parties focused on rebuilding the Shi'a religious authority on new basis in line with the new political reality. It aimed to play a leading role in society and step out of the era of seclusion of the past caused by the oppression, exclusion, and marginalization by the political regime that ruled and governed Iraq. In pre-2003 Iraq and pre-1979 Iran, only a handful of women were taught in Hawza. The Shi'a political authority supported women's participation in the public sphere and allowed them, for the first time, to join the Hawza "Ilmiyya" in the cities of Najaf, Baghdad, and the rest of the provinces. This "space" was exclusive to men since the establishment of the Hawza in 460 A.H.–1067 A.D.

Interviews with female MPs revealed the depths of the political division within Iraqi society because all women joined the hemicycle based on their sectarian and ethnic affiliation. In every interview, my identity as a Sunni woman was a riddle to the interviewee/responder. Based on my identity, she would approve or reject some of the questions, and she would determine the level and kind of information she is willing to reveal. The same happened again during my PhD field study. This time my sect and feminist/secular tendency was the riddle many Islamic women tried to expose. The level of caution and worry increased in my PhD field study because all of the women shared the same sectarian identity.

Hawza: Prickly Religious–Political Context

I raised doubts and mistrust in every Hawza that I visited about the motives and objectives of the research. Why this research? Who is behind this research? And for whom? The sensitivity of the situation, status, and role of the Hawza for Shi'as influenced the conduct of the field research, and even greatly influenced the results of the research. I felt that I was bound by political determinants rather than religious or cultural ones. Religious holiness mixed with politics, and it became difficult to differentiate between them. What makes the Hawza so complex when researchers attempt to study it?

Since 1067 A.D. the role played by the Hawza is of great importance in the history of Shi'a; it is linked to holiness in the Shi'a tradition. All Shi'a (contrary to Sunni) are obligated to perform *Taqlid*, which literally means to follow someone, to imitate. In Islamic legal terminology, it means to follow a *mujtahid* (an interpreter) in religious laws and commandment as he has derived them from the Qur'an and Hadith. Of all clerics/ulama who study in the Hawza schools, only one of them became a religious reference, Marja'a Taqleed. The Hawza became an intellectual and social establishment and a link between the religious reference Marja'a Taqleed and Shi'a imitators/followers and had an influence on the political positioning of Shi'a historically (Awad 2013, 47).

It was not possible to ask questions and get answers about Hawza before 2003 due to the intellectual and existential absenteeism imposed by the Ba'thist political regime on the Shi'a religious reference, Marji'iya, and the Hawza since the Ba'th took power in 1968. Hawza schools were a platform for hidden political opposition. Any research about Shi'a was often done for security issues in order to uncover any attempt by Hawza students to threaten the security and stability as well as the authority of the regime. The problematic of security-based studies continued after 2003, but this time for reasons different from previous ones, after the status and role of the Hawza represented by the Shi'a religious reference Marji'iya had changed and had become the facade of the new political system.

Studying women in the Hawza was thus a challenging project, all my theoretical research before my field studies did not give me a real perception of the meaning, status, and holiness of Hawza among Shi'a. Given this historical and political context, it was understandable that my experience of Islamic women's study in the Hawza school would certainly be regarded with suspicion. I often feared that the purpose of my research would be misinterpreted. Even now after my research is complete, when I am asked about the subject of my thesis, I stop for a moment to think about the orientation of the person who is asking, are they Shi'a or Sunni? Are they religious or not? Then I answer the question.

The Hawza, for Shi'a, means sacred constants that cannot be criticized. One day, during my field studies, one of the representatives of the Marja'a Sistani—the most important Marji'iya for Shi'a inside and outside Iraq—warned me directly not to write anything against the Hawza, because it has historically suffered enough. Then, he started giving me instructions on how to talk about the Hawza, and the Marji'iya and its holiness, noting that the Marji'iya had nothing to do with the bad events happening in Iraq.

The contradiction between my position as a researcher who is keen to deal honestly and responsibly with the results of the research, and the delicate and tense situation I was in, impacted the course of my field studies. My caution—or rather the direct and indirect warning from others to me—led me in many situations to avoid any questions that might be understood to offend the Hawza or the religious reference Marji'iya. It also made me avoid questions that seemed to be trying to learn the secrets and mysteries of the religious establishment. For example, questions about the funding of the Hawza schools or that addressed the body responsible for the administration of the Hawza, especially if it was an influential political party, were not possible. I did my best to make clear to folks that the subject of my study was about women, not Hawza, and that somehow allowed me a space to help reduce my anxiety. Over time, I learned to start by introducing myself and my research, in a defensive position by simply summarizing the purpose of my research, that is, the women's experience in the Hawza, without being asked to do so. Then, I used to repeat that my research was not about the Hawza but about women. This helped me a lot to stop being tense and anxious and made women inside the Hawza feel comfortable.

The Academic Study and the Dichotomy—Sacred versus Secular

My first moments in any Hawza were always the hardest. When I introduced myself as a PhD student and a specialist in anthropology, I put the first boundary or distance between the women in the Hawza and myself, because my academic studies are totally different from jurisprudence topics and sciences in the Hawzas. Natural and human sciences are often described as mundane sciences, whereas jurisprudence topics and the interpretation of the texts of the Qur'an and the Hadith are considered divine sciences, one is of lower order and the other higher. Women's education in Iraq had historically suffered from structural, cultural, economic, and political stumbling blocks. However, Islamic Shi'a women had additional challenge that Shi'a establishment had had a special attitude toward formal/governmental education, because it promoted secular thought. One of the reasons behind the establishment of the Islamic Da'wa Party—the first Shi'a Islamic political party—was to respond to the communist, secular, nationalist, and other materialistic ideas that dominated the intellectual and political orientations of Iraqis in the 1930s. The position of the Shi'a religious establishment had not changed much in terms of preferring religious sciences over natural sciences (Khursani 1999, 96–98).

Juxtaposing the divine versus the earthly and preferring the divine over the earthly has in many cases put me in a position of vulnerability, fragility, and inferiority. My secular academic education, in the perspective of Hawza, is earthly and mortal, contrary to the immortal divine religious education provided by the Hawza. I noted this attitude among women who had not been in the Hawza for a long time and who were unable to complete their formal education in public schools due to political and gender norms restrictions. However, the position of most women who have been in the Hawza for many years and those with official and university education was very different. They appreciated formal academic education and considered religious education as an added value that gave them a prominent place among their families and in their community. I even became for them an example and a model they sought to imitate.

Identity: More than Social Category

The protection of Islamic religious identity was not limited to protecting the Shi'a community from secularism but from any other religion or sect. The name Saint Joseph University (where I was studying for my PhD) or "Jesuit" was a great challenge for me during fieldwork because the name itself carried a symbol of the Christian religion. The administration in some Hawzas feared that my research was for religious purposes—to distort the image of Islam. I suffered in many instances from suspicion and mistrustful looks and from uncomfortable reactions by women once I would mention the name of the Jesuit university. I often had to say that it was a large and inclusive university that offered all scientific and humanitarian disciplines. This explanation did not stop them from questioning me, that is, if there was direct guidance from the university to students to conduct research in certain subjects, such as Islam. The purpose of the question was of course the Hawza and not Islam in general, that is, whether there was a plan or intention to choose the Hawza as a subject of research. I was also asked if I had been subjected to "evangelization" to leave the religion of Islam and become a Christian, as one of the conditions for granting the certificate.

Most of these fears and doubts dissipated for the women with whom I had a friendly and close relationship. As for the rest of the women in some Hawzas, they continued to feel worried about me, my identity, my university, the topic of my studies, and my independence—all aspects that made me unwelcome. This concern had a political dimension because some of these Hawzas were affiliated with Shi'a political parties. For these political parties, the Hawza establishment constitutes one of the strategies and defense lines for Islam and Shi'a identity against another sect, especially Sunni and other religions, as well as to earn political gains. During the sessions there is a direct and indirect political socialization that trains women to be the protectors of this new Shi'a political authority and positions of power. The most conservative Hawza, where women reached the last phases of their studies becoming diligent *mujtahid*, was in Najaf. It was one of the first Hawzas established for women in 2003. It belonged to a historically Islamist political party with power and authority among the Shi'as. Its power grew steadily after the overwhelming victory of the Shi'as in the 2005 parliamentary elections. At first, I was not allowed to visit the Hawza because the administration rejected my demand. Then I was able, through my contacts with known persons in Najaf, to obtain the support of a well-known cleric—the grandson of a supreme Marja'a—who introduced me to the director of the Hawza. While the director was the one behind the rules around prohibiting any visits by strangers to the Hawza, relationships between clerics overrode that and thus I benefited by being granted admission.

But my visit to the school was restricted in a way I did not expect. I was not allowed to wander around the Hawza nor to directly mix with the women. All interviews took place under the administration's direct supervision and I was not able to meet any woman alone. The plan was to have a collective interview, so that the women "police" each other in case I asked a question about the Hawza and its orientations. On the third day, the principal told me that she could not meet me anymore. She was very sorry and explained that the decision was not hers.

"These are the instructions of the director," she stated. She explained that she wished she could or had the ability to take the decision and host me as much as I wanted in the Hawza and then she offered to host me at her house if I wished so. She explained that our discussions were interesting and broke her daily routine because we had tackled new topics. Every time I used to mention that "I got fired" from one specific Hawza after the third day, all the women/students in the rest of the Hawzas had a single reaction: "Very good. You were lucky that they hosted you for three days." This Hawza is known to be too conservative and is firm in dealing with women/students. One of the women/students said that the director—who is a very famous *mujtahid*—used ways and practices similar to the security practices adopted by Baʿth regime. It became clear, then, that the patriarchal and male hegemonic system had only changed its name, while the content and the tools remained the same, violating women's human rights and limiting their choices.

Feminist Methodology of Scientific Value

Another important challenge in working on feminist research through institutions that do not have feminist theoretical or methodological training is the utter rejection of such methodologies and the assumption that these are simply unnecessary qualifiers. My supervisor for the PhD program categorically rejected the idea that there is something as feminist methodologies for research. She would argue that observations, interviews, focus groups, and case studies were not discovered by feminist methodologies but existed in the disciplines prior. Despite her objections, I felt that feminist methodologies were essential to my project. In the end, I cannot imagine I would have been able to conduct my research successfully and with academic rigor without learning from the ethical considerations and practices of feminist researchers in women and gender studies. The important thing that I am sure of is that the results of my research would have been quite different.

My advisor's question seemed similar to that of Sandra Harding's question: Is there a distinct feminist approach to research? (Harding 1987, 2). Harding was building a case for feminist methodologies. She had used some or all of these disciplinary techniques to collect information, but what distinguished feminist research was its remarkable different use of these tools. For instance, researchers listen with great attention to women being interviewed and look for areas of power relations in the field research experience. Feminist researchers observe settings differently, ask different kinds of questions, and pay close attention to power dynamics interested in hearing silences and understanding refusals; all of these techniques had a huge impact on my research process and results.

Changing My Question and My Assumptions

The rapid denunciation of unfamiliar beliefs and practices, especially religious ones, is one of the dilemmas that are not easily recognized by researchers when studying other cultures (Gross 2004, 22–23) and even when the researcher studies their local culture as in my case. Avoidance of pride, the sense of cultural and values superiority, and postponement of prejudices are important rules to consider in conducting field research. My assumptions and perceptions of Islamic women before conducting my field study reflected research processes that produced power differences in terms of: Who defines the research project? Who defines what counts as a problematic situation? Whose concepts, questions, and hypotheses are the focus of the research? My assumptions were ready-made projects on what women should do to overcome the constraints and challenge obstacles. I drafted my main question based on this assumption: Is there Islamic feminism in Iraq? I postulated that Islamic women in the Hawza schools are working toward the production of alternative, gender-sensitive religious knowledge that engages with Islamic sacred texts (the Qur'an and Sunnah). Like other Muslim women scholars from different countries who are committed to their religious faith, this scholarship I presumed consisted of studies that critically revisit and unpack dominant religious interpretations that are patriarchal and discriminatory against women, and aim to produce new knowledge that makes the case for gender equality and justice from within an Islamic paradigm.

In the field, I discovered that my question was naive and superficial because it was built on two presuppositions. First, I expected that the challenges I faced as a woman from the same community who lived and faced the same circumstances (political, economic, and cultural) were going to be the same for all women in Iraq. However, my field studies proved that I was entirely wrong. For example, my family did not support or encourage me to go to school. "There is no benefit from the education of girls," my mother—widowed and poor at age 30 with eight children—kept telling me and my sisters. She never asked me how my studies were going and she almost never knew in which grade I was. At the same time, she often encouraged my brothers to go to school and get a job hoping they can financially support her. However, because all public schools were free of charge and poor families were not charged extra costs, my mother did not prevent me from getting my education nor did she stop me from going out of the house to school. Nonetheless, this was not a common experience with other girls; many of the women I interviewed mentioned that their families prevented them from going to school because they considered it a boycott or political dissent against the Ba'th regime. Other families' reasons tied to gender norms, particularly not wanting their daughters to be in coeducational schools, especially in the rural areas.

Second, my background research and literature review mostly based in Western feminist literature also impacted the assumptions I was making about these women in particular. This literature often portrayed particularly Muslim women as subordinate and submissive, assuming that all women had a similar liberal desire of being free from subordination. Feminist scholars criticized, argued, and problematized assumptions about resistance, freedom, agency, authority (Abu-Lughod 1990; Mahmood 2005) that sharply limited our ability to understand and interrogate the lives of women who believe in nonliberal traditions, women involved in patriarchal religious traditions. "We should learn to read in various local and everyday resistances the existence of a range of specific strategies and structures of power. Attention to the forms of resistance in particular societies can help us become critical of partial or reductionist theories of power" (Abu-Lughod 1990, 53).

In realizing that my assumptions and preconceived conclusions were potential pitfalls, I decided to focus on a feminist scholarship that was in line with what I was observing in the field and to let my data guide my analysis instead. The deep conversations with women helped me understand why women believe in those doctrines and practices and what their goals are. I worked to identify what women use to improve their lives, what are their options, what alternatives are "available" to them, and what are the "costs" incurred in relation to their actions; sometimes it costs them their own lives.

I knew that when I decided to abandon the main research question and my initial assumptions, it would take me longer and would require more reading and identifying a new analytical framework. I decided to allow the data to guide me rather than be guided by premature assumptions. The feminist approach had emerged ethnographically as the most fitting solution for analyzing the complexities of my body of spoken data and helped me to address a particular research methodology problem, which is a pivotal part of the analysis.

The Hegemony of Quantitative Research and Feminist Perspectives on In-Depth Interviewing

I faced a difficult challenge in working with my university due to the hegemony of quantitative research methodologies in the region. My PhD advisor had only conducted quantitative research. She warned me against challenging the importance of quantitative research in my methodology chapter because the discussion committee will include professors specialized in quantitative research and this may affect the evaluation of the thesis. But I was convinced that statistical data cannot bring to the surface the voices of marginalized and oppressed groups that have been silenced, in which women are the majority. Sensitive details associated with feelings and affect may also provide important analytical insights into the self-aspect of the individual. Capturing this requires time and probing questions that encourage the respondents to speak freely without worrying about only answering exact questions. It was important to let the respondent discuss deeply the topics she wished and felt were important to raise from her point of view (Hesse-Biber and Leavy 2015, 197). All this is not possible with quantitative research methods.

My insistence on conducting interviews according to the feminist approach and letting the respondents decide which subjects were important to discuss opened up doors that would not be opened if I were committed only to specific questions and if I did not listen to women's feelings and concerns. My advisor was won over when she saw the final product and the quality of the research and she is now a champion of qualitative feminist research methods.

It became clear quiet early on that in-depth interviews would be the most important strategy to gain more rigorous and complete data and enable the respondents to share their stories. As Sharlene Hesse-Biber (2007) stated, "A feminist perspective regarding in-depth interviewing would see the interview process as a co-creation of meaning. The researcher must stay on his or her toes and listen intently to what the interviewee has to say, for the researcher must be prepared to drop his or her agenda and follow the pace of the interview" (132). The in-depth interviews provided me with an opportunity to build trust with the women and allowed a safe space for mutual dialogue, without any third person intervening. Most women stopped talking when someone entered the interview place. Respondents made sure not to be heard by other women if the interview did not take place in an isolated location. They expressed their opinions, issues, and beliefs that are of particular concern differently, when they were in individual interviews isolated from people. Gaining confidence, becoming more familiar with the space, and my constant presence in the Hawza school somewhat broke women's reservation. In some cases, my interviews with women were not limited in time and were a series of dialogues.

On one occasion, I shared my personal opinion about the challenges that women face in Iraq and the obstacles during their lives, and how women still had to be polite and patient. I shared that I felt all of this was hard to handle and that we can fall apart at any moment. Two hours later, I was surprised as one woman approached me asking to go speak in a more private space. She had been listening to me. Although she was very friendly to me when I first met her, she was also one of the most reserved women in talking about her life and studies in the Hawza. She was one of the most active women committed to the public discourse of the Hawza and its new call for the dissemination and consolidation of Shi'a identity. She started the interview by repeating the sentence I mentioned earlier, which seemed at the heart of her suffering. She then went on to recite in detail violent practices that she faced every day from her family, and at the same time marginalization and lack of interest from clerics responsible for managing

Shi'a religious institutions. After the interview, I pondered over the conversation for a long time and thought how much it would have been impossible for me to gain access to this information if I had not shared a personal story. Depriving women from human rights, exclusion, marginalization, and violence are practices that women face every day. This is what feminist research attempts to address by criticizing and analyzing the roots of historical and political discrimination against women as an integral part of the feminist struggle.

Power Relationships between the Researcher and the Respondent

One of the most important lessons I learned during my field research was paying close attention to minimizing the power relationships. Although I was careful to avoid the hierarchical relationships between me and the participants by establishing a level of intimacy in our relationship, I was in countless cases at the other end of the power relationships, that is, the participants were those who exercised power over me. My relationship with many women was markedly strained. I was like someone walking in a minefield. I did not know what the reaction of the women would be to my position and role as a researcher and what I had to do to be accepted by them. The most likely reason for this is my higher education, the university name and location outside of Iraq, my financial independence (because I am an employee), and my personal independence, as I have the ability to move, travel, and control my life. This information was known to most women in any school I visited, that is, information about a strange visitor moving quickly between women in the Hawza. For me, it was not easy to create a friendly atmosphere with some of the women. Many women were not interested in talking to me, some of them were annoyed by my presence, and others commented aggressively on some of my views. I heard this from one of the respondents in one of the Najaf Hawzas. "There are some women who are upset about your presence and are wondering why and what is behind it," she said. She spoke of herself saying frankly, "whenever I met you, I would say 'this girl is hated,' but when I have spoken to you, my feelings changed completely towards you."

My studies at Saint Joseph University caused mixed reactions. In some instances, I was highly accepted among women, as a student at a prestigious university outside of Iraq. In fact, the level of education in general has witnessed a marked deterioration in Iraq since 1980, as a result of wars and the imposition of harsh economic sanctions between 1990 and 2003, during which the infrastructure of educational institutions was destroyed. In addition, large groups of women—especially women within the scope of my field research—were deprived of education for political, economic, and cultural reasons. Therefore, studying at Saint Joseph University in Lebanon and working for a doctorate degree was a privilege that made me deserve additional recognition. A college degree or the diploma for women was a sign of social status and capital. My privileges were a source of admiration and curiosity for some women but were also a source of annoyance for others. My presence reminded them of the opportunities and choices they were deprived from.

In other instances, I seemed to hold less power. The principal of the Hawza was the one who exercised authority over me and the women. In one of Baghdad's Hawzas, I immediately felt the hegemony relationship between the teachers and the principal. The Hawza was managed by the agent of reference of the Marja'a al Sistani (the most important Shi'a reference in Iraq) and the principal was his sister. She looked very firm and cautious toward me; however, she agreed that I meet the women and decided that I meet the teachers only, not the students. When I stepped in the room, she introduced me to the women, and I mentioned that I was a PhD student. She warned the women to be cautious during the interviews. But she suddenly left the room because she had something to do. In the meantime, I had a discussion with one of the teachers. She asked about the nature of my studies and specialization and I started asking her about joining the Hawza. Then the principal stepped in, and when she saw us talking, she yelled at the teacher saying: "Who allowed you to talk? I did not give you the permission to talk to her!" Then, she addressed me: "And you, why were you talking to her? I am the one who decides when to talk and with whom."

I cannot describe what happened to me at that moment. I felt confused and scared. I did not know what kind of situation I was in and if I would cause any harm to the teacher I was talking to. I started apologizing in a tense way. I did so more than once and told the principal that it was my fault and that she did not talk to me, but I talked to her. I took responsibility, as if we were committing a crime. The principal gave a short speech to all the teachers in the room about the instructions, recommendations, and orders that she mentioned earlier about what women at the Hawza should possess, the most important of which is being cautious when talking to anyone. Then, she asked a teacher to have the interview with me. The teacher was about to leave the Hawza at that moment, because of a family emergency. I noticed that she was very upset, and I told the principal that she had to go out. However, the principal insisted that she should stay and continue the interview, because it will not take much time. But the teacher's face showed that she was upset. I became confused, I felt anxious and nervous, the teacher and I were in the same situation, under the authority of the principal; I lost the ability to control my decision whether to do or cancel the interview! If I had the choice, I would have cancelled it! I apologized for delaying her departure, and had the following discussion with her:

Me: I am sorry for delaying your departure.
The teacher: There is no problem. The most important is to do the interview as the principal has asked.

Me:	The interview is not important; it is you who is important. What is important is that you feel comfortable. If you are preoccupied, we can do it on another day. (Here her face changed, and she felt comfortable about what I said, and she regained control over her time).
The teacher:	It is ok, we can do the interview.
Me:	So how much time would you give me so I can figure out what is most important to ask you?
The teacher:	Maybe fifteen minutes.
Me:	Very good. This is fine for me.

The interview lasted more than 45 minutes, and throughout the interview, I watched her body language if she was worried or disturbed. We were able to engage in a friendly and smooth discussion. I knew she was an architect who had practiced her profession for some time but was at the moment a housewife. She talked about her desire and relentless attempts to join the Hawza. I apologized at the end again for having in essence forced her to talk to me, even if inadvertently, but she smiled and said that time passed quickly and that she found the discussion interesting. My feminist anthropological training helped me recuperate the situation and gain her trust, thus allowing me to an extent to shift the power dynamic that we had found ourselves in.

In one of the schools in Baghdad, I asked for an interview with a teacher, of whom I had heard from the rest of the teachers that she was excellent and had the educational ability to teach more than one subject at the Hawza. She agreed to do the interview and seemed interested. However, I had to postpone the interview twice because she was busy, and when I had the opportunity to do the interview with her, she refused to answer my questions and asked to see them in writing to study them at home and write her answers accurately. I told her that my questions were general and did not need thoroughness. She was surprised by this answer, and how I did not prepare the questions before the interview. I told her that my specialty was in anthropology and that the researcher had general questions in his or her mind. At this point, she became the interviewer and I became the respondent. She spent more than 20 minutes asking me about my life, my studies, my job, and how I got the approval to study outside Iraq at the government's expense. Suddenly, she stopped talking and laughed at the changing roles between me and her, and how she became the interviewer and I became the respondent. She was interested to know about my life because she was personally interested in women's education, employment, and financial independence that she missed and is still missing in her personal life. This interview was very instructional, and she became an important resource for my study. Our relationship became more collegial and continued to grow over time.

Findings, Anthropology, and Feminist Research Ethics

My fieldwork allowed me access to a wide range of sensitive information and data about the Hawza schools I visited. I had to make decisions about what I would be comfortable publishing and what could put me or my respondents in a compromised or dangerous position. Given the political climate in Iraq and the growth of the various religious political factions and their armed groups sometimes, and given my identity as a Sunni woman researcher who at times would be perceived as a spy, I had to consider my safety in what I would publish. I needed to make sure that what I wrote was not seen as being critical or exposing inside information.

Since my dissertation was filed in Lebanon, it still needed to be submitted and approved by the Iraqi Ministry of Education and I was worried about what that process may entail. I work for the Ministry of Education as a teacher, would this cause me any problems in my job? I felt it was my responsibility to ensure the safety of the women first who were the sources of my data. The first principle in the Principles of Professional Responsibility developed by anthropologists is "do no harm" (American Anthropological Association 2020). In reflecting upon my research findings, I concluded that in the new political formations where Shi'a political groups have become more dominant, there is little shift in the violence and other life challenges experienced by the women, meaning that patriarchy remained intact. I did not include this in my dissertation even though the stories the women shared with me exposed the contradiction between the public discourse for the Shi'a establishment and the real conditions of women's lives. I believed that this statement would not contribute to improving the conditions of the women but may to the contrary cause them more harm and may lead to calls for them to be removed from the Hawza, which has become a place and a way to enable disadvantaged women to make choices and improve their life.

Bibliography

Abu-Lughod, Lila. 1990. "The Romance of Resistance: Tracing Transformations of Power through Bedouin Women." *American Ethnologist* 17 (1): 41–55.

Altorki, Soraya. 1988. "At Home in the Field." In *Arab Women in the Field: Studying Your Own Society*, edited by Soraya Altorki and Camillia Fawzi El-Solh, 51–59. Syracuse, NY: Syracuse University Press.

American Anthropological Association. "Principles of Professional Responsibility." *AAA Statement on Ethics*. https://www.americananthro.org/LearnAndTeach/Content.aspx?ItemNumber=22869&navItemNumber=652, accessed 13 March 2020.

Cline, Lawrence E. 2000. "The Prospects of the Shia Insurgency Movement in Iraq." *Journal of Conflict Studies* 20 (2). https://journals.lib.unb.ca/index.php/JCS/article/view/4311.

Gross, Rita M. 2004. "Where Have We Been? Where Do We Need to Go? Women's Studies and Gender in Religion and Feminist Theology." In *Gender, Religion and Diversity: Cross-Cultural Perspective*, edited by Ursula King and Tina Beattie, 17–27. London Continuum International Publishing Group.

Harding, Sandra. 1987. *Feminism and Methodology: Social Science Issues*. Bloomington: Indiana University Press.

Hesse-Biber, Sharlene N. 2007. "The Practice of Feminist In-Depth Interviewing." In *Feminist Research Practice*, edited by Sharlene N. Hesse-Biber and Patricia L. Leavy, 110–48. Thousand Oaks, CA: Sage.

MacLeod, Arlene E. 1992. "Hegemonic Relations and Gender Resistance: The New Veiling as Accommodating Protest in Cairo." *Signs* 17 (3): 533–57. www.jstor.org/stable/3174622.

Mahmood, Saba 2005. *Politics of Piety the Islamic Revival and The Feminist Subject*. Princeton, NJ: Princeton University Press.

Arabic Bibliography

أبو بكر، أميمة. 2012. مترجم. النسوية والدراسات الدينية. مصر، القاهرة: مؤسسة المرأة والذاكرة.
(Abubakar, Omaima. 2012. *Alniswih Waldirasat Aldiynih. Misr, Alqahirih: muasasat almar'a waldhaakira*.) (Abou-Bakr, Omaima, ed. 2012. *Feminism and Religious Studies: A Reader*. Translated by Randa K. Aboubakr. Cairo, Egypt: Women and Memory Foundation.)

البزري، دلال. 1996. أخوات الظل واليقين، إسلاميات بين الحداثة والتقليد. بيروت: دار النهار للطباعة والنشر.
(Albazri, Dalal. 1996. *Akhawat Alzili walyaqin, Iislamiaat bayn Alhadatha Waltaqlid. bayrut: Dar Alnahar liltibaea walnashr*.) (Al-Bizri, Dalal. 1996. *Sisters of Shadow and Certainty: Islamist Women between Modernity and Tradition*. Beirut, Lebanon: Dar Al-Nahar for Printing and Publishing.)

الخرساني، صلاح. 1999. حزب الدعوة حقائق ووثائق، فصول من تجربة الحركة الإسلامية في العراق خلال 40 عاماً. دمشق: المؤسسة العربية للدراسات والبحوث الأستراتيجية.
(Alkhirsani, Salah. 1999. *Hizb Aldaewat Haqayiq wawathayiq, Fusul min Tajribat Alharaka al'iislamia fi Aleiraq khilal 40 eamaan. Dimashq: Almuasasa alearabia lildirasat walbuhuth Al'ustratijiati*.) (Khursani, Salah. 1999. *Da'wa Party Facts and Documents, Chapters of the Experience of the Islamic Movement in Iraq in 40 Years*. Damascus, Syria: The Arab Foundation for Studies, Research and Strategy.)

النفيسي، عبد الله. 2011. دور الشيعة في تطور العراق السياسي الحديث. الكويت: آفاق للنشر والتوزيع.
(Alnafisi, Eabd Allah. 2011. *Dawr Alshiyeat fi Tatawur Aleiraq Alsiyasii Alhadith. Alkuayt: Afaq Lilnashr waltawziei*.) (Alnafisi, Abdullah. 2011. *The Role of Shi'as in Iraq's Modern Political Development*. Kuwait: Afaq for Publishing and Distribution.)

عوض، عبد الرضا. 2013. الحوزة العلمية في الحلة، نشأتها وانكماشها، الأسباب والنتائج. بغداد: دار الفرات للثقافة والإعلام.
(Euad, Eabd Alrida. 2013. *Alhawza Aleilmia fi Alhilati, nash'atuha wankimashaha, al'asbab walnatayija. baghdada: Dar Alfurat Lilthaqafa wal'iielam*.) (Awad, Abdul R. 2013. *The Scientific Estate in Hilla; Its Origin and Contraction, Causes and Results*. Baghdad, Iraq: Dar Al-Furat for Culture and Information.)

نقاش، اسحاق. 1996. شيعة العراق. سوريا، دمشق: دار المدى للثقافة والنشر.
(Niqashu, Ashaq. 1996. *Shieat Aleiraq. Suria, Dimashqa: Dar Almadaa Lilthaqafa walnashr.*) (Niqash, Ishaq. 1996. *Shi'as of Iraq*. Damascus: Dar Al Mada for Culture and Publishing.)

هاشم، عزة جلال. 2007. المشاركة السياسية للمرأة الإيرانية. دولة الإمارات العربية المتحدة: مركز الإمارات للدراسات والبحوث الإستراتيجية.
(Hashim, Eazat jalal. 2007. *Almusharakat Alsiyasia Lilmar'a al'iirania. Dawlat Al'iimarat Alearabia Almutahida: Markaz Al'iimarat Lildirasat Walbuhuth al'iistratijia.*) (Hashem, Azza G. 2007. *Political Participation of Iranian Women*. United Arab Emirates: Emirates Center for Strategic Studies and Research.)

هيسي، شارلين ناجي وبايبر باتريشا لينا ليفي. 2015. مترجم: هالة كمال. مدخل الى البحث النسوي ممارسة وتطبيقاً. القاهرة،مصر: المركز القومي للترجمة.
(Hisi, Harlin Naji Wabaybar Batrisha Lina Lifi. 2015. *Mutarjimi: Halat Kamal. Madkhal ala Albahth Alnaswiu Mumarasatan Wttbyqaan. Masir, Alqahirat: Almarkaz Alqawmia Liltarjama.*) (Hesse-Biber, Sharlene N., and Patricia L. Leavy. 2015. *Introduction to Feminist Research Practice and Application*, translated by Hala Kamal. Cairo: National Center for Translation.)

PART 3

KHALEEJ (ARAB GULF)

11 EMBEDDEDNESS IN THE FIELD: NAVIGATING FAMILIARITY

Sarah Shaer

Introduction

This chapter draws on my experience conducting fieldwork in Dubai in 2018. I had begun my MA thesis research interested in examining the institutions of the *majlis* (ruler's council) and the *diwan* (ruler's court) in the United Arab Emirates (UAE).[1] I was interested in interrogating the kinds of "intimacies" that these institutions facilitated between rulers and citizens. I was concerned to investigate the sorts of practices of "citizenship" and claim-making enabled or foreclosed by these "intimacies" and the implications for the kind of political authority and governmentality operating in the country. I was reading against conventional rentier state theory—the theory through which most political economists and even political scientists have chosen to understand the politics of the Gulf (Beblawi 1987; Davidson 2008; Luciani 1987).

This chapter reflects on my role as an "indigenous researcher" and the ways in which occupying that position has come to bear on my fieldwork. The questions that occupied me, as well as the networks that enabled my research, were the direct result of my having grown up in the UAE and working alongside the UAE government for many years. As a Jordanian citizen resident in the UAE, and someone who worked for a UAE government-affiliated think tank, my interest in studying the Emirati state and its structures of rulership had been cultivated through many years of experience and observation before pivoting into the field of anthropology.

In this chapter, I reflect on the fieldwork encounter as familiar rather than strange and the ways in which my personal investments and histories, some of which I shared with my interlocutors, came to shape what it meant for me to be "in the field." The field for me was not about "encounter[ing] difference by going elsewhere" (Gupta and Ferguson 1977, 8), it was about interrogating the familiar by going home.

As Altorki and El-Solh (1988) observe, there is no consensus about the relevance of indigenous status to data collection. In fact, it might even be difficult to ascertain who might or might not count as an "indigenous" or native anthropologist. This is especially true in the case of the UAE. The UAE has a population of 8.3 million people, more than 90 percent of whom are non-nationals (UAE Government Portal 2020).[2] The country is home to people from more than two hundred nationalities (UAE Government Portal 2020), many of whom will leave the country for good, out of choice or out of necessity, at some point in their lives. South Asian and Arab residents have a long-standing history of migration to the Gulf. South Asian residents, in particular, form the majority of the country's population. These dynamics, as well as the complex interplay of class, race, citizenship, linguistic affiliation, and divergent regimes of governance make any insider/outsider, native/non-native binary difficult to hold. One need not belong to UAE society to feel like an insider. In their reflections on their own fieldwork in Dubai, Neha Vora and Ahmed Kanna (2020) draw attention to the ways in which the composition of UAE society and its histories of migration enabled each of them (scholars of Indian and Iraqi descent respectively) to feel like insiders (and at times outsiders) in the field.

My own reflections here are about the ways in which a project of studying my own home and my own state was always an endeavor laden with the opportunities and pitfalls of personal investments and histories. I reflect on the experience of doing research in a place with which I share a lifelong history, in whose future I am deeply invested, and which I do not intend to exit (or at least not for long). Doing fieldwork at home flips the script of the traditional imagination of fieldwork as "expressed in the standard anthropological tropes of entry into and exit from 'the field'" (Gupta and Ferguson 1977, 12). Flipping this script runs the risk of threatening the image of the researcher as an objective and distant observer (Gupta and Ferguson 1977, 17), but as Suad Joseph (1988, 47) reflected, decades prior to my beginning my own work, "I find myself now wondering how people do research on questions or people far afield from themselves." My embeddedness in my field and in my work predated my still nascent academic career and, I hope, will always exceed and outlive it.

Shared Experience in the Field

I met Maha and Afra, two young Emirati women, at a café in the newest wing of the Dubai mall.[3] It was wintertime in Dubai. We sat outside on a terrace overlooking the Dubai fountain. The "interview" was a casual conversation about Maha and Afra's experiences with the ruler's *majlis*. As they described to me the role of the *majlis*, as well as their experiences and desires to interact with rulers in that space, the conversation became emotional. Maha talked about the kind of devotion and love she feels rulers show citizens in the country. She recalled the death of Sheikh Zayed bin Sultan al Nahyan, one of the founding sheikhs of the UAE. She explained how devastated she was to hear of his passing. She talked about how, weeks after his death, she was still unable to stop crying and how her mother would console her. I remember the death of Sheikh Zayed vividly. I was still in high school at the time and have memories of my teachers standing in hallways crying. I remember the general feeling of gloom washing over that day. Even before being told that Sheikh Zayed had passed, it was clear that something was wrong. Parents were called to pick their children up from school early. When my mother arrived, she too had been crying.

As Maha recalled that time, she began to tear up. When she began to tear up, so did Afra and I. Leaning over a short table and holding warm cups of tea, we shared experiences of a time long ago, experiences that, while different and from different positionalities, were nonetheless shared. Within the space of the interview, sharing this experience enabled a kind of intimacy between interviewer and interviewee. I was not a UAE national. Yet, I was not a foreigner or a stranger to the experience they were describing. I had inhabited the same time with them in a very small city, in a very small country. What was the same and what was different about our experiences could be read by Maha and Afra, as well as by me. The ability to observe and analyze our interaction was not limited to me alone. We each understood our relation to one another as nationals and non-nationals, as people "from" different emirates, as people from different class and family backgrounds, and spanning different ages. There was a legibility, however limited, that was possible due to each of our familiarity with Dubai and its social and economic relations. What we understood about one another was not a kind of sameness or difference but rather our place in a web of relations, historic and present, that was visible and legible to each other. We also understood something about what it meant to live in the UAE and be ruled in the UAE.

This was something that I wanted to write about—palpable yet elusive. The affective relations of rulership and subjecthood—the practices and institutions that made them possible, and the kinds of power, politics, and citizenship that was operating there. The reason that this display of emotion was notable to me was precisely because I understood that Maha was not peculiar in her emotional reaction to the death of the ruler. This knowledge was drawn not only from my own experience but also from decades of listening to apocryphal stories about the rulers of the Emirates and from having witnessed displays of emotion at the sight of rulers many times before—sometimes from unexpected sources. What I was seeing anew, as I did my fieldwork, connected with what I had seen before I came to call it "fieldwork." The stories I was hearing reminded me of stories I had heard before, when I was not "in the field" but was just in life, at home, in Dubai.

Sharing in this moment offers an uncomfortable space of reflection, as it complicates my role as a distant observer. I had intended to critically interrogate the place of affect in relations of rulership, but in that moment, it was not possible to take distance and be an observer, critical or otherwise. In this moment that I shared with Maha and Afra, I was not just someone studying how "other people" related to their rulers. I was relating to my rulers also. Even while I wanted to analyze these relations of power, affect, and intimacy, I could not but feel with Maha. I could not but remember.

This is the thorny space of being both the subject and object of one's own study. My familiarity with my field afforded me the ability to see patterns and significance faster and more easily than if I had been encountering it for the first time. However, there was always, as it was pointed out to me countless times by mentors and advisers, the concern that my closeness to my field might make it more difficult to distinguish between what I considered important and what was important to the people with whom I was speaking. It also always offered the possibility that I might not see patterns that I was not socialized to see. These are, of course, some of the risks that are always present when studying one's own community (Altorki and El Solh 1988, 7).

The ability to relate and shed tears for passed-away rulers made my own position in relation to my "home" painfully clear: I was an Arabic-speaking resident brought to the UAE through a series of migrations to escape economic conditions in my parents' native Jordan. Though my family's hopes for economic prosperity never came to fruition, my experience of the UAE was mediated through my parents' own imagination of the UAE as a place filled with potential. Even as a child, my father used to tell me stories he had heard about how Sheikh Zayed negotiated to create the union of the UAE. How he had insisted on citizens benefiting from oil wealth. Despite the flaws of the UAE and the hardships my family experienced living there, my father's vision of its potential went hand in hand with his criticism of its failings. It was through this history of migration, this imagination of an Arab home away from our native country, this experience of my father and countless other Arab residents of the UAE that my conversation with Maha and Afra unfolded.

It was also through this history that I was able to witness two women's affective relations to their rulers with an understanding that this was not about being duped or brainwashed. My ability to relate to their experience brought to the fore some of the most salient questions of my research. It allowed me to take seriously their feelings while also holding my own commitment to understanding these affective relations as an extension of a particular form of authority and power. Conversations I had with noncitizen residents who were critical of rulership practices in the UAE were set against the ideal of a particular form of care in rulership and informed by the perception of its failed promise. The significance I placed on these questions could only have been the result of my own socialization and experience and my own understanding that there was something here worth thinking about. In that moment, as well as throughout my research, I was always reminded that I do not stand outside of the relations that I wish to study. I am embedded within them. Affective relations were accessible to some categories of people in the UAE and not others. My background and history in the country made it possible for me to have shared this experience with my interlocutors.

The stakes of this research were not just in understanding the ways in which particular relations of dependency and intimacy made some kinds of politics possible while foreclosing others, for other people, but also how these animated my own relationship to authority and politics in the place I call home. The stakes of the research were not just about how other people may inhabit a future politics amid unpredictable geopolitical change and tensions but also about how we might inhabit such a politics. How we might live together and do politics together were questions that the field imposed on me because I was from this place, of this place. In this place, I was, with others, entangled.

This story, though banal, offers a point of departure for addressing the place of shared experience in my fieldwork. It offers the space to consider how the stakes of the research became configured and reconfigured.

Remembering Space in the Field

The role of memory in fieldwork is not often talked about. Yet, when writing in the UAE after living in the UAE for two decades, memory intrudes on everything. Memory intrudes in a place where, year after year, streets, neighborhoods, and coasts transform. This is the tragedy, the wonder, and the puzzle of the Gulf, and Dubai in particular. Like a magic trick, observers are not always sure what they are seeing. What happened here? When was this building erected? Where did that store go? Where did this bridge come from? But the change in landscape makes up so much of the sense of this place. The mix of memory, nostalgia, and spaces unrecognizable from ten years ago is indivisible from Dubai.

Memory intrudes also in a place where much goes undocumented, where information is hard to come by and much of it travels through the grapevine. What was happening at any particular moment in history can sometimes be found in books and newspapers and other times can only be found in the stories that were told in hushed tones over a cup of coffee after a big dinner. Squabbles between political figures, changes in plans for infrastructure developments, corrupt activities at the height of the economic boom in Dubai, new surveillance technologies, unexpected deportations—these things can only be remembered as hearsay.

I sat down one day with Joud, a young Emirati woman.[4] We had been introduced to each other through a friend for the purposes of this and subsequent interviews.

She was young and enthusiastic. We met in a coffee shop in Jumeirah. We sat indoors to escape the scorching heat of the Emirati summer. Even as we sat inside, I could feel the warmth of the sun's rays on my skin. I did not have a fixed set of questions for what Joud and I were going to discuss. I was primarily interested in the ways in which someone as young as she is might think about or discuss the state, citizenship, and her relationship to rulership in the context of conscription requirements, geopolitical tensions, and war efforts. I told Joud what my research was about. As we discussed nationalism and citizenship, Joud began to tell me a story about her grandfather. She showed me a poem that he had written to his newest grandson. In the poem he talked about the bounty of the UAE and the bright future it offered this family's youngest member. He recalled the hardships and scarcity of his generation. He recalled a UAE that was unrecognizable to his granddaughter. It was unrecognizable even to me, although it was only 30 or 40 years ago. As she talked to me about national duty, the conversation wove back and forth between the topics of nationalism, change, and sacrifice. Joud's grandfather walked in a city whose streets, walls, buildings, and homes bore little to no resemblance to anything in his past. There was little he could point to beyond the coast and the sea that could document to his granddaughter what his young life had been. This was a sacrifice made for development—a sacrifice of which his granddaughter was extremely aware.

Joud's grandfather was not alone in this. Generations of residents from the Middle East and South Asia have faced the same ever-changing cityscape. Even the oldest parts of the city have not been protected from the constant rise of shiny new buildings and outdoor malls. I always asked myself, when sitting down to write about Dubai, how do I describe this place? How can I capture a past that cannot be seen but that drapes over the reflective glass of multistory buildings like an invisible layer? My own memories of Dubai always informed the way I wrote about it. Yet it seemed almost impossible to talk about what I remembered.

Memory extended the temporality of the field for me. The field stretched into my childhood and back again. I made a visit to the ruler's court one day. I was interested to know what the building was like, to see where the stories that people told me took place. I walked around the area it was located, on the creek in al Fahidi district. Considered to be a historic part of the city, this area was gentrifying quickly. A new outdoor mall, styled after wind-tower buildings, had just opened in the area. I was walking there with an old friend and we were marveling at how different everything had become. We remembered the creek of our childhood, where we came with our parents, parked near the street, and took long walks by the water. On the other side of the creek was the Deira corniche and the Dubai Fish Market. The fish market had recently closed in favor of a newer more "state-of-the-art" air-conditioned version. I recalled taking trips with my father to the market on Friday mornings when the day's catch was still fresh. The smell of fish filled the senses and humidity hung heavily in the air as early as 8:00 a.m.

In an address presented in 1985, Adrian Mayer discussed field "revisits" as an emerging trend in anthropology. He discussed memory and the role of memory when an anthropologist visits the same field site after many years or even after short stints away. He examined the relationship between "factual" data represented in fieldnotes, images, or recordings and the fieldworker's memory. For Mayer, memory influences an anthropologist's experience of a field revisit, and an anthropologist's interpretation and analysis of her field notes, after the fact. Memory is unreliable and yet unavoidable. Despite its unreliability, memory of previous visits aided Mayer in noticing differences over time in the village he was studying. Memory allowed him to better understand what he was observing in the past. The anthropologist, particularly one who revisits his site, he noted, is always dealing with a mix of observation and memory (Mayer 1985). Despite this, Mayer insisted on a distinction between memory and factual data. Whatever intangible observations were facilitated by his memory, he contended, were also corroborated in some way by facts. Memory was held as largely unreliable, without supplementary evidence. Importantly as well, memory for the anthropologist is only discussed in relation to previous fieldwork and field notes. What about memories that span a longer period of time? That do not come attached to field notes? That might be even more unreliable?

The unreliability of memory was not lost on me. I tried to keep my own memories silent but was keen for the memories of others to speak. To bring to life a temporality of the city that can only be felt if one knew the layers that lay underneath. But I also quickly realized that my own observations were necessarily mediated by my memories. My memories were necessarily unreliable, partial, imperfect, as any form of knowledge is. Yet they were significant to my encounter with the field. They became subjects of interrogation in themselves and points of departure for conversations with others.

Managing Myself; Writing the Field

These experiences and many others like them posed a problem for me as I tried to describe my experiences in "the field," whether in writing or in discussions held later in my university. I was worried that I could relate too closely to the stories that people were telling me. I was worried about how much that would manifest in my writing. I felt that it was my task as an anthropologist to question the terrain of power in which I lived but worried sincerely that my implication in my "field" would handicap me.

One day after having returned to campus, I met with a faculty member to discuss this dilemma. I explained that I did not want to get written off as uncritical, or worse, sympathetic toward one regime or another. I did not want to be read as overly "charitable" in my interpretations (Gellner 1970). It was important to me to complicate relations between rulers and subjects without dismissing them. I was not interested in presenting an uncritical account of politics in the UAE, but I was equally uninterested in painting a picture of people who were themselves uncritical.

I was warned that if I did not take enough distance, at least in the process of analysis, I might risk projecting my own feelings onto the people with whom I was talking. The worry was that I was risking my own objectivity and criticality, potentially vacating an appropriate discussion of power relations from my work. Relating too well became a kind of liability. In understanding and accepting that I do not stand outside of the dynamics I wish to observe lay the task of extricating myself just enough to be able to see those dynamics and attend to their power relations. This required me to pay very close attention to my own positionality, thoughts, and feelings so that I could ensure that they were not projected onto the work. I had to take care that I could see the similarities and the differences between my own position and that of my interlocutors. I had to dwell reflexively on myself to bring myself to the fore and make explicit the ways in which I was "implicated in the field." By doing so, I was to draw myself into the background. This tension is a tension that always already informs the practice of ethnography for anthropologists.

Despite the now general acceptance of "native anthropologists" and a turn to anthropologists studying Western societies (Clifford and Marcus 1986, 23), I still felt the burden, self-inflicted or not, of proving an adequate amount of "objectivity" to be credible. These gestures toward academic distance became a kind of anxious performance. It was a way to embody a kind of "outsider" perspective, an "objective" perspective, the sort conjured up by a romantic imaginary of anthropology. This, potentially self-inflicted, demand relied on the insider/outsider binary and on an imagination that identity and investments in the field can be mapped and bounded. This was, of course, impossible. Such a performance, I feared, was an acceptance of my alignment with a discipline enmeshed in a colonial and orientalist past, one that I was now entangled with whether I liked it or not. It was an occupational hazard, one that asked me to be an anthropologist at the exclusion of something else. In their own reflection on fieldwork in the Gulf, Vora, Kanna, and Le Renard (2020) suggest that the excesses of field experience ought to be taken seriously as "epistemological openings" instead of being "excised in the process of producing neat categories and maps" (54).

Managing myself, the way that an anthropologist ought to, felt like a kind of violence not only against myself but also against the friends and interlocutors who engaged in the conversations that were to become my thesis. This was the result of my own anxieties as a young scholar who was new to anthropology and my own worries about the kind of scholarship that I might someday produce. These anxieties were also the result of a discipline whose assumptions about itself often go unquestioned (Gupta and Ferguson 1977).

In the field, I was understood as someone who shared in the worlds of the people with whom I talked, even if partially or imperfectly. In the academy, I was suddenly distancing myself from them, writing them without myself, and playing the role of the Western anthropologist. It felt like a betrayal of what was shared between us. I felt that I was betraying the trust of those with whom I spoke under the assumption that I shared their concerns and empathized with their positions. They spoke with me precisely with the assumption that my own investments would not be excised from my work. In the field, I cast myself as someone who was "from" the UAE. In the university, I cast myself as a "critical" anthropologist who could, with an appropriate amount of objective distance, translate the field to the unquestionably white, imperial, Western academy. This was not a bargain that I was bound to make. It was the experience I had as an unsure 20-something, entering the Western academy and being evaluated by its standards.

Writing "the Other" for an Other

I have since wondered why so many such betrayals feel inevitable. What was so inevitable about casting myself within the academy as an anthropologist writing about the UAE for a Western audience, where the UAE was simply the stage in which more interesting and important "conceptual" questions played out? The UAE itself was merely a backdrop. Rightly or wrongly, it felt as though to speak appropriately from within an academic environment required this kind of orientation to the work that I was doing. This is particularly true of the discipline of anthropology. It is worth quoting Gupta and Ferguson at length here as they note the "Faustian bargain" that some anthropologists have to make.

> Although it is widely recognized that this is not how most of us choose our field sites, the vocabulary of justification employed in grant proposals, books, and research reports requires that such choices be cast in terms of the theoretical problems that the research site is especially suited to think about. Such a view privileges those who have no compelling reason to work in particular localities or with particular communities other than intellectual interest. (1977, 118)

Attempting to speak about my research within the norms of anthropology, which continue to assume a default white male anthropologist, was an alienating experience for precisely the reasons outlined above. Take, for example, the process of applying to academic programs in the United States or writing an academic research proposal. In each instance in which I was tasked with describing my research within an academic context, I could not say that my work was motivated by love and commitment to my home and the people who live there. I could not say that the questions I was asking were significant because they allowed me to understand that place better and to understand its politics better. These were not the kinds of motivations that were of value in the academy. I was advised always to focus on my conceptual questions, how they spoke to debates or conversations within the discipline, and how they could be of use to the work of other scholars irrespective of their geographic interest. The UAE's value was in its ability to illuminate larger questions. It was a place in which particular dynamics could be appropriately observed. This recasting of myself, my work, and my "community" felt to me to be deeply extractive. I nonetheless played this game and wrote proposals that were not bogged down by a loyalty to a single geography, however much that loyalty was undeniable to me and inextricable from my work. It allied me to the academy and to all of the legacies of my discipline, many of which I did not wish to be allied with.

The process of writing came with its own kind of betrayal. After months of conducting research in Dubai, making use of conversations with the people, histories, and streets of my city, I was producing something that I knew was never intended for them or for it. In representing my fieldwork textually, I inevitably produced an academic document that I knew was written with my academic adviser in mind. It was written for a group of people sitting in offices in red brick buildings covered in vines. I took experiences that were first rendered in a language that I shared with the people I interviewed and transformed them through analysis into discourse only professional colleagues wished to engage in.

I was recasting my home into an object of study for the consumption of a Western academic audience. I was talking about the people I interviewed to others knowing that they may never get the chance to enter that conversation. I felt guilt. I had to come face to face with the kind of power that I held as a researcher, even if only a student, in an American university, able to write and render a group of people to others for the purpose of discussion in closed rooms and papers. In those moments I had severed ties, I stood outside of my relations and wrote from a distance. The stakes of the research were suddenly reoriented and the research I was doing was, at worst, just a way to earn a degree and, at best, a way to contribute to academic conversations. Especially as a young scholar with incomplete training and a desire to write and produce work that might one day look like that of anthropologists I admired, participation in this form of academic writing was an important rite of passage. These constraints, though they may in some ways be imaginary (I could probably have written a very different kind of thesis if I tried), still exert a power.

Conclusion

In this chapter, I discussed the experience of doing fieldwork in Dubai, the place where I grew up and where I intend to continue to live. I wished to reflect on the field as a space of the familiar rather than the strange and the challenges and opportunities that presents. I focused on sharing experiences with my interlocutors, even as they were experienced from different positionalities, and the way that complicated, for me, requirements of distance and objectivity. I talked about the ways in which embeddedness in my field, past and present, and the closeness I felt to my subject matter became problematic, within the academy. I reflected on the kinds of tensions that I had to navigate to become a fieldwork researcher in the place I call home.

Notes

1   The *majlis* refers to an open forum held by the sheikh or a member of his family.
2   These numbers are based on a 2010 census and are the only available numbers on the percentage of noncitizens as a part of the total population.
3   Maha and Afra are fictitious names.
4   Joud is a fictitious name.

Bibliography

Altorki, Soraya, and Camilla F. El-Solh. 1988. "Introduction." In *Arab Women in the Field: Studying Your Own Society*, edited by Soraya Altorki and Camilla F. El-Solh, 1–24. Syracuse, NY: Syracuse University Press.

Beblawi, Hazem. 1987. "The Rentier State in the Arab World." In *The Rentier State*, edited by Giacomo Luciani and Hazem Beblawi, 49–62. London Croom Helm.

Bloch, Maurice. 2017. "Anthropology Is an Odd Subject: Studying from the Outside and from the Inside." *HAU: Journal of Ethnographic Theory* 7 (1): 33–43.

Chung, J. 2009. "Ethnographic Remnants." In *Fieldwork Is Not What It Used to Be*, edited J. Faubion and G. Marcus, 52–72. Ithaca, NY: Cornell University Press.

Clifford, James, and George E. Marcus, eds. 1986. *Writing Culture: The Poetics and Politics of Ethnography: A School of American Research Advanced Seminar*. Berkeley: University of California Press.

Davidson, Christopher M. 2008. *Dubai: The Vulnerability of Success*. New York: Columbia University Press.

Gellner, Ernest. 1970. "Concepts and Society." In *Sociological Theory and Philosophical Analysis*, edited by Dorothy Emmet and Alasdair MacIntyre, 115–49. London: Palgrave Macmillan.

Gupta, Akhil, and Ferguson, James. 1977. "Discipline and Practice: 'The Field' as Site, Method, and Location in Anthropology." In *Anthropological Locations: Boundaries and Grounds of a Field Science*, edited by Akhil Gupta and James Ferguson, 1–46. Berkeley: University of California Press.

Joseph, Suad. 1988. "Feminization, Familism, Self, and Politics." In *Arab Women in the Field: Studying Your Own Society*, edited by Soraya Altorki and Camilla F. El-Solh, 25–47. Syracuse, NY: Syracuse University Press.

Luciani, Giacomo. 1987. "Allocation vs. Production States: A Theoretical Framework." In *The Rentier State*, edited by Giacomo Luciani and Hazem Beblawi, 63–82. London: Croom Helm.

Mayer, Adrian C. 1985. "Anthropological Memories." *Man* (New Series) 24 (2): 203–18.

United Arab Emirates' Government Portal. 2020. "Population and Demographic Mix." https://u.ae/en/information-and-services/social-affairs/preserving-the-emirati-natio nal-identity/population-and-demographic-mix.

Vora, Neha, Ahmed Kanna, and Amélie Le Renard. 2020. "Space, Mobility, and Shifting Identities in the Constitution of the 'Field.'" In *Beyond Exception: New Interpretations of the Arabian Peninsula*, edited by Ahmed Kanna, Amelie Le Renard, and Neha Vora, 26–54. Ithaca, NY: Cornell University Press.

12 PERSONALITY AND PERCEPTION: ASPECTS OF THE RESEARCHER'S IDENTITY AND THEIR IMPACT ON FIELD RESEARCH WITHIN DIVERSE LOCATIONS

Kholoud Al-Ajarma

Introduction: Access to Ethnographic Fieldwork

Research is a multifaceted activity and inevitably involves reflection not simply on the wealth of data gathered but also on factors that may affect both the process of collection as well as the analysis of those data. We are all the products of our environment: we are encultured into identities and roles developed within contexts of the family, nation, political/religious orientation, educational experiences, and gender self-identification inter alia. None of these influences operates independently of the others and none is static. All these factors, which shape and influence the researcher, often at a subliminal level, have the potential to impact on the field of research in multiple ways.

My first experience of anthropology, albeit as an amateur, was at the age of 14, when I worked with a group of fellow Palestinian refugees, collecting oral narratives from survivors of the Nakba, the mass expulsion of more than

700,000 Palestinians, in 1948. Our intentions were multilayered. Collectively, we youngsters felt the simple need to capture and preserve the memories of an aging generation, whose lives warranted the dignity of a written record. On a different level, their stories offered us an explanatory political narrative, a gateway to understanding the situation in which we, the younger generation of Palestinian refugees, lived. The methodology was simple: observation and interview.

The years which followed my first encounter with anthropological inquiry, my university education, and fieldwork-based research (in Palestine, Chile, Morocco, and Saudi Arabia) have broadened my understanding of ethnographic methodology in the field in order to embrace questions of positionality, reflexivity, and the impact of my insider/outsider status on my interlocutors. I developed an awareness of varied techniques of social interaction and of the complexity of communicative strategies people employ, and I became increasingly aware of the need for mindfulness. Ethical principles must be observed, including the imperative to do no harm and to protect the autonomy, dignity, and safety of research participants. Essential too is a degree of understanding of the local communities and their cultures.

However, I have become more and more acutely aware of matters related to the identity of the researcher as a significant factor in fieldwork. As was the case with the contributors to *Arab Women in the Field* (Altorki and El-Solh 1988), my gender and indigeneity have been central aspects in determining how the fieldwork positionality affects my ethnographic and epistemological practice (cf. Al-Ajarma and Buitelaar, forthcoming). Against the realities of the everyday lives that I experienced in various places and among diverse communities while conducting fieldwork research, I attempt to examine the intricacies of access to the field, conceptualizing it as a fluid process that requires sensitivity to social issues and questions related to the ethical choices faced by researchers conducting ethnographic fieldwork. My particular contribution to this matter, I believe, lies in examining ways in which the identity of the field researcher influences the research process, data gathering and analysis, as well as negotiating the variety of inherent challenges faced during fieldwork.

Reflecting on aspects of conducting anthropological research in various geographical locations and in different sociopolitical contexts, including Palestine, Chile, Morocco, and Saudi Arabia, I do not simply discuss how the different facets of my identity influenced my access to the field, but I ask how best to understand the significance of the conditions and the social reality in these different locations. In the process of my enquiries, I am hoping to contribute to a discussion about the myriad ways in which the identity of the ethnographer is situated in relation to the field and to explore what ethnographic experience can tell us about circumstances that simultaneously affect the lives of both researchers and research participants.

Before I deal with the question of multiple identities in relation to place and their impact on my fieldwork and data analysis, I shall set the scene for my ethnographic encounters.

At Home and Away: An Ethnographer— Insider or Outsider?

In 2012, I returned to Palestine to conduct fieldwork on arts-based resistance to the Israeli occupation among refugee youth. I had been away for one year studying for a master's degree in Peace Studies and Conflict Resolution. I was returning home as a Palestinian, born and raised in a refugee camp, looking at my community from an insider's perspective (cf. Narayan 1993). I was familiar with the camp's life, knew the people, understood their everyday experiences and practices. However, I was soon enduring, with considerable irritation, the continuous Israeli invasions of the camp, in addition to night-time army raids, tear-gas attacks, and shootings. I did not readily resume the position I had held prior to departure; I felt that I was no longer a fully integrated community member. People become acclimatized to their situation and context: while refugee camp members do not accept military invasions and attacks, they adapt to and resist them. Residents live within a matrix of control to which they become accustomed, even as they strive to resist it in numerous ways, from collecting and displaying tear-gas canisters to throwing stones. I knew all of this intellectually and from my lived experience, but the emotional impact of reacclimatization took its toll on me. I both admired the resilience of my community and, at the same time, found myself bitterly resenting and complaining about events that had seemed quite routine before I studied abroad. My points of reference had changed through exposure to different social and political contexts and, in my own home environment, I had assumed something of the "outsider" status as a result.

The realization that I should question my assumed insider perspective came home to me one afternoon when I met some of the children who participate in the daily activities at a local community center in Aida refugee camp. The children were collecting tear-gas canisters left on the street after an earlier raid on the camp. I asked the children if they could still smell the tear gas, as I could at that time. A little girl said, "This is normal! We have this every day!" I became aware of the changes wrought on my perception by separation from such "normal" experiences; to me, these were no longer the norm.

Researching home was challenging. It required continuous reflection on, and interrogation of, my positionality in the field. My relationships with the people and my identities were complex. Here, I was a member of a local family, I knew the people and was familiar with the life in the camp—the insider. I was therefore expected to be "normalized" within the daily life, to accept and to be part of a communal experience of oppression and ongoing resistance that I had physically left behind for a while in Europe, imbuing me with some outsider status and experience. I occupied an ambiguous position at home.

In 2013, I conducted fieldwork among the Palestinian Diaspora Community in Chile as part of a second master's degree, this time in Anthropology and International Development. I was conducting fieldwork in a country whose culture and people were unfamiliar to me. However, my fieldwork was among the Palestinian community, more than 300,000 people, a community that had been in the country for over a century. Among this community, traditions of Palestinian music, dance, and food had survived and were featured in both private and public spaces. The people themselves were very diverse. First, there was the older Diaspora, the majority Christian and largely upper middle class or upper class. They are well established and have been in the country since the early 1900s. The second group were Palestinian Nakba refugees originally settled in Iraq, then displaced during the Iraqi Civil War, and relocated in Santiago de Chile in 2008; these interlocutors were Muslim and mostly working class. Among the Palestinians in Chile, I was welcomed and often referred to as paisana, based on the Spanish word for "fellow compatriot." Research participants told me that it represented the homeland and reminded them of places they longed for. The people whom I lived with in Chile did not feel alien to me; their hospitality, openness, and the nature of their discussions reminded me so much of home. The aspects of the Palestinian identity which had lived with the first generation of the Diaspora and were passed to the subsequent generations, such as the decorations of people's houses, Arabic songs loudly played in the restaurants of Recoleta, Palestinian cuisine found almost everywhere, and traditional debkeh dance learnt and performed by young people in celebrations and cultural events, made it easier to bridge the social gap between me and my interlocutors.

Despite the mostly positive encounters and hospitality of both groups, there were numerous occasions when I felt alienation caused by assumptions and questions about my identity. One such question was asked by a woman I met in Santiago who asked, "I still wonder, since you come from the homeland, how did your parents let you go? How did they accept your travel alone? Are people in Palestine that 'liberal/modern' now?" What the question implied, I believe, is that as a Palestinian, and single woman, I was expected to conform to social and cultural norms that this woman associated with the people in Palestine. It seemed to me that my interlocutor was applying stereotypes of Palestinian families and their attitudes, which are increasingly outdated. When I reflected on other encounters during my fieldwork in Chile, I found myself constantly trying to define my positionality as either "insider" or "outsider." I came to realize that these categories are not clearly defined and that I should not limit myself to identifying as one or the other. It is my understanding that the context, the situation, the relations I developed in the field, my interactions with research participants in addition to my position and reflexivity, all contribute to my positionality and my perception.

Between Researcher Detachment/ Independence, Integration into Family Structures, and Gender-Based Traditions

While working in Palestine, I was predominantly aware of my gender identity as an individual operating within patriarchal settings. At home, I was the youngest of fourteen children, so both my ranking as the youngest and my gender were problematic. I was lucky, however, that my parents valued equality and education over gender differences. Within social setting, however, my position was not always straightforward. For example, what I was able to grasp in conversations with my friends both at home and elsewhere was that, for those who identified as secular or not religious, I was too conservative. On the other hand, I was too liberal for those who were more conservative. I was too political and a rather strong-minded woman.

In the field, my gender identity shaped the opportunities available to me in a number of ways, including access to the social networks of my interlocutors. In Morocco, for example, where I conducted field research of twenty months' duration, seeking to examine the significance of Muslim pilgrimage, Hajj, in the everyday lives of Muslims, I lived with a local family, which meant that I was given preferential access to the public and private spheres of the people whose lives I was trying to understand. This helped me to perfect my Moroccan dialect and learn about local culture and traditions, and allowed me access to family networks. Conducting the first single-country ethnographic study of the Hajj, my aim was to explore both its performance as well as its significance in everyday Moroccan life. Therefore, the principal method of data gathering during my fieldwork was participant observation (cf. Al-Ajarma 2020). Living with the family allowed me rapid and unhindered access to observe and participate in the local community, specifically because I was often introduced as a close friend, sister, or daughter by my hosts, offering me powerful linguistic passports to interaction. In Fes, for example, my host mother accompanied me around the neighborhood, introduced me to the shopkeepers on the street, and talked about me to neighbors. On Fridays, I was asked to carry several plates of the traditional dish, couscous, which was made by my host mother in huge quantities, to the local café, the bank, and the tailor's shop. This practice of gift-giving allowed me to interact with the local community and to connect further to local traditions. These interactions allowed enjoyable conversations and discussions. In short, the family structure itself was a crucial and integral element within my fieldwork: on a personal level, I enjoyed their company and appreciated their care for my safety.

In the field, I aspired to be someone interlocutors could trust. Trust and confidence are qualities that encourage disclosure of sensitive information, even of truths or attitudes and values people would normally prefer not to disclose to a wider audience. I was a good keeper of people's secrets, read people well, and my opinion was often trusted, I felt. I had access to both male and female research participants. Such friendships and personal relations with research participants call into question the very boundaries of the field and the ability to truly draw lines around what constitutes "the research." I developed an awareness of "accidental" research and findings. By this I mean that, by listening attentively to a casual conversation, one not prompted by a research question or opener, I could discover an unpredictable gem of knowledge or information. Mixing with the community on a daily basis—after some time—normalized my existence to the extent that people shared intimate details of their daily life with me.

Although I recognized the importance of living with a family during the fieldwork, I sometimes felt restricted. Those with whom I lived felt great responsibility for me, including for my safety within socially and politically problematic situations. Mostly this took the form of insisting that I should be accompanied by a friend or a family member when traveling long distances or going to unfamiliar places. One example of this paradoxical experience is when I wished to visit a pilgrimage site near the city of al-Hoceima, a city on the northern edge of the Rif Mountains and on the Mediterranean coast. During the period of my field research, protests over economic and social problems in the region escalated into a mass protest movement, which came to be known as ḥirāk al-Rīf or the Rif Movement, following the tragic death of Mouhcine Fikri, a local fish vendor. Worried for their safety and mine, none of my friends in Fes, Casablanca, or Rabat agreed to accompany me on a trip to the troubled region. I was further advised not to risk my safety by going to al-Hoceima alone. At the time, I listened to my friends and waited until I had successfully made connections with locals in al-Hoceima. Then, I was able to visit the city and observe the pilgrimage.

It seemed to me that my friends' concerns were not only connected to my gender, worrying about a young woman traveling alone, but also to their feelings of concern over my safety due to the political unrest in the country at the time (cf. Al-Ajarma, 2022b). Therefore, when I finally managed to visit al-Hoceima, I also lived with a local family. I was often warned, nonetheless, that I was being watched, this time not by the family or the locals but by the surveillance of secret police. At the time, it struck me as ironic, my being warned to be careful of the police, when I was coming from a country where the daily lives of millions of Palestinians are monitored by Israel's colonial surveillance systems (Al-Ajarma, 2022a). Nonetheless, this experience of being regarded protectively by my interlocutors made me reflect on other kinds of injustice and the lack of civic security in both Morocco and Palestine.

National Identity, Political Affiliation, and Researcher Positionality

Conducting fieldwork in both Chile and Morocco, I found that my Palestinian identity was a highly significant identifier, both for my interlocutors and for myself as researcher. As I grew up in Aida refugee camp, I was accustomed to the daily struggles of refugees and the collective oral narrative of the Nakba and the displacement of Palestinians. However, I had experienced few encounters with the Palestinian diaspora (apart from some who were able to visit Palestine as tourists and the Palestinians I knew in the UK) when I represented Palestine and Palestinians on different platforms. Since I was 18, both my photographical work and films have been on show locally and internationally. I also led dance and cultural tours in Europe and have by now spoken to thousands of people about Palestine, refugee rights, and our collective aspirations for freedom. However, there was a qualitative difference between these performative encounters and my more intimate conversations during fieldwork. I was constantly aware of the sense of displacement and loss among the people of the Diaspora—fellow Palestinians with whom I lived and who helped me conduct my fieldwork.

The Palestinian refugees of Iraq with whom I worked in Chile made me more aware that, despite our shared refugee status, their experience was inherently different from mine. Those refugees had been displaced multiple times, from Palestine, to Iraq (and before that for many people, to Jordan), and thence to Chile (which for many was not the final destination but a place of settlement until a better option was available). I realized that, as an individual, I was blessed: although I was a refugee and lived in a colonized land, I was living in the homeland to which those people longed to return. Being a Palestinian refugee myself allowed me to identify with research participants who shared with me their struggles in Iraq, their displacement, and the journey from Iraq to Chile.

Thus, coming from the "homeland" allowed me to be a reference point for many people who wanted to talk about Palestine. I was often asked about daily life in Palestine, the refugee camps, Jerusalem, the Right of Return, the 1948 Nakba, and many other related topics. Longing for and belonging to Palestine seems to be a powerful emotional connection and a political need. Since the theme of my research concerned diaspora formation, representation of identity, and the politics of belonging, these conversations were crucial in allowing me to understand the participants' struggles to build new lives for themselves, to narrate their own history, to negotiate their relationship with the "old diaspora," and to make sense of their own diaspora experience. Participant observation further allowed me to see how a group of refugees build new lives for themselves in a complex and challenging context. The dilemma for many, it seemed to me, is to sustain a positive and constructive life pathway in a new land, becoming settled and fully involved citizens while also, at the same time, maintaining the personal desire and the political aim of asserting the refugee's Right of Return.

Being Palestinian in Morocco was somewhat different. Here, people manifested abundant support for Palestine that reached beyond the sense of nationalistic belonging or personal identity and became more politically meaningful. I was often told that in Morocco, "Palestine is considered a national cause," and that Moroccans supported the political struggle of the people of Palestine. People often referred to the Moroccan quarter of Jerusalem and the historic relationship Moroccans had with Palestine, a connection that dates back to the thirteenth century. Often people wanted to hear about Palestine through me, creating a natural and easy starting point to many conversations. Many Moroccans told me that they wished to visit Jerusalem and wanted my opinion on how to realize that ambition. Others, like a local governmental officer, stated that he would help me simply because I come from Palestine, which he described as a sacred place that was dear to his heart.

The significance of my Palestinian identity became a paramount aspect of my experience in Morocco. When introducing me to others, Moroccans used my nationality as a Palestinian as the first identifier after my first name. People often responded to that with *miskina*, the denotation of which is poor; the word can often be used to describe someone who is the epitome of misery. In Morocco, however, the expression is used colloquially to express acquired connotations, signifying sympathy and empathy with the other. Being the *miskina* from Palestine allowed me to gain access to larger number of contacts within the local community. Many Moroccans were also fascinated by the fact that I excelled in the local dialect, which is distinctively different from Palestinian Arabic; my dialectal accomplishments were seen very positively, and I was occasionally told that I had become a local *maghribiyya* (Moroccan) myself. This interesting combination of being distinctively Palestinian, yet linguistically in harmony with the local Moroccan culture enhanced my access to research opportunities.

In September 2016, I wanted to visit the coastal city of Safi to observe and document a local pilgrimage practice known as the "pilgrimage of the poor." This pilgrimage takes place once a year on the day preceding ʿīd al-aḍḥa, the feast of sacrifice. Being new to the city and having no contacts was problematic. One friend offered to ask a distant female relative to assist me. Later in the evening he called me with good news. He explained that the woman had welcomed me to her house upon learning that I was Palestinian. Even though the feast is often seen as a family occasion, I was welcomed not only to visit the family before the feast but also to spend the days that followed with them in order to witness the preparations, rituals, and customs of the 'id. To the woman I was, in fact, a stranger, but being Palestinian was my access point.

Despite the generally positive experience of being a Palestinian researcher in Morocco, there were a few occasions when people felt at liberty to tell me that they thought Palestinians did not resist enough or that we had surrendered our rights. In these occasions, I felt that I was responsible to defend my people and explain the many forms resistance can take. Upon reflection, such encounters obliged me both to reflect on where we Palestinians stand today in terms of our pathway to national liberation and, at the same time, to understand the ways in which our struggle is seen, understood, and supported by other Arab nations. At the same time I needed to ensure that I explained as clearly as possible the political conditions in Palestine. Nonetheless, my "Palestinian-ness," to coin a phrase, continued to be of paramount importance to my interlocutors, offering a point of reference, a connection based on a sense of solidarity, and an automatic entry qualification.

The Challenges of Carrying Out Research as a Woman

When I conducted my first fieldwork in Palestine, I was not a feminist, at least not consciously. Aware of the history and struggle of African American women through the work of Alice Walker, however, I often identified as a "womanist," a person who believed in women's equality. I did not fully grasp at the time the meaning of the term nor its inclusion of race and class-based oppression as necessary concomitants of gender oppression. So, in my early days of working, during my high school years in the camp, I strove simply to be accepted as a professional person, without the more complex and important aspects of self-awareness and gender consciousness that came later. For me, empathy and respect are essential in any relationship, whether that is within social interactions, within political movements, or with people in the field. Certainly, in the field, research participants possess greater knowledge about the subject of study than does the researcher (cf. England 1994); therefore, it is important for the researcher to reflect on interactions with others, specially in relation to challenges presented by power imbalances between the researcher and research participants, and between the researcher and others.

The greatest challenge during fieldwork was how to be accepted as both outsider and a woman. However, as a result of my upbringing and experience in male-dominated fields in Palestine, I have learnt how to navigate my way around obstacles and prove my abilities. I had learned strategies of active observation, techniques by which to direct or redirect conversation, deflecting attention in other directions, and subtly asserting both my rights as a woman and my skills as a researcher. Underpinning all this, in common with many women in male-dominated fields, I retained the belief that my work was of value, that my anthropological training gave me the tools I needed, and that my work mattered, whatever obstacles I encountered.

During my fieldwork, the fact that I claimed professional status came into question, especially in conversations with professional men. One specific encounter was the subject of much reflection on my part. At the time I was participating in a conference in Casablanca and had numerous discussions with both Moroccan and international researchers. In a discussion on French Philosophy, a male academic, also a teacher at a local university, complained about English translations of Michel Foucault. As a non-native speaker of French and English, I mentioned that Foucault is challenging to read. His comment then was that if I found Foucault difficult to understand, my place "should be in the kitchen." I felt offended by the comment, first by his lack of appreciation of my honesty but mostly because of the derogatory "kitchen comment." When I objected to his remark, he retracted it, denying that it was personal, but claiming it rather related to his comment regarding translations of Foucault. I took this to be a diversionary tactic, deflecting attention from a comment he knew to be sexist. Regardless of his explanation of his words, an explanation that seems illogical, I was intrigued by his revealed attitude. Power dynamics obviously came into the situation. He had a position of multistranded authority: his status as teacher, his position as an academic leading a course, his local identity as a Moroccan and, crucially, as a man. He was also a speaker of the highly valued, often by the upper middle class, language of French, which, despite its being the colonial oppressor's language, in Morocco functions as "symbolic capital" since it is related to being well-educated. The nature of his riposte to me could be seen as demonstrating that he prioritized his status as a man, rather a conventional one, above all other aspects of his identity in that encounter. I am sure he instantly regretted what that remark revealed about him: my challenge forced him to reflect and retract. However, I doubted that he would have made a similarly dismissive comment if his response had been to a male researcher. Such encounters within a patriarchal structure profoundly conflicted with my understanding of my identity as an independent woman and, I must add, the restrictions on my mobility were part of my encounter with this patriarchal structure, resulting in inner tensions. I came to understand the dilemma faced by many independently minded women in modern-day Arab society—arguably in most societies to some extent.

On a personal level, another experience was troubling to my sense of womanly independence, during my short fieldwork in Saudi Arabia. In order to establish a deeper understanding of the pilgrimage experience of Moroccans who travel to Mecca, I made an attempt to conduct part of my fieldwork among Moroccan pilgrims in Saudi Arabia. Under Saudi Arabia's male guardianship system (*mahram*), however, every woman applying for a visa must have a male guardian—a father, brother, husband, or even a son—to accompany her during the visit. This *maḥram* provision is only relaxed for women over 45 years of age, traveling in organized groups. Therefore, I had to ask my father (aged 80) to accompany me and since my father does not travel without my mother, I had to be accompanied by both of my parents on this trip.

I deeply appreciated and valued the generosity of my parents who were willing to accompany me on this journey. However, these encounters within a patriarchal structure profoundly conflicted with my understanding of the essence of Muslim pilgrimage: equality between all people. As for the research experience, these trips to Saudi Arabia helped me to reflect on the experiences of research participants. I witnessed examples of the stories told by the women about their visit to the Prophet's mosque, for instance, where the authorities have restricted women's access to the place where the Prophet Muhammad is buried (together with Abu Bakr and Umar, the first and second caliphs) and only allowed to the Rawḍa (al-rawḍa al-nabawiya), where, after hours of waiting, they were rushed to pray two rakʿas of prayer under the strict surveillance of female guards (Al-Ajarma 2020b). Men, privileged by their gender, were able to see the tomb of the Prophet and often took pictures of it to share with their female relatives. According to my interlocutors, the gender privilege of men, the time limitations on women's visits, and the control by guards were felt by some to militate against a spiritually satisfying experience.

The constraints, the controlling encounters that Moroccan and other female pilgrims had to experience, nonetheless, did not mean that they were passive recipients of Saudi regulations. Both in Morocco and during the pilgrimage, research participants reflected on aspects of Hajj that they found discriminatory (cf. Alajarma 2020b). Rumination and criticisms of restrictions, albeit made in women-only company, can be seen as a form of resistance; through their critiques, they showed that they had refused to internalize the limitations created by a patriarchal system (cf. Al-Ajarma 2020a).

Conclusion

My ethnographic fieldwork in Palestine, Chile, Morocco, and Saudi Arabia was an attempt to understand aspects of the everyday lives of groups of people in these settings. While conducting fieldwork, there are enabling factors, some of which reside in the personal identity/identities of the researcher, which smooth access to the field and to people of different backgrounds. At the same time, many boundaries and limits exist that one may encounter when conducting fieldwork.

These can be either formal or informal, related to one's identity, to national or religious background and gender, and, in addition, to rules and mechanisms that enable or constrain research.

It has long been argued that it is impossible for the anthropologist always to remain impartial in relation to the politics and ethics of conducting participant research (Armbruster and Laerke 2008). During fieldwork, I often had to alternately follow, read between, or even cross the "lines" imposed upon me by local regulations or gender restrictions. However, having said that, I do not underestimate here the importance of the people among whom I lived and worked and their role in facilitating or otherwise affecting my research in different ways.

As a student of anthropology, I understood that I should be highly sociable, interested, questioning, and enthusiastic. As a gendered individual, I tried to adapt to local norms, even those that conflict with my understandings of my self as independent and equal. As a Palestinian, I discovered that my national identity offered a passport or mode of entry into many conversations and situations that would otherwise have been more problematic. The fact that many of my informants identified with my place of origin, either because of their ethnic origins or from a political motive (sometimes because of an interplay between them both) was a major aspect in my research. There were also many moments of inspiration during fieldwork: participating in social and cultural events in multiple locations, observing research participants' expressions of solidarity with the Palestinians, and witnessing women's resistance to patriarchal systems.

As a corollary to these positive aspects of the fieldwork experience, I should add that these encounters were not without complexities. Conversing about stereotyped expectations based on assumed cultural patterns was challenging and so was responding to gender-related assumptions and rigid views on the Palestinian political resistance. In these occasions, I questioned how much a researcher should "disclose" her personal views during participating in the everyday lives of other individuals. Because of my professional position as a researcher, I found it impossible to respond as I might otherwise have done.

Inasmuch as the field researcher's subjective experience continues to shape ethnographic knowledge, I hope that I have been able to reflect on, and to discuss, some aspects of the way in which the field marks its imprint on the researcher and, in turn, the researcher's identity impacts on the data gathered, as well as the ethical, political, and cognitive registers of fieldwork.

Bibliography

Abu-Lughod, Lila. 1990. "Can There Be a Feminist Ethnography?" *Women & Performance: A Journal of Feminist Theory* 5 (1): 7–27.

Al-Ajarma, Kholoud. 2020a. "Mecca in Morocco. Articulations of the Muslim pilgrimage (Hajj) in Moroccan everyday life." Unpublished PhD thesis, University of Groningen.

Al-Ajarma, Kholoud. 2020b. "Power in Moroccan women's narratives of the Hajj." In *Muslim Women's Pilgrimage to Mecca and Beyond: Reconfiguring Gender, Religion, and Mobility*, edited by Marjo Buitelaar, Manja Stephan-Emmrich, and Viola Thimm. London: Routledge, Taylor & Francis Group.

Al-Ajarma, Kholoud. 2022a. "Subverting Israeli Surveillance Systems: A Note on Palestinian Resistance." Special Issue e-Magazine on Feminist Digital Justice. Suva, DAWN.

Al-Ajarma, Kholoud. 2022b. "'Pilgrimage of the Poor': Religious, Social and Political Dimensions of Moroccan Local Pilgrimage." *Anthropology of the Middle East* 17(1).

Al-Ajarma, Kholoud, and Marjo Buitelaar. Forthcoming. "Studying Mecca Elsewhere: Exploring the Meanings of the Hajj for Muslims in Morocco and the Netherlands." In *Approaching pilgrimage: Methodological Issues Involved in Researching Routes, Sites and Practices*, edited by Mario Katić and John Eade. London: Routledge.

Altorki, Soraya, and Camilla F. El-Solh. 1988. *Arab Women in the Field: Studying Your Own Society*. Syracuse, NY: Syracuse University Press.

Armbruster, Heidi, and Anna Laerke, eds. 2008. *Taking Sides: Ethics, Politics and Fieldwork in Anthropology*. Oxford: Berghahn Books.

Davies, James, and Dimitrina Spencer, eds. 2010. *Emotions in the Field: The Psychology and Anthropology of Fieldwork Experience*. Stanford, CA: Stanford University Press.

Deeb, Lara, and Jessica Winegar. 2012. "Anthropologies of Arab-Majority Societies." *Annual Review of Anthropology* 41 (1): 537–58.

England, Kim V. L. 1994. "Getting Personal: Reflexivity, Positionality and Feminist Research." *Professional Geographer* 46 (1): 80–89.

Fechter, Anne-Meike. 2003. "Cultures in the Classroom: Teaching Anthropology as a 'Foreigner' in the UK." *Anthropology Matters* 5 (1). https://doi.org/10.22582/am.v5i1.128.

Guillemin, Marilys, and Lynn Gillam. 2004. "Ethics, Reflexivity, and 'Ethically Important Moments' in Research." *Qualitative Inquiry* 10 (2): 261–80.

Narayan, Kirin. 1993. "How Native is a 'Native' Anthropologist?" *American Anthropologist* 95 (3): 671–86.

Tillmann-Healy, Lisa M. 2003. "Friendship as Method." *Qualitative Inquiry* 9 (5): 729–49.